"*Free Trade and Freedom* throws down the gauntlet to contemporary theories of globalization. By exploring how St. Lucian banana farmers confronted deleterious shifts in international trade policies, Slocum reveals the degree to which local and global processes are mutually constitutive. Challenging the idea that globalization ought to be understood as a homogenizing process in which flows of capital and culture overwhelm local communities, she writes brilliantly about social movements that, while pitted against global forces are ultimately shaped by local conditions, traditions, sensibilities, cultures, and ideologies."

> —Robin D. G. Kelley, William B. Ransford Professor of
> Cultural and Historical Studies, Columbia University,
> and author of *Freedom Dreams: The Black Radical Imagination*

"Slocum's thoughtful study of the mobilization of banana growers in St. Lucia in the 1990s shows how globalization intersects with national and local spheres. Their movement, which integrated class and cultural factors, was based on local values and practices rooted in their history. 'Freedom,' for them, does not mean 'free trade,' but freedom to work and live in ways they choose. Slocum's careful anthropological analysis deserves wide circulation because it challenges some widely held assumptions about globalization."

> —O. Nigel Bolland, Charles A. Dana Professor of Sociology
> and Caribbean Studies, Emeritus, Colgate University

"A fascinating study of the survival of place-based identities despite the loss of the Windward Islands banana market. Essential reading for those interested in the local impact of WTO rulings."

> —Janet Momsen, Department of Human and Community
> Development, University of California, Davis

FREE TRADE & FREEDOM

*Neoliberalism, Place,
and Nation in the Caribbean*

Karla Slocum

The University of Michigan Press Ann Arbor

Copyright © by the University of Michigan 2006
All rights reserved
Published in the United States of America by
The University of Michigan Press
Manufactured in the United States of America
♾ Printed on acid-free paper

2009   2008   2007   2006   4   3   2   1

A CIP catalog record for this book is available from the British Library.

Library of Congress Cataloging-in-Publication Data

Slocum, Karla, 1963–
Free trade and freedom : neoliberalism, place, and nation in the
Caribbean / Karla Slocum.
        p.   cm.
Includes bibliographical references and index.
ISBN-13: 978-0-472-09935-1 (cloth : alk. paper)
ISBN-10: 0-472-09935-3 (cloth : alk. paper)
ISBN-13: 978-0-472-06935-4 (pbk. : alk. paper)
ISBN-10: 0-472-06935-7 (pbk. : alk. paper)
1. Banana trade—Saint Lucia.   2. Banana growers—Saint Lucia.
   3. Globalization—Economic aspects—Saint Lucia.   I. Title.
HD9259.B3S167   2006
382'.41477209729843   2006003036

A portion of the royalties for this book are being donated to The St.
Lucia Folk Research Centre, an organization in St. Lucia that focuses
on the cultural development of St. Lucian citizens.

Dedicated to the world's farmers, who envision freedom

Contents

Illustrations

Tables

Abbreviations

ACP   African, Caribbean, and Pacific countries (under the Lomé Agreement)
BFA   Banana Framework Agreement
BSC   Banana Salvation Committee
CARDI   Caribbean Agricultural Research and Development Institute
EC   European Community
E.C.   Eastern Caribbean dollar
EEC   European Economic Community
EU   European Union
FRC   Folk Research Centre
GATT   General Agreement on Tariffs and Trade
GDP   gross domestic product
IMF   International Monetary Fund
MVDP   Mabouya Valley Development Project
NBR   New Banana Regime
OAS   Organization of American States
PLC   Geest Public Liability Company
SEM   Single European Market
SLBA   St. Lucia Banana Association
SLBC   St. Lucia Banana Company
SLBGA   St. Lucia Banana Growers' Association
SLBGA Ltd.   St. Lucia Banana Growers' Association Ltd.
SLP   St. Lucia Labour Party
SLWCU   St. Lucia Workers' and Cooperative Union

WIBDECO   Windward Island Banana Development and
          Exporting Company
WINBAN   Windward Island Banana Growers' Association
WTO   World Trade Organization
UK   United Kingdom
U.S.   United States
USAID   U.S. Agency for International Development
UWP   United Workers' Party

Acknowledgments

THIS BOOK HAS BEEN a long time coming. As such, over the years I have interacted with a variety of people who have provided generous and critical support to me.

My strongest and deepest gratitude is to the banana growers of Morne Verte, who opened up their homes, their farms, and many other aspects of their lives to me during some very tense and trying times in the banana industry. It is because of the growers of Morne Verte that I had my richest research experience, out of which this book has grown. I feel indebted to them.

More broadly, I am also thankful to the residents of Morne Verte (the family members of banana growers, those who collected my mail for me at the post office or helped me navigate the mail system, those who stopped to point me in the right direction as I tried to find someone's house, those who offered me food, those who gave me rides) for making me feel welcome in their community.

While conducting my data collection, I worked with an excellent research assistant. Angelina Phera Polius was more than a translator of Kwéyòl during my interviews or a transcriber of some of my interview material. She was a dedicated *researcher* who put herself in the work alongside me as if it were her own. My research benefited from her investment, top-quality skills, and support.

I also received interviewing assistance from Sally St. Juste and Jamine Baptiste, and I also received assistance with interview transcription from Ms. Armelle Mathurin.

In St. Lucia, a variety of institutions and their staff members were pivotal in my work for this book. I was hosted by the Caribbean Agricultural Research and Development Institute (CARDI), whose then director, Barton Clarke, graciously agreed to have CARDI facilitate my research by making the organization's resources fully available to me. At CARDI, I am also thankful for input and guidance from Gary Melville, Sylvester Frederick, and Lystra Fletcher-Paul.

The staff at the St. Lucia Banana Growers' Association was also helpful to me, including Mr. Fremont Lawrence, who was very generous in providing me with access to many SLBGA documents; Mr. Tony Jean Pierre of the Communications Office, who also made SLBGA materials in the Communication's Office available to me; and Mr. Cuthbert Joseph, operations manager of the SLBGA.

At the Windward Island Banana Growers' Association (WINBAN) and the Windward Island Banana Development and Exporting Company (WIBDECO), I received help from the staff librarians and my research also benefited tremendously from my interactions with Dr. Errol Reid, who provided generous assistance and often shared his keen insights into St. Lucia's banana industry.

Additionally, I spent extended time going through archival material at the St. Lucia Archaeological and Historical Society, whose director, Ms. Margot Thomas, was diligent in helping me locate key materials. Ms. Thomas put me in touch with Professor Leonard Glick in the United States, who also made some archival material he had obtained available to me.

The library at St. Lucia's renowned Folk Research Centre (FRC) was also important to my study. There, I am especially grateful to Mr. Kennedy "Boots" Samuel, who not only gave me access to the FRC library but who also arranged for me to present my research findings to the broader St. Lucian public. The gesture, which enabled me to bring my research results back to St. Lucia in an accessible way, was important to my overall research experience.

Finally, also in St. Lucia, other individuals assisted me with information and/or accommodated my research needs, including Mr. David Demacque; Mr. Kerde Severin, former director of the Mabouya Valley Development Project (MVDP), and other MVDP staff; and Mr. Henry George. I am very grateful to Terencia Kyneata Joseph for sharing her very important research on Indo-St. Lucians with me.

In the United States, a variety of institutions helped support my research. This included financial support from the Fulbright Program, the Inter-American Foundation, the Carolina Minority Postdoctoral

Fellowship at the University of North Carolina-Chapel Hill (UNC-CH), and the Department of Anthropology at UNC-CH. To assist me with the writing phase of this book, I also received fellowship support from the Woodrow Wilson National Fellowship Foundation and UNC-CH's Institute of Arts and Humanities. I am grateful for the funding, as well as the important assistance of several staff members at these institutions, who helped coordinate and organize the logistics for my fellowships.

At the University of Michigan Press, I was also fortunate to work with Raphael Allen, whose candor, keen editorial eye, and intellectual engagement with my project were invaluable during the final stages of putting the book together. His assistant, Julia Goldstein, also provided much-needed information during the manuscript preparation and production process.

Because the research for this project grew out of research for my dissertation, I must acknowledge essential guidance from my doctoral committee: Marianne Schmink, Anthony Oliver-Smith, Helen Safa, Barbara McDade, and Peter Hildebrand. Marianne deserves special mention, as I believe my work continues to benefit from the professional integrity that she both demonstrated and demanded of me.

Additionally, I consider myself to have had three other senior mentors to whom I owe so much. Feedback from Arturo Escobar, Faye Harrison, and Catherine Lutz has been critical to me not simply for the development and production of this book. Their assistance also has been significant for the larger professional context in which a project such as this (a first book for a tenure-track junior faculty member) is necessarily situated. All three have been tireless in extending their time, advice, and support to me on so many levels and, in some cases, over several years. I am fortunate to have them as mentors, colleagues, and friends.

Colleagues formerly and currently at UNC-CH and also at neighboring Duke University have provided useful encouragement and, in some cases, critical eyes for drafts of my work during the process of putting this book together. They include especially Michele Berger, William "Sandy" Darity Jr., Judith Farquhar, Dorothy Holland, Jerma Jackson, Norris Johnson, Donald Nonini, Rosa Perelmuter, Orin Starn, Lorraine Taylor, and Deborah Thomas. Leslie Calihman Alabi was a careful and fine graduate assistant whose work was critical in helping me to prepare the book's references and figures. I also owe many thanks to Karin Reese of UNC-CH's Center for Teaching and Learning, for her keen technological skills and resourcefulness, which enabled me to prepare several of the images in this book. Finally, my work on this book has also benefited from my participation in some meetings of the engaging Social Movement Working Group (SMWG) at UNC-CH. I especially thank the graduate students of the group for their inspiring vision and dedication to the SMWG's project and possibilities.

Further, a network of friends has helped me with book logistics, inclusive of moral support. Whether working in academic or nonacademic fields, they have read, heard, and/or edited drafts of my work, but they also have been available for lengthy phone calls as I worked through different dimensions of this project (which sometimes seemed to have nothing to do with the project at all but almost always did). I could not have succeeded without the spirit of generosity, camaraderie, and support from my dear friends Keith Clarke, Maria Franklin, Karen Gibson, LisaGay Hamilton, Kimberly Nettles, Karolyn Tyson, Robin Vander, Rachel Watkins, and Maria Zerr.

Finally, due to the nature of anthropological fieldwork, I have been fortunate to be part of (at least) two families that have been very important to me and without whose warmth, guidance, and support (including at times reading, editing, and checking my written work) I could not have managed to bring this book into fruition. In St. Lucia, my host family of Chrispina Augustus, Colleen "Nealia" Augustus, and Collins Lynch provided me with a wonderful home and space during my research, as well as useful daily conversations that helped orient me to St. Lucia and Morne Verte. I cherish the time I spent living with them and the time spent keeping up the ties. In the United States, members of my immediate family, Suzanne Elsoffer, John Elsoffer, Robbin Slocum, and Cheryl Slocum, have been supportive and encouraging of me in ways that I cannot repay. Above all, they have been patient with what I am sure seemed like an endless and curious process, and I hope they are as glad as I to see this book reach completion after so long.

1. *Locating the St. Lucian Banana Industry*

*I*N 1990, I WENT TO St. Vincent and the Grenadines to research the domestic and professional lives of women who purchased agricultural goods from local farmers and then shipped and sold the products in neighboring Barbados or Trinidad. Several years later, my exposure to this area of women's work in St. Vincent became the motivator for my interest in St. Lucian agricultural producers, who form the subject of this book. While my study of the work of Vincentian women traffickers (as they were known) did not focus on the meaning traffickers attached to the specific crops that they traded, I was keenly aware of traders' concerns about the future of their work related to one crop: bananas. I often heard them talk of "Europe 1992," a term I confronted repeatedly as traffickers forecast a kind of impending doomsday for themselves. Their fears were that in 1992 the European market to which most Vincentian bananas were exported through a local state organization and a foreign shipping company might no longer be accessible to Vincentian farmers. This would have been due to the formation of a Single European Market (SEM), which threatened to annul St. Vincent's (and other Windward Islands') preferential access to the United Kingdom's (UK) market. Traffickers talked with sheer dread of what this would mean for their own work since they relied on Vincentian bananas grown for export to the UK market. The goods they brought to Barbados and Trinidad were those considered to be of subquality for European tastes and therefore were available for sale in local and regional markets. To the traffickers, the end of the banana export industry to the UK possibly meant the end of their inter-island trade within the Caribbean because if Vincentian

farmers stopped cultivating bananas for Europe, production of the crop
might drop off entirely and leave traffickers without one of their most
important trading items. Moreover, I inferred, this would affect
traffickers' livelihoods since their incomes and their families' survival
drew heavily on the regularity of trading goods across Caribbean
islands.[1]

By the time I left St. Vincent and completed my relatively short project four months after I began it, ideas about a future study on the status
of the Windward Islands banana trade swirled in my head. The ideas
were boosted by a proliferation of reports, studies, and news articles
affirming that the advent of the SEM was one of the most pressing cases
of economic uncertainty and global economic trade striking the
Caribbean in the late twentieth century. The SEM was, by most
accounts, a quintessential example of contemporary globalization
because it could usher free trade policies into the region's local industries, which previously had been organized around preferential market
access. The report *Time for Action* authored by the West Indian Commission cited shifting terms for the banana trade as a major issue before
the Caribbean islands (West Indian Commission 1993), while other
independent studies (Fitzpatrick and Associates 1990; Neff and Raney
n.d.; Daisley 1991) performed predictive analyses of what such a policy
shift might mean and how Windward Islands governments could prepare. Back in the United States, I also read stories in major U.S. newspapers about the forecasts for vulnerable Caribbean industries caught
between tough competitors (especially in Latin America) and a soon to
be liberalizing market in Europe.

Buoyed by these predictions and my investment in another study on
the Windward Islands, I crafted and set out to conduct research on producers' responses to transformation in trade policy (particularly the
intensification of liberalized trade). St. Lucia came to me especially
because it was the largest banana-producing country of the four Windward Islands and it also was the site of the major institutional apparatus
around which all of these four islands' production was organized. St.
Vincent introduced me to the topic of trade policy and producers'
responses; St. Lucia would be the test case for exploring it. I was, then,
curious about the ways in which a decline in trade preferences, an
intensification of neoliberal economic policies such as free trade, and a
related increase in market competition might prompt producers to
rework how they organized production at an individual and household

level. I especially was interested in the ways in which assignments of farm tasks and domestic responsibilities might shift by gender given the significant number of female-headed households and farms in the eastern Caribbean.

Armed with these questions, I was settled in St. Lucia by October 1993, three months after Europe handed down the first of its many changed policies on banana trade. The first new policy, the New Banana Regime (NBR), restricted the Windward Islands banana trade to Europe by setting a quota for the volume of bananas that could be exported to Europe. While the quota allowed higher quantities of bananas from the Caribbean than from other world regions such as Latin America, it still reduced trade from the unlimited quantity that previously had been permitted. As this development sent shockwaves through the urban-based agricultural agencies in St. Lucia and also was talked up in local papers, I was immersed in interviewing and working alongside banana growers on their farms in the eastern St. Lucian community of Morne Verte.[2] It was there that I encountered what I considered to be an oddity. When I asked producers what they felt changes in Europe's trade policy meant for St. Lucian banana growers, almost uniformly I received blank stares, comments that people did not know to what I was referring, or statements that they had heard something about this policy but really did not understand. In one instance, a banana grower, Christie,[3] told me she knew this was something important, and, as we sat in her living room after a day working on her farm, she leaned closer to me with an intense look of curiosity and a desire to learn. Focusing her eyes squarely in my direction and revealing her perception that I had more information about this topic than she did, she asked that I explain to her what this market issue was all about. Her bewilderment about market policy change in Europe resonated throughout Morne Verte. In daily life and on the farms, I heard people talk often of their hardships trying to make ends meet through banana sales, but very few spoke of global trade policies or the SEM as related to their problems. When I interviewed more than fifty producers in the area and asked directly what European trade policy meant for their lives, my question was met with a resounding and repeated "I don't know" or a common and more emphatic "I *really* don't know." The peculiarity of this grew even stronger as I listened to producers tell me of the freedom they experienced while farming and as I saw them invest in work practices deemed by some industry analysts to be unsuitable for successful competition in global markets. With me, producers spoke favorably of farming as a flexible occupation that afforded them autonomy and individual achievement, qualities that they were committed to engendering among family and close friends. Puzzled in the first months by comments about freedom and observing over time producers' emphases on freedom and work, I developed my own curiosity about this conundrum: a disconnect between what I read in policy papers, what I heard in urban St. Lucian institutions and the popular press, and what I listened to in a rural farming community.

My confusion grew even more as I started to follow the work of a rapidly developing banana growers' movement that swept the country from just weeks before I arrived on St. Lucia through my departure in November 1994. Calling itself the Banana Salvation Committee (BSC), the group was organized to protest declining prices for St. Lucian bananas and the corruption that its organizers claimed was rampant in the state-run banana growers' association. Taking to the streets, sports playing fields, banana boxing depots, and city market steps across the nation, the BSC forcefully claimed before crowds of listeners that farmers' problems were the result of issues internal to St. Lucia: organizational corruption, state power, and even social and cultural divides and labels among St. Lucia's population. Unlike the policy analysts and local journalists, the BSC barely talked about the global market context in its repeated and detailed dissection of the industry, industry actors, and the industry's current status. Talk of European trade policy and what it meant for the national banana industry seemed to pervade much of St. Lucia, but I did not find that talk in one of the largest rural banana-producing areas of the country or among the most vocal and publicly present groups agitating for change in the industry in 1993 and 1994.

The meaning of the disconnect between the more "official" analyses of the industry and producers' own analyses is the focus of this book. More specifically, the book examines the reasons why banana producers in Morne Verte and elsewhere did not cite the pressures of global free trade as "their" problem when all around them global markets were referenced as the most pressing issue. How and why did producers evade discussion of "Europe 1992" while Vincentian traffickers had highlighted it actively a few years prior? And, if they did not draw attention to the weight of free trade policies, of what else did they talk when assessing obvious economic and structural changes in their daily lives growing bananas in 1993–94? If global events were not privileged by the banana producers I encountered in Morne Verte and by the BSC, which events proved important to them and why?

While they are explored here through the case of St. Lucia, answers to these questions have implications for issues that are theoretically and geographically far reaching. They inform us about the crucial importance of particular interfaces between global spheres and local spheres. A popular and ubiquitous position holds that globalization is a homogenizing process in which flows of capital, culture, and finance overpower local communities, but there are other ways to conceive of a global-local nexus. Indeed, global and local spheres must be considered as mutually constitutive, shaped by one another, and asymmetrically organized (Inda and Rosaldo 2002a; Friedman 2003).[4] This was true in St. Lucia, where in the initial stages of a shift in banana trade policy during the 1990s, the local (e.g., St. Lucian producers) intersected with the global (e.g., the SEM and attendant liberalization policies) rather than the former being entirely consumed and displaced by the latter. This is not to say that policy changes were inconsequential for producers' lives. Rather, it is to say that the SEM was not all-encompassing because, by their actions, growers accentuated their own conceptual disagreement with the expectations of liberalized trade.

In what follows, I show how: (1) in a variety of ways, global processes and discussions of globalization pervaded the daily context where St. Lucian banana producers operated; and (2) during the early stages of a global trade policy change producers wrestled with those discussions and those processes by foregrounding the meaning of specific local places and cultural practices in their lives. Around these places were built practices, conventions, histories, interactions, and meanings specific to St. Lucia and sites within St. Lucia. I argue that, whether in everyday practice, public discourse, or collective organization, growers engaged with these places more so than they openly engaged the processes and logics of global economic integration. From the late 1980s (when "Europe 1992" was a developing policy concern) through 1994, the St. Lucian state and foreign corporate actors attached to St. Lucia publicly and repeatedly profiled and announced the primacy of the global market context. Yet, during this time growers did not give equal credence to this context since they offered and accentuated alternative models of engaging the economy within local places.

The time frame is important here. The context discussed in this book

concerns the period when market integration measures were unfolding
and being debated but the dire policy impacts from market shifts were
not firmly in place. Thus, my focus is on the context where there was
heightened concern about what free trade *would* do to the Windward
Islands rather than a context where there were clear results from market
policy change. The St. Lucian state, I assert, was invested in reorganizing the banana industry within this period of heightened concern, leading to a public emphasis on global markets and their potential impacts.

During this period, media analysts also devoted concerted attention
to trade policy and growing competition in banana trade. There was also
the finessing of a contract labor arrangement between Windward
Islands' producers and a foreign transnational company, popular and
institutional organizing in St. Lucia around European market development, and negotiations before multilateral agencies regarding preferential versus liberalized trade policies for banana exporting. All the while,
the BSC openly and publicly analyzed the industry by examining, critiquing, and redesigning social and political formations at a national
level. Morne Verte growers anchored themselves in notions of work
freedom embodied through daily practices and principles historically
and culturally linked to their residential and rural community. I argue
that during these early stages of unfolding events in a transitioning
industry this signaled an investment in the meaning of place at the same
time that it revealed a political refusal of specific global processes as the
sole means of understanding and shaping the banana industry. While
their lives were necessarily situated in the developments of global trade,
producers' own forms of organizing (farms, movements) called attention
to the significance of the place of Morne Verte and the place of St. Lucia.

Place is not to be confounded with "the local" (Escobar 2001; Dirlik
2001), although the two are related. Arif Dirlik (2001) prefers to think of
the local as defined primarily by its otherness to or its distinction from
"the global." Local is not a physical site but an abstraction signifying that
which is not global. As sites divergent from all that we think of as global,
places can be local but often are simultaneously situated globally. That is,
as geographically located sites, they exist amid those processes we understand as both global and local. The place invoked by St. Lucian growers
discussed in this book calls up a scale other than global but it also calls up
practices that necessarily are organized amid global processes. Growers
produced for foreign markets, worked under contract for a state organization and a transnational company, were informed of British consumers'

tastes and preferences, and were asked to produce accordingly. But, by failing to address these processes in their discourses and practices, and by unpacking how they were situated vis-à-vis the state or how they were free to organize their working lives in specific ways that were historically and socially significant to their community, producers were more apt to examine the place of the nation and the place of Morne Verte. Thus, this case reveals how the local can engage with and even willfully participate in the global by recentering the local.

It is common for someone to ask whether a subordinated group's tactics, such as asserting forms of local engagement in the face of global integration processes, actually "worked." Did growers' movements and forms of organization around place result in changed state policies and reduced state surveillance, the retreat of the transnational corporation, or, even broader, fairer trade conditions? Did they secure higher incomes in a long-range way? Did producers succeed in dismantling market liberalization as we know it? The answer to this latter question is an unequivocal and probably an obvious no. Free trade persisted as a pervasive global economic paradigm of the late twentieth century. The answer to the former questions, however, is a tempered and yet ironic yes. As will be discussed in chapter 8, state influence was reduced in growers' lives by 1995. Geest Industries, the transnational company that steered banana production on St. Lucia for decades, did pull out of its role in shipping Windward Islands production by 1995 (although these shifts appear to have brought a new set of problems for banana growers). Still, because the answer to these last questions is not entirely affirmative, this does not mean that growers failed to succeed in their efforts. Despite short-term political and economic transformations in producers' positions within the St. Lucian banana industry, this book is not about whether banana growers' movements or challenging discourses succeeded or failed to engender revolutionary change. The focus here is not on outcome, then, in a traditional sense. Rather it is on demonstrating local processes by which alternative perspectives and practices became inserted into a context of intensifying global integration measures. Instead of asking how neoliberal agendas were transformed, I ask: how did producers' perspectives on work, economy, culture, and nation *converse with* and *rethink* neoliberal policies? What alternatives to neoliberalism did producers raise by sheer virtue of the way that they organized and conceived of their everyday lives? By posing these questions, we underscore that movements are as much about alternative possibilities as they can be about tangible material change (Kelley 2002). Thus, if we shift our notions of success away from looking solely for material outcomes or even ideological transformation, we can consider the kinds of possibilities that exist for imagining alternative worlds and forms of organization that movements, counterdiscourses, and unconventional practices offer and perhaps seek among their goals.

PLACE & GLOBALIZATION

How Caribbean banana industries were situated within changing global markets was the subject of much media attention in the early 1990s and continues to be a focus of many social science studies (Grossman 1993, 1998; Raynolds 1994a; Raynolds and Murray 1998; Nurse and Sandiford 1995; Sutton 1997; Lewis 2000).[5] Several developments led to this, including: (1) the extension of agribusiness and contract farming in parts of the Caribbean; (2) the threat faced by some Caribbean countries of losing their longstanding, preferential trade status with Europe amid the European Community's (EC's) economic integration and negotiation toward a single EC trade policy; (3) disputes at the meetings of General Agreement on Tariffs and Trade (GATT) between the United States and Europe regarding Europe's protected trade policy vis-à-vis producers from Africa, the Caribbean, and the Pacific (ACP); and (4) a growing belief that Latin American countries could outcompete Caribbean countries if trade protections for the latter were annulled. Added to this was the dependence on banana exporting that marked many eastern Caribbean economies for over forty years and that also touched the lives of thousands of smallholder banana growers. Thus, in varying ways, a question was often raised: how could economically vulnerable Caribbean farmers survive a transition to free trade? In answering this question, media analysts and some academic researchers tended not to be optimistic. With an emphasis especially on transformations in global trade protocol and their expected impacts on the economic and political policies of Caribbean governments, several observers drew attention to the long-term uncertainty, weakening, or vulnerability of Caribbean economies, livelihoods, and political interest groups due to receding trade preferences (Nurse and Sandiford 1995; *Economist* 1990, 1997a, 1997b; *Newsweek* 1997; Sutton 1997; *New York Times* 1999b; Clegg 2002; Anderson, Taylor, and Josling 2003).[6] However, this focus on global market impacts left out equal consideration of how national and local dynamics could shape the global banana industry (Slocum 2003).

The approach I follow in this book departs from an emphasis on how global trade policies threatened to obliterate local economies. Although the economic, social, and political impact of such policies are important, I consider here how local processes rethought the shape, direction, and possibilities for specific forms of global processes in particular places. This approach draws on producers' own arguments about economy, society, culture, and nation. It thereby allows us to consider how the local entered into a conversation with the global, by redirecting focus away from global markets to place-specific relations, practices, identities, and possibilities.

It represents a move away from the analysis that first brought me to St. Lucia when I was interested in the economic impacts on and responses from farm households and collective groups living amid global economic change. Trained in studies of gender and development, I started this project interested in household economies and shifting social arrangements (such as gender roles) within farm households operating under impending pressures of globalization.[7] My project was formed within a defining area of social science inquires from the 1970s to late 1980s, as it considered intersections of gender, work, and household organization within the context of development processes and macroeconomic shifts.[8] Yet, as I was unexpectedly confronted with the BSC's active agenda from the first day of my arrival in St. Lucia, I necessarily expanded my work to consider the national public sphere as a key domain of contest and collective agitation amid the global changes I had come to explore in St. Lucia.[9] However, two phenomena needed to be considered beyond this: the broader structural base of the BSC movement; and the various vocal, politically pointed, and simultaneously subtle narratives about the industry that banana producers developed. This led me to explore growers' responses to the industry beyond the reorganization of household responsibilities and roles and also beyond public, open, and organized protests. I shifted to consider how growers' responses occurred also in place-inflected organizing tactics of everyday life. My recognition of this, stemmed from what I observed in producers' narratives and forms of social organization. The observation moved me away from a strict focus on households and public spheres as sites of globalization's impact or sites for responses to globalizing economies to an investigation of the organization of daily life made meaningful through appeals to place within globalizing processes.

As I listened to growers who were reformulating the globalization arguments around them, I was also led to acknowledge that power (in their working lives) occurred in ways more complex than through the extension of market integration policies. It occurred in their reformulations, and thus rejections, of certain assumptions about the saliency of market dynamics in their lives. Labor studies of banana industries in the Americas have been important in detailing the forms of inequality under which producers and laborers operate, especially through forms of labor control and manipulation by corporations and states (Moberg 1997; Bourgois 1989; Purcell 1993). These dynamics also were a significant feature of the Windward Islands industries where corporate domination has been evident (Trouillot 1988). Yet, in the St. Lucian industry, I argue that power flowed in multiple directions. It flowed from "global forces" (such as markets and transnational companies that defined what and how producers could market and from state actors who were partial companions to the transnational), to farm households. It also flowed from politicized, place-based acts that were in conversation with these forces and that refused to privilege the forms of social organization that such forces engendered through banana production.

Reflective of my rethinking of theories of globalization and my argument about power, this book focuses on three intersecting questions that take us beyond strict household, political-economic, and resistance analyses. The questions help us comprehend how and where people confront, shape, and interpret power and politics under globalization. First, how is power inflected in everyday life within a context of changing global economies? Second, what are the specific historical and social experiences that exist in an economically globalizing context but simultaneously are attached to particular places (where everyday life plays out)? And, third, how are such places sites for enacting politics within these globalizing contexts?

Everyday Life, the State, and Power through Neo-liberal Paradigms

The anthropology and sociology of the everyday zeros in on how people are situated in their worlds, derive and express meaning, formulate identities, and construct and participate in relations through regularized practices across time (Lefebvre [1947] 1991; Goffman [1959] 1990; Highmore 2002). And, while everyday life constitutes the forms of quotidian practice that we observe in work, play, and a variety of common social interactions, power and agency also mark these settings (see Willis 1990; Hebdige 1979; Genovese [1974] 1976; and Scott 1985). Michel Foucault (1977), for instance, showed that power exists within the repeated and ubiquitous maneuvers of institutions, which survey "subjects" continually to oversee and discipline behavior in all the details of daily institutional life. But power is also part of everyday life, in less obvious and overt ways, in the more micro contexts of what we do on a regular basis. We can, for instance, observe how individuals resist power through the tactics that they enact in the minutiae of life (such as reading, talking, eating, and so on) when such tactics fail to conform to conventional expectations (de Certeau 1984).

Quotidian practice inheres in certain contemporary forms of economic organizing. This is true of contract work, which some consider to be one of the key forms of capitalist accumulation in agriculture in the late twentieth century (Little and Watts 1994; Watts 1994; see also Collins 1993; and Carney 1988). As an "agreement" between the contractor (often a transnational company), which owns or buys the crop from the producer-worker, a contract stipulates production responsibilities and terms. Here, capital accumulation and labor use under it are considered "flexible," due in part to the ways in which the contract pulls on multiple individual laborers and their families, inserting smallholder households into new globalized production systems (Watts 1994). This type of labor arrangement is organized in diffuse microsettings and involves expansive yet sometimes regularized and structured practices across numerous small farms. Moreover, transnational corporations, the purveyors of labor contracts, become part of the power base behind such flexible production strategies. Their contracts "define the social space of autonomy and subordination that the grower occupies in relation to the labor process" (Watts 1994: 27). But, although transnationals are the agents that bring these production schemes to the corners of the world, nation-states are also critical in this global economic configuration (Berry 1989; Harvey 1991). Motivated by international capital flows (Harvey 1991), nation-states contour forms of administration, legislation, and party politics, which often are mobilized around the (contract) work of transnational companies. In this capacity, they are "neoliberal states," legislative bodies whose policies reflect global restructuring organized around a neoliberal economic agenda.[10] To be sure, states increasingly play a role in coordinating the activities of foreign capital or they adopt the policies of privatization and social service reductions that multilaterals promote (Berry 1989). There is, then, a recognition that states working in these ways take on or work alongside neoliberal policies. Even in quotidian practice, various forms of state apparatus function within forms of global economic restructuring. States are not fixed within political and national institutions but rather are embodied within a range of people's lived experiences and, as with the contemporary spread of processes for global integration, so, too, has the embodiment of the state expanded (Trouillot 2001).

In the St. Lucian case, the state was part of a legal and political apparatus applied to everyday farm work and thereby brought the contract between growers and a transnational shipping company into concrete existence. For over forty years, banana production on the island was an occupation in which legally mandated and quotidian work tasks were defined and enforced by a statutory organization known as the St. Lucia Banana Growers' Association (SLBGA). From the 1950s on, the SLBGA held a contract with the British shipping company, Geest Industries, to provide the company with bananas according to a given schedule and given product specifications. By the 1970s, in its work with local farmers, the SLBGA was overseeing weekly stages and routines of preharvest, harvest, and postharvest work tasks performed by multiple producers. With cultivation occurring on as many as ten thousand individual fields at any one time, banana production was decentralized. Surveillance responsibilities, consequently, were spread out across multiple SLBGA representatives, who fanned out across the expanse of banana fields. Due to this monitoring role, which was set according to a production schedule, there were regularized and habitual interactions between producers and SLBGA monitors. Guided by state law, the interactions were designed officially to ensure that producers' farm practices fit the SLBGA specifications, which included expectations of global markets around which much SLBGA policy was built through its contract with Geest Industries. Therefore, through the statutory organization, the state was a key player in this regularized mode of linking foreign markets (conceptually embodied in the contract) to growers' fields. In this way, the state was an agent of global processes in everyday life and power was effected through forms of state surveillance as well as in the hierarchical notions of agricultural knowledge that such monitoring of producers by the SLBGA presumed.

Banana producers interpreted the production context in ways that differed from how it was officially structured. For example, while the SLBGA mandated a restrictive and regimented schedule for harvesting and postharvesting activities, Morne Verte producers set parts of their work schedule not overseen by the SLBGA according to principles of freedom and alternative notions of flexibility. Their shifting and pliable uses of labor and land, as well as their belief that agricultural work should and can be a source of personal and familial freedom, spoke directly against the rigidity of the routine tasks organized and surveyed by the SLBGA. Further, the BSC challenged and reconstituted hierarchies between growers and state/SLBGA representatives due to the ways that the BSC organizers structured its repeated and weekly movement activities within and *against* class and cultural formations within the national space. The BSC also filled its speeches with symbols that reinterpreted the notion that cultural and social superiority lay within the SLBGA and its representatives.

Thus, I argue that growers' labor and land use tactics as well as the BSC speech and organizational tactics constituted alternative discourses that were not only about the routine organization of work but also about producers' and state representatives' social and cultural identities and positions. These tactics complicated growers' full adoption of the SLBGA discourse about the need to work rigidly and restrictively to compete within liberalized markets. The tactics also threw into question the SLBGA's authority and "expert (agricultural) knowledge," which justified producing according to a particular schedule. In this way, growers' tactics not only envisioned and offered alternatives to production but they also shaped the possibilities of power attached to the discourse on globalizing production.

Amid Placelessness, Places as Cultural Referents

Based on market liberalization policies, the extension and extensive work of multinational and transnational corporations, the accentuation of multilateral organizations such as the World Trade Organization (WTO) and the International Monetary Fund (IMF), and the general mobility of capital, we have indeed witnessed an overarching "globalization discourse" (Kelly 1999). In this "capitalist script" (Gibson-Graham 1996), global capitalism is associated with deterritorialization, selective placelessness, and flexibility, as capital moves away from being territorially fixed (Appadurai 1990; Basch, Glick Schiller, Szanton Blanc 1994; Harvey 1989; Trouillot 2003). This particular spatiality and dislocation of capital occurs through the vast and vigorous mobility of capitalist ventures, which seek to occupy new and multiple productive spaces (Harvey 1989).

But what alternatives to this form of economic organizing and the context of capital flows exist? An example could be the global justice movements that, in part, refuse global capitalism and its related discourses by protesting at multilateral meetings that advocate and negotiate for the advancement of global free trade; organizing their own bodies framed around inclusivity; and, as with the World Social Forum, forging nonhierarchical "learning, networking, and political organizing" (Callinicos 2003; Fisher and Ponniah 2003: 6). Yet, places are other sites of alternative organizing around economic practice. Within them exist everyday practices that, like the global justice movements, can be structured on a different scale, with a different intent and organization than global integration projects. Such practices are called up out of the logics, meanings, histories, and politics of individual places. Like the global justice movements, place-based practices indeed operate within the global sphere because they are not bounded by but rather are connected to other places far and wide (Massey 1993). Yet they are attached to so much more.

Places are a "source of life and reference point with which people may identify from their particular position in the more global network of human relations" (Hastrup and Olwig 1997: 12). Places are where we can ascertain how people relate to, perceive, and experience specific locales (Low and Lawrence-Zúñiga 2003); they are sites where individuals and groups form their identities and out of which they derive meaning through their experiences with particular landscapes (Feld and Basso 1996). And, while places may be symbolic, changing, constructed and cannot be generalized as stand-ins for the culture or social organization of particular areas (Gupta and Ferguson 1997; Rodman 1992; Appadurai 1988b), they nonetheless are part of where people locate and situate themselves culturally and economically (Escobar 2001). How people create meaning in and through places, therefore, should be of consideration within studies of globalization that seek to situate and understand how people's lives take shape amid a variety of global processes (Hastrup and Olwig 1997; Olwig 1997).

Contemporary global processes give places an added meaning and importance. For places are sites targeted by nation-states engaged in furthering the work of global capitalism (Prazniak and Dirlik 2001: 10). But, perhaps more importantly, with accelerated global integration processes that break down or shift boundaries, place-based identities become significant as a source of reinforcement against the social dislocation and placelessness prompted by forms of global integration (Adams, Hoelscher, and Till 2001). Thus, places do not necessarily lose their place—become obliterated or evacuated—amid processes of deterritorialization and fluid national and community boundaries. Moreover, people might be inclined to affirm places instead of retreating from them (Escobar 2001). People might, as Dirlik says, place discursive (rather than geographical or historical) boundaries around particular places to distinguish place-based discourses from the "placeless abstractions such as capital and national status and their discursive expressions" (Dirlik 2001: 23). Indeed, as Stuart Hall (1991: 35) has argued, the amorphous, almost ungraspable quality that globalization exhibits against the "familiarity" of individual locales prompts people to accentuate place as something they know:

> It is a respect for local roots which is brought to bear against the anonymous, impersonal world of the globalized forces which we do not understand. "I cannot speak of the world but can speak of my community." The face-to-face communities that are knowable, that are locatable, one can give them *place* (emphasis mine).

As such, there is a reinforcement of logics drawn out of the meanings and discourses of particular locales that people know, a reinforcement that suggests a type of place-based consciousness (Dirlik 2001).

It should be obvious by now that, whether participating in the BSC movement or talking individually in Morne Verte, banana producers did not "speak [directly] of the world" or global issues when assessing the banana industry. Indeed, Morne Verte growers and the BSC exhibited a glaring avoidance of discussing and accentuating global markets, Geest Industries, or competition from other banana-producing countries. Instead, producers' analyses were centered on national, regional, and local issues. In its speeches and the organization of its activities, the BSC critiqued the banana industry by analyzing the problems associated with St. Lucian social practices and relationships. Morne Verte producers engaged in farming practices that were particularly meaningful to the history of agricultural production in their village and also connected to histories of farming among Afro-Caribbeans in other parts of the West Indies. This participation in and analysis of everyday farming life in Morne Verte and in everyday social interactions was how growers emphasized meanings related to place instead of focusing on the primacy and features of global economic processes.

Places as Sites of Political Contestation

Forms of place-based consciousness are projects enacted amid such crises associated with the (flexible) reorganization of labor and the expansion of global capital (Dirlik 2001). It is from such projects that people engage local politics, which end up in conversation with global processes. We have seen this dynamic with the proliferation of place-based movements from Chiapas (Nash 2001) to Quito (Sawyer 2001) to Queens, New York (Gregory 1998), where protestors and activists rally around a local or national identity as well as environmental, economic, and political rights. This has occurred in the midst of encroaching markets, corporations, and "development" models that destroy and reorganize uses of lands, community composition and boundaries, and forms of work. Through organized action in these cases, people assert a defense of place and/or openly privilege a place-based consciousness.

Identity often is at the intersection of place and politics in two key ways. First, people are invested in what places mean. Thus, place-based struggles frequently are identity struggles over how and by whom places situated in cultural politics, political economies, and relations of power are defined (Gregory 1998; Escobar 2001; Harvey 1993). Second, places are sites within which people organize and form identities that then become points from which place-based political claims can be leveraged (Lovell 1998: 4). Identities are constructed and profiled strategically around place, particularly when conflicts over place (e.g., land, territory, and territorial boundaries) emerge (Low and Lawrence-Zúñiga 2003: 24; see also Radcliffe 1993). Regardless of how subtle or overt, claims enacted through place draw on, engage, or accentuate an identity and cultural politics of place, the ever-present politics that gives them their meaning (Escobar 2001; Moore 1997). Therefore, as it is played out under globalization, continual participation in place-based discourses and identities might reveal a type of political defense of place. That defense is political because of its reinforcement of discursive practices and perspectives and its insistence on defining place by means of certain discourses and not by others. It is also political because of its strategic mobilization and assertion of identities contested by a global integration project that is built on discourses that highlight a particular scale and space.

Through these measures that engage places as political around globalization, we must see place and locality as part of (rather than responses to) globalization processes (Dirlik 2001; Friedman 2003). For Friedman (2001, 2003), the dynamic between local and global is not one of simple stimulus and response: capitalism does not invade and cause the development of new social realities such as protest movements. Instead, capitalism and anticapitalist protests are part of the same system. They are connected by their existence within an "underlying structure" where there is a "hierarchy of constraints and dynamic processes that link global processes with . . . local structuring" (Friedman 2000: 655). Even though we often think of globalization and locality as opposed, critiques rendered *through place* and *around place* are in continual conversation with efforts that appear geared toward undoing place. They are mutually constitutive.

Indeed, St. Lucian banana producers' emphases on place were political discourses of alternatives to globalization because they overtly rejected discourses around the need to organize work for global markets. But we also must understand them as dynamics within globalization processes. Producers' discourses were not unconscious or inadvertent, and they also were not locally or nationally bounded events. Because their work as banana growers linked them to the global circuits of capital, St. Lucian producers' practices around farming were necessarily inserted within those circuits. Yet, to the extent that the BSC's work and banana growers' cultivation practices were purposeful and implicitly spoke against a script about the primacy of economic globalization, especially free trade, they were political projects. Further, following from Friedman's point, their practices were part of the "local structuring" linked to "global processes." These forms of local structuring, enacted through and around everyday interactions and formations, were ways of conceptually challenging a globalization discourse.

BANANAS, GLOBAL PROCESSES, & CARIBBEAN WORKPLACES

Research in small communities, villages, and residential settlements has been a hallmark of anthropological research, including Caribbeanist studies. From the 1920s through the 1960s (the early years of Caribbeanist anthropological research), several projects focused on such issues as social organization and economy in peasant villages (Horowitz 1967; Mintz 1960), family patterns in rural communities often peripheral to plantations (Clarke 1966; Smith 1956; Gonzalez 1969), and survivals of African culture within Caribbean religions practiced in particular Caribbean valleys (Herskovits 1937). This work was largely rural and village centered in its scope (although a few studies of urban areas also exist), with a focus especially on family, religion, performance/dance, ethnic and other forms of stratification, Creole cultural development, and peasant production. It also always considered these formations as features of broader patterns such as colonialism, the plantation system, slavery, and urbanization (Slocum and Thomas 2003). However, during these years, researchers spent far less time analyzing how these broad patterns operated than how people in villages and valleys did. The notion of Afro-Caribbean culture as bounded and confined to (rural) places was obvious and problematic here, but the work did reveal rich ethnographic detail on specific cultural forms as seemingly place driven.

Second, the more recent work on contemporary patterns of Caribbean migration points to the depth of people's engagement with geographic Caribbean places amid the transnational connections that envelop their own movement. Indeed, the research connects with Sidney Mintz's (1998: 121) observation that "people can be bilocal [or transnational] in identity and highly mobile . . . [but this] does not mean that the unilocal communities have stopped existing." When people migrate out, such communities, he says, "are what they come back to." Consider, for example, Caribbean migrants who reside physically in the United States and who are simultaneously and heavily invested in participating in Caribbean places and practices.[11] Helping to augment their cultural and social capital in the Caribbean places where they used to reside, they invest in those sites by political, social, cultural, and symbolic means (Basch, Glick Schiller, and Szanton Blanc 1994; Hintzen 2001; Kasinitz 1992; Olwig 1997). This occurs as they send remittances to help fund projects in Caribbean communities or as they purchase and send "home" material items of status that help *place* the migrants socially in the communities where they do not physically reside. But it also occurs when they accentuate generations of migratory narratives by participating in migration patterns that form the identity of extended family members and that also are attached to specific "sending and returning" sites (Chamberlain 1998). In these ways, migrants make material, social, and symbolic investments that become part of their social and cultural identity formation linked to the patterns of particular Caribbean places.

Were their attachment to those places not significant, one assumes, they would not invest so heavily and so readily in them.

Third, research on Caribbean nationalist and other social movements shows how the movements have been informed by and been expansions of pan-Caribbean political projects as well as extra-Caribbean projects. It also shows that movements have been simultaneously located and organized in specific Caribbean countries and communities. For example, the 1930s and 1950s labor movements, as well as the 1970s independence/nationalism movements, which dotted many Caribbean countries (Knight and Palmer 1989), were pan-regional, reflecting a broad trend toward decolonization and independence as well as a crumbling plantation economy throughout the Caribbean. The movements grew and developed, then, in conversation with one another, yet they were always centered as individual projects (e.g., Jamaica's independence movement, Trinidad's Black Power movement, Guyana's Working People's Alliance movement, and so on). They were attached to individual nations, often invested in nation-building processes, and centered in particular areas of nations as workers and citizens pressed for specific changes in labor conditions and the creation of specific governmental formations "at home." Indeed, labor historian Nigel Bolland (2001) has argued that labor movements that appeared in one Caribbean locale tended to draw on the structure and arguments developed by movements in other parts of the region, given the migration of particular movement leaders and organizers throughout the region and beyond. At the same time, some individual movements that fit within wider regional movements and ideologies were decidedly national in their frame, rarely ever developing as pan-Caribbean movements decentered from particular nations and colonies.[12] Thus, even if notions of nationalism, black power, anticolonialism, and labor rights contextualized many intersecting Caribbean movements of the mid- to late twentieth century, organized political action sometimes has been place specific in terms of the way it has played out and the issues it has profiled relevant to particular nations and locales.

Caribbean people attached to banana industries also know globalization through their experiences within given places. Caribbean banana production has always been situated on plantations or small farms in rural areas typically considered "banana-producing regions" so designated due to the concentration of producers engaged in cultivating

bananas for export. In the eastern Caribbean, there exist numerous valleys—often former plantation regions as well as massive hillside settlements—where banana production has occurred on a relatively large
scale. Here connections to external markets are strong, but this is not the
only evidence of these banana-producing regions' connections to "elsewhere." Migration, tourist flows, indirect foreign finance, and mass
media all circulate through these areas. And, as a number of studies show
(Moberg 1997; Grossman 1998; Raynolds 1994a), banana production
sites interact with, interpret, negotiate, and redirect processes associated
with foreign markets and products. Yet, because the sites develop
specific cultural, political, social, and economic dynamics within a given
setting, we are reminded that the specifics of place matter in this global
context.

SITUATING ST. LUCIA & MORNE VERTE

However imagined (Anderson 1991), nations are sites of identity formation and cultural politics (Radcliffe 1993). St. Lucia officially became a
nation in 1979, although the formation of identities and other political
and social interactions on the island started during the long period of colonization that began in 1635 (Breen 1970). From this point, the island,
comprising 238 square miles (27 miles long and 14 miles wide) and
located in the Caribbean Sea, was a European colony. It was first occupied by the French, who several times battled the British over possession
of the territory. The succession of territorial conquests by the two European powers resulted in the island's exchange between them fourteen
times before a final British occupation resulted in 1814 (Breen 1970).
Thus, in the final analysis St. Lucia was a British colony, but the stamp of
France remained, as French nationals continued to reside on the island
and formed part of its local politics, economy, and culture.

The French role also included the decimation of the Carib Indians by
the middle of the seventeenth century; however, other non-European
groups were subsequently brought to St. Lucia. African slaves were
imported in the late eighteenth century (Breen 1970), and, like elsewhere
in the region, they worked on sugar plantations run by European planter
families. Following the emancipation of slaves in 1838, indentured servants from India were brought to St. Lucia to make up for some of the
loss of enslaved African labor (Joseph 2004). Thus, due to these various

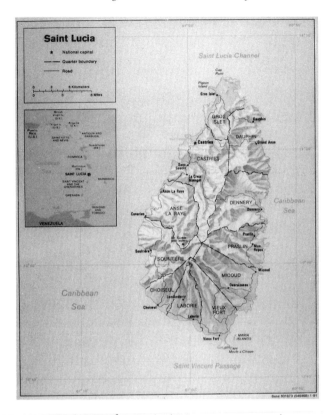

Fig. 1. Map of St. Lucia. (U.S. government map.)

migratory streams organized by the colonial project, St. Lucia was necessarily a British, French, African, and South Asian place.

In the 1940s, the United States also entered the island directly when it
set up a naval base that replaced the colony's southernmost plantation.
The American presence on the island also occurred following and during
earlier out-migration streams from different Caribbean territories to the
mainland United States and from U.S.-sponsored projects such as the
building of the Panama Canal (Richardson 1989, 1992; Kasinitz 1992).
Much later, the American presence on St. Lucia accelerated as tourism
from the United States became important to the island's late twentieth-
century experience, as was capital from U.S. corporate ventures and offshore finance industries (Maurer 2004).[13]

The legacies of the various populations and flows to St. Lucia were
important in shaping the relations around race, color, class, and nation of
the early 1990s, when the banana industry was enduring its newest pol-

icy shifts. First, the 1991 census showed a large "African"/"Negro"/ "Black" majority (87%) and far smaller populations of "East Indians," "Syrian"/"Lebanese," "Chinese," "Portuguese," and "Whites," who comprised as much as 3% of the population and as little as .01% (de Albuquerque and McElroy 1999: 8).[14] A group classified as "Mixed" represented 10% of St. Lucian residents, but this classification emerged only when racial self-identification was added to the 1991 census and might reflect an attempt by Afro- West Indians to raise their status through color identification (de Albuquerque and McElroy 1999). Chinese and Portuguese residents of St. Lucia in 1991 were relatively recent immigrants, as were some Indo-St. Lucians migrating from within the Caribbean to St. Lucia in the 1980s, whereas the other groups' presence grew out of the early migrations during colonialism.

In terms of occupational diversity by ethnicity, Chinese residents were employed in the Taiwanese agricultural missions and also as urban business owners; whites, Syrians/Lebanese, and Portuguese also formed the business elite working in the lucrative tourist industry and other retail industries; Indians or Indo-St. Lucians worked as "skilled craftsmen" (e.g., masons and carpenters) and in agriculture, most likely as large scale farm owners;[15] and the Afro-St. Lucian population, inclusive of the "mixed" population, had more of a bifurcated class status, with its elite entrepreneurial segment and its strong working class and rural peasant population (de Albuquerque and McElroy 1999). Whites, then, continued to form the wealthy elite, though through urban industries rather than ownership of plantations, while Afro-St. Lucians and Indo-St. Lucians took on a more diverse occupational and class position.

Along with race and occupation, social difference also has been marked by rural and urban designations. Geographically, rural and urban areas of St. Lucia are barely separated, sometimes distinguished by a matter of ten miles. Yet, socially, politically, and sometimes economically, they feel and are considered light years apart. From the colonial period, the island's capital, Castries, was the site of administrative development while the rural valleys were areas of significant economic ventures in agriculture (Breen 1970). Export agricultural production occurred on the valley's plantations, such as the one in Morne Verte, around which residential, social, and informal economic life was built (Breen 1970; Adrien 1996). Yet, by the late twentieth century, rural areas remained agricultural sites, but urban centers, especially Castries, had become areas for commercial development and residential life for the island's middle class and urban elite. It appears that whites, Chinese, and Portuguese tended not to live in the rural valleys, yet Afro-St. Lucians and Indo-St. Lucians resided in both urban and rural areas. People in rural areas such as Morne Verte sometimes acquired income that, economically, might have placed them among a middle class, but socially the rural connotation obviated against a rural resident being considered of the same status as an urban middle-class dweller.

Banana production fits into this rural-urban dichotomy. The rural-based Afro-St. Lucian and Indo-St. Lucian populations historically were attached to peasant banana production and/or wage labor on banana plantations, especially from the 1950s through the late 1970s. Indeed, by the early 1960s, at least half of banana export production was estimated to be led by smallholders, who increasingly became an important defining feature of production in rural valley life (Biggs, Bennett, and Leach 1963). Yet, during this time, the industry was also made up of urban administrators, who played a role on the board of the Castries-based SLBGA and who often hailed from St. Lucia's wealthier classes, larger-scale farming population, and/or political and economic elite (Welch 1996; Biggs, Bennett, and Leach 1963).[16] Therefore, through the industry, rural and urban sites both intersected and were distinctly demarcated. This was so even after the SLBGA board of directors shifted to include smaller growers because managerial positions in the association tended to be held by wealthier, middle class, and formally educated St. Lucians (Welch 1996; Biggs, Bennett, and Leach 1963). Occupation, class, and residency thus often distinguished most SLBGA administrators from the bulk of producers, but there was also overlap between the two. Obviously, both administrators and producers were attached to the SLBGA, but in some cases, administrators also possessed banana farms of their own. Further, the growth of the banana industry, especially from the 1970s on, led to what many saw as an economic and social improvement of rural areas as producers' incomes rose and they were better able to purchase new homes and vehicles. From this development, there was an active late twentieth-century discourse suggesting that the poverty associated with the rural valleys had significantly diminished and narrowed the gap between St. Lucia's social classes thanks to the banana industry.

Situated south of St. Lucia's capital in the eastern coastal district of Dennery, Morne Verte, is considered one of the places where these developments occurred. With a total population of 1,434 in 1991 (GOSL

1990), it was one of the largest banana-producing communities in the larger Mabouya Valley,[17] where one of St. Lucia's oldest large plantations also was located. The Dennery Estate was the first European-owned plantation to take up banana production after sugar production declined, and it was associated with St. Lucia's 1950s' push out of sugar into bananas. Since the estate dominated the most fertile and productive lands, it also was linked to problems of land scarcity for the majority of the area's non-European residents (Organization of American States 1991). Further, historically, ethnic/racial and class divisions in plantation and other forms of farm work, land distribution, residential life, and local social interactions marked people's experiences in the valley (Adrien 1996; Organization of American States 1991; Breen 1970). During the colonial period, the valley was seen as distinct and "lesser than" the urban areas (Breen 1970), while Afro-St. Lucians and Indo-St. Lucians existed on the margins in terms of their access to the bulk of the area's productive land base and their employment status within this context.

However, while social marginalization and social division defined the area, so, too, did the prospects and possibilities for improved class status among the non-European populations. After the slaves were emancipated, there was growth in the Afro-St. Lucian and Indo-St. Lucian peasant farming class, including in the Mabouya Valley (Adrien 1996; Joseph 2004). But the primacy of the plantation and its domination of land also shifted in the late nineteenth century and again in the mid-twentieth century, opening up land to smallholders for squatting and purchase (Meliczek 1975). Further, different land tenure systems such as forms of sharecropping created the prospects for economic growth among the community's socially and economically marginal populations (Adrien 1996). Here, small-scale farming was important and became a defining feature of Morne Verte and the larger Mabouya Valley (as it was in other plantation valleys). At the same time, in the mid-twentieth century, the valley's laboring population that worked on the plantations was active in worker protests, revealing itself as an active and vocal force for social and economic change through land acquisition, independent employment pursuits (e.g., peasant farming), and outward agitation (Jackson, Pounder, and Leacock 1957; Malone, Hagley, and Pearson 1952).

While the area's predominant Afro-St. Lucian and much smaller Indo-St. Lucian peasant populations were considered to have been mar-

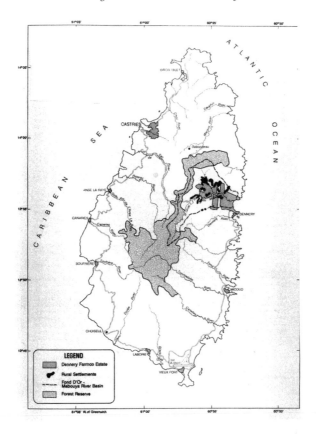

Figs. 2a and 2b. Map showing the Mabouya Valley. (Map by the Organization of American States.)

ginalized for centuries by the Dennery Estate's domination, many credited agriculture generally, and the banana industry specifically, with an improvement in the economic and social status of many of the valley's non-European residents. This was especially the case by the end of the twentieth century once the plantation sector became less prominent and small-scale farming increased. At the time of my research in 1993 and 1994, 67% of Morne Verte's working population worked as small-scale independent farmers and 81% of all households in the area had at least one resident who was a banana grower. Thirty-one percent of Morne Verte's working-age population held the status of banana producer (Slocum 1996: 84). At the same time, by 1991, 86% of Morne Verte residents owned their own homes and more than half (53%) owned the land on which their homes were built (Department of Statistics 1991). An overwhelming majority of the houses (66%) were built after 1970. Agri-

culture's prominence thus has often been considered to explain the relatively high incidence of property and home ownership in the area. This
coupling of the two—small-scale farming and property acquisition—
has helped define Morne Verte as an agricultural place, a banana-producing place, a rural peasant place, and a place of economic and social
growth all at once. As I will show in this book, definitions and meanings
of Morne Verte were important to how freedom became inserted into the
ways that free trade and broader neoliberal discourses were processed by
Morne Vertian banana growers.

OUTLINE OF THE BOOK

This book is divided into four parts, which emphasize the intersections
of global, regional, national, rural, and local processes and projects
within St. Lucia's banana industry. In part 1, "Neoliberalism Globally

and Nationally," I provide background on the debate that developed in the early 1990s over market liberalization policies and the global banana industry, and that initiated the link between St. Lucia's banana industry and neoliberal policies. This debate, discussed in chapter 2, took place before the General Agreement on Tariffs and Trade. It involved Latin American banana-producing nations, the European Union (EU, representing various European nations), and African, Pacific, and Caribbean banana-producing countries that were invested differently and contentiously in whether free trade should be applied liberally with respect to the trade of bananas to Europe. The chapter also illustrates the St. Lucian state's policies, which, in pushing growers to advance production for a more globally competitive industry, reinforced aspects of the neoliberal agenda.

In part 2, "Global Integration and the Local/Regional Valley," attention is on the insertion and negotiation of the neoliberal agenda in the Mabouya Valley area, especially in everyday life, and how producers confronted that agenda. Chapter 3 demonstrates how St. Lucian state representatives, who worked through the SLBGA, promoted production for liberalizing markets and meeting foreign consumer demands. This was conveyed overtly and subtly through regularized and structured interactions between association staff and valley banana growers. In chapter 4, I discuss how, despite the heavily regimented production practices, as set especially by the SLBGA, Morne Verte growers considered their work as a source of their own freedom. Looking at the conceptualizations and practices that beset this freedom of work discourse, as well as the nuances in the discourse according to growers' different social identities, I show how the discourse was a challenge to the conceptual foundations of the industry as it was organized for global market integration. I argue that the concept of freedom of work resonated with the history of the economy, society, and culture within the valley and the larger Afro- and Indo-Caribbean populations in the British West Indies.

Part 3, entitled "The Rural Nation," is meant to signal the ways in which the globalization discourse that operated in St. Lucia was challenged by the BSC movement, which brought St. Lucia's rural producing regions into the center of the nation. Chapter 5 discusses the history of the 1950s and 1970s agricultural movements in St. Lucia and points out that the question of a (possibly) independent St. Lucia and politics were at the center of the early protests that inserted rural agriculture into the nation-building process. The chapter situates the BSC's work within these earlier movements. In chapter 6, I focus on the work of the BSC, in particular the group's tactics for: rearranging conventional social uses of space in St. Lucia, which delineated a distinction and hierarchy of rural versus urban, and analyzing and reworking cultural and social categories and representations regarding producers and nonproducers/urban dwellers. My argument here is that the BSC's organizing and conceptualizing strategies disrupted conventions regarding the distinction and definition of rural versus urban sites in the nation. In so doing, the group reinforced the nation as a place and an important site for organizing for social and political change from the rural vantage point within a globalizing context.

In part 4 "Placing the Global," I conclude the book by emphasizing three major points. First, I underscore that, rather than becoming obsolete in the presence of global processes, local sites—places—are arenas around which people organize. Second, to return to my point about how and whether to measure movements' success and purpose, I emphasize how movements should be understood as formed around questions of both class and culture. Our purpose should be to ascertain under which conditions and how class or culture becomes more significant to the motivation and mobilization of a given movement's project. Third, I contend that we can see St. Lucian banana growers' efforts as part of an interplay between a globalization discourse and a counterdiscourse, the latter crafted by growers and invested in a political project of theorizing globalization in alternative ways.

Finally, chapter 8 is an epilogue that briefly discusses developments in the St. Lucia banana industry following the 1993–1994 period profiled in the book.

I. NEOLIBERALISM GLOBALLY & NATIONALLY

2. *Negotiating Neoliberalism*

GLOBALIZATION, NEOLIBERALISM, & DISCOURSES

*I*N MARCH OF 1999, five years after completing my year of doctoral research in St. Lucia, I gave a lecture at a U.S. university on the ways in which banana growers challenged globalization through their discourses on work, especially in 1993–94. By chance, during the same week as my lecture, news stories broke to announce that the United States was applying stiff tariffs on European imports. The move was cited as a response to the European Union's (EU) policy on banana trade that disadvantaged U.S. companies with banana holdings in Latin America and favored Caribbean nations by granting protected trade only to the latter. For a few short days, Caribbean bananas were part of headline news in the United States and Europe. The focus of most of the stories was not merely on how the tariffs would impact U.S. businesses that relied on the sale of European goods. It also concerned how the general U.S.-EU dispute over banana trade would affect small-scale banana producers in the Caribbean. Many of the stories profiled the plight of small-scale farmers who were cast as producers with few alternatives other than bananas. But, the stories also stressed that, despite these problems, freer trade (the kernel of the U.S.-EU dispute) was preferable and inevitable in a contemporary world. Indeed, while the word *neoliberalism* almost never appeared in the stories, conventional ideas about market liberalization as a form of globalization and an inevitability did.

That the stories broke on the eve of my lecture gave the presentation unexpected currency and probably helped draw in a crowd larger than usual. The overlap between the stories and my lecture was evident and made even clearer when an audience member, who happened to be from St. Lucia, pressed me about my argument that producers' forms of organizing work were compromised by new global production policies. "But," this person asked, "don't you agree that banana growers must comply with international market trends, or get out of the industry altogether, in order to survive and make Caribbean industries competitive." Spoken with urgency and frustration, his words reflected ideas similar to those underpinning the news stories. They were ideas about the necessity of a specific definition and meaning of economic globalization, where competition and liberalized markets are viewed as a given. They are ideas that I sought to analyze then and now.

As in the news stories and this individual's question, economic globalization is often paired with neoliberalism, which I take to refer to policies that promote laissez-faire economics and trade, expansion of exports, privatization, flexible production, and a reduction of the role and sovereignty of the nation-state.[1] One could call it a discourse, as geographer Philip Kelly (1999) and sociologist Saskia Sassen (1998) do, based not merely on the ideas and language that describe and conceptualize contemporary economic formations. It is also based on various institutions and forms of organizing economic activity that privilege, prioritize, or sanction market liberalization. Understood this way, forms of economic organizing—economies—are crafted and conceptualized out of institutional processes and through social and economic practices. Anthropologist Karl Polanyi (1944) made a similar point about earlier economies when he analyzed mid-twentieth-century European markets as planned projects produced by political organizations and states rather than as deregulated and natural. Looking at a more contemporary scene, Kelly (1999: 380) put it this way: the relatively recent expansion in the spatial organization and scale of activities that we associate with globalization has been "socially produced rather than [constituting an] absolute entity." In other words, when we pinpoint various and specific economic configurations as spanning the globe, we refer to processes that have been constructed, politically and socially, not to formations that developed "naturally" or merely through market forces, as Polanyi also pointed out.

If we agree with Polanyi that markets are necessarily regulated and with Kelly that globalization is created based on specific ideas about spatial and temporal organizing, we might ask how these dynamics emerged in the Caribbean banana trade problem that so often is described within a market liberalization framework. Indeed, developments in the Windward Islands banana industries during the 1990s drew broad attention among policymakers, economic analysts, and the media, who almost always couched such events as the U.S.-EU dispute or competition between Latin American and Caribbean banana-producing nations within markers of neoliberalism (Slocum 2003). The intersection of talk about global market dynamics, ideas about what characterized that change, and the set of practices and policies connected to the ideas made up this specific globalization discourse.[2]

Many overlapping and divergent perspectives contributed to the discourse, and, as we will see, they also charted out individual subdiscourses or alternatives to the overall neoliberal model of globalization applied to banana trade. For instance, the notion that neoliberal economics should motivate banana trade was upheld by many Latin American banana-producing nations (which were eventually backed by the United States). Arguing twice in 1993 before the General Agreement on Tariffs and Trade (GATT), the body established in 1947 to promote and regulate trade among member nations, these nations disagreed with the EU's policy to restrict trade from non-Caribbean countries and to grant preferential trade to Caribbean producers. At the same time, a decidedly *anti*-neoliberalist stance emerged from the Caribbean countries, which argued for maintaining trade preferences to assist their small island economies. Before GATT, all parties participated in a debate in which the fairness and feasibility of unfettered trade was hotly contested. Talking across divergent perspectives about the appropriateness of preferences within Latin American and Caribbean economic trade, participants in the debate were negotiating neoliberalism and engaging in the type of globalization discourse of which Kelly (1999) speaks.

CONTESTED PREFERENCES

Bananas have been of great, yet specific, significance within the worldwide trade of fruit. This is especially true with respect to export volume and value, corporate profit, the relationship of labor to foreign capital, and income provided to banana workers and producers. Studies show that high-volume exports destined for foreign markets became especially important during the late nineteenth century, emerging amid the initial interests and efforts of North American merchants and seamen who exported Caribbean bananas into the United States (Kepner 1936; Striffler and Moberg 2003). This was followed by the work of a U.S. entrepreneur, Minor C. Keith, who arrived in Costa Rica in the 1880s to help build a railroad. Granted land by the Costa Rican government as part of his contract terms, Keith eventually set up a banana plantation operated with Costa Rican and West Indian laborers. Not long after, he established the United Fruit Company (now well known as Chiquita Brands), which was incorporated in 1899 and worked in direct banana production and exporting (Kepner 1936; Purcell 1993). Keith's work thus was central to the crystallization of a long-standing banana export industry through which foreign capital, corporate profiteering, and Caribbean and Latin American labor were essential dynamics. That legacy spawned a global banana industry of wider proportion, marked by competition for international markets among various corporate actors who developed after United Fruit.[3] Production for domestic use and sale was indeed the most important means by which bananas were produced and marketed by the late twentieth century—a century after Keith's work began (Arias et al. 2003). Yet, the work of transnational corporations on banana plantations and through smallholders' own farms in Latin America, the Caribbean, and Africa remained extremely significant to the entry of bananas into North Atlantic markets. In fact, by the mid-1980s, bananas represented the highest volume and value of any fruit traded globally (Arias et al. 2003).

Laura Raynolds (2003) describes the organization of banana production in the Americas as linked to two different production and exporting systems arising out of divergent colonial histories: indirect colonial rule by the United States in Latin America and direct colonial rule by European powers in the Caribbean. In one system, which she terms "the Latin American/US system," production and distribution have been concentrated since the mid-twentieth century among three major corporations: United Fruit, Dole, and Del Monte. As part of a vertically integrated system, these three companies owned banana plantations across South America, Central America, and parts of the Caribbean (Jamaica and Cuba) and employed regional laborers to cultivate bananas that the companies then exported to the United States and, to a lesser extent, parts of Europe. The corporations were so inserted into the regions where they set up operations that they were known for having strong influences on local political formations throughout Latin America (Raynolds 2003; see also Striffler 2002). By contrast, "the Caribbean/European system" was organized through French and British colonial administrators, who incorporated peasant-led banana trade into their models of economic development for Europe through crop exports.[4] Supported by the British government, British shipping companies eventually became attached to the banana trade from Jamaica, Belize, Surinam, and the Windward Islands and, in some cases, engaged both in distribution and production after purchasing plantation lands on particular islands (see Trouillot 1988; and Slocum 1996). Their work was also channeled through local producer associations (e.g., the SLBGA) that helped organize peasant production of bananas and that were financially and legislatively backed by the colonial state. Thus, as Raynolds (2003) points out, the Caribbean/European system was decentralized, led by small-scale producers whose products were routed to Britain through a British company with support from the colonial state. This contrasts with the more vertically organized Latin American/U.S. system, wherein an influential corporate apparatus was the impetus and coordinator of banana production and trade from Central and South America, especially to the United States.

While export banana production extends across East Asia, Africa, Latin America, and the Caribbean, the role of Latin America (i.e., Central American and South American countries) cannot be understated, as 78% of total world bananas exported came from these regions between 1988 and 1995 (Arias et al. 2003: 8). This compares with 3% to 4% of total exports from Africa, 14% from Asia, and 4% from the Caribbean (8). Further, the major transnational corporations distributing the largest volume of banana exports were Chiquita International, Dole, and Del Monte, all of which are U.S. corporations whose primary activities were concentrated in Latin America, especially Costa Rica, Guatemala, Panama, and Honduras, as well as Ecuador and Colombia, between the late 1980s and the mid-1990s.[5] Most bananas controlled by these corporations and produced in Latin America were destined for the U.S. market, although Latin American nations also had secondary importing agreements with various countries in the European Union. Chiquita, Dole, and Del Monte competed for European markets against smaller banana-exporting companies, especially Fyffes International, Noboa, and Geest Industries. Geest channeled Windward Islands bananas into specific European markets where Caribbean countries had privileged access given their status as former colonies of Europe. In the pre-1993 arrangement, Latin American bananas handled by the three major distribution companies were exported to Germany, the Netherlands, Belgium, and Denmark while Caribbean bananas were destined for France and the United Kingdom.

Historical dimensions of different countries' positions within the world banana trade, the developing terms and contours of their trade patterns, also give the trade a particular and specific resonance. Indeed, during the forty years in which Windward Island countries sold bananas through their contract with Geest Industries, they were also linked to a protected trade agreement with the UK.[6] In part, that agreement was made possible in 1975 by an international accord known as the Lomé agreement. Upheld as a model of development for former and then existing colonies of Europe, the Lomé agreement promoted preferential market access through lowered tariffs and price stabilization for ACP territories that were trading commodities to specific European countries, particularly France, the UK, Spain, Italy, and Portugal (ACP-EU Council of Ministers 1979; Nurse and Sandiford 1995). Renewed in four- to six-year increments, Lomé granted preferential access and price advantages for bananas and other products exported from ACP countries and colonies to several EU countries, including France, the UK, Spain, Italy, and Portugal. Lomé contained trade terms for the specific commodities, including bananas, and the terms were addressed in the agreement's clause, Protocol 5, where it was stated that:[7]

> in respect of its banana exports to the Community markets, no ACP State shall be placed, as regards access to its traditional markets and its advantage in those markets, in a less favorable situation than in the past or at present. (ACP-EEC Council of Ministers 1992: 224)

Bananas from ACP suppliers thus had a privileged and guaranteed outlet in the EU, over suppliers from non-ACP countries, through the implementation of a licensing system that granted licenses differentially to ACP and non-ACP banana-producing nations (Sutton 1997; Nurse and Sandiford 1995).

Protocol 5, also known as "The Banana Protocol," and the differential positioning of ACP and non-ACP countries within the EU's consumer market were at the heart of the banana dispute in the 1990s. At the fourth renewal of the Lomé accord in 1990, a problem was raised regarding Lomé's fit with efforts to create a Single European Market in Europe in 1992, as well as broader global trends for free trade (Sutton 1997). The dilemma concerned whether to maintain trade protection for ACP banana-supplying countries when suppliers from elsewhere (particularly Latin American) had trade relationships with EU countries that did not participate in Lomé but would participate in the SEM. Thus, maintaining Lomé would have meant applying and maintaining different trade terms for different (ACP and non-ACP) banana-supplier countries. Yet this contradicted the goals of a unified European market as well as the terms of the General Agreement on Tariffs and Trade, to which EU, Latin American, and ACP member states belonged.

Debating Discrimination before the GATT

The EU's consolidation of various national importing and exporting regimes into a single EU regime opened the way for non-ACP producer nations to argue against some of the national policies permitting trade preferences that would be integrated into the EU's trade arrangement. This argument played out at first when, appearing before GATT panels in April 1993 and again in October 1993, Venezuela, Colombia, Costa Rica, Guatemala, and Nicaragua collectively challenged the EU's trade policies. They contended that the policies were inconsistent with the GATT's terms because trade preferences discriminated against different suppliers. Also represented in a much reduced capacity at the hearings were "third contracting parties" such as ACP suppliers and other non-Latin American countries with investments in world banana production, importing, and exporting.[8]

Based on the arguments brought by the participating parties, the GATT panels signaled broad conflicts over forging a uniform trade policy out of an import-export system that previously had been bifurcated and, in many ways, managed by individual European nations for decades. Specifically, Latin American complainants, who for decades had found outlets for their banana exports within individual European countries, were threatened with having to compete with ACP suppliers. Yet that treatment would have been extended to the entire EU rather than solely for the UK and France, as in the past, leading to open objections from Latin American countries.

GATT Panel I

At the first GATT panel meetings, held in April 1993, Latin American complainants charged importing discrimination while the EU held that discrimination was permissible under a variety of legal and historical conditions. One lobbied for freer trade while the other contended that mitigating factors justified a restrictive trade regime. Specifically, the Latin American side charged that the EU's import policies ran counter to the GATT by: (1) restricting imports through applying quotas and tariffs to non-ACP banana suppliers, (2) providing tariff preferences to ACP suppliers, and (3) permitting disproportionate supplies of bananas into EU markets for domestic vis-à-vis nondomestic suppliers. These policies, they argued, discriminated against non-ACP banana-producing nations by offering differential import policies to different suppliers in ways that reduced imports to the EU and thus violated the GATT's policies. In its response, the EU claimed that discriminatory restrictions were justified because it needed to "protect the economic interests of suppliers" with whom [EU member nations] had a historical relationship and because legislation within individual EU nations that predated the GATT granted preferential market access to specific non-EU nations or European domestic suppliers (GATT 1993: 20). Further, the EU contended that, through Lomé, it had created a free trade area between the EU and the ACP and also that the GATT allowed for preferential treatment to "less developed countries." Following up on this latter point, the EU argued that ACP nations held a disadvantaged position vis-à-vis Latin American countries, noting especially the gap in material conditions of production available to the former over the latter. The panel noted:

> The EEC [EU][9] replied that . . . [t]he ACP bananas were, generally speaking, smaller in size than the Latin American bananas. Banana plantations in ACP countries were in most cases small and run on a family basis. In many cases, these plantations were cultivated on volcanic soil which did not lend itself to large plantations. The bananas were harvested by hand and grown in a way respecting the environment. Latin American bananas usually came from very large plantations often run by a small number of multinational companies. Their bananas were mostly cultivated on an industrial scale. This meant that Latin American bananas could be produced at substantially lower cost. . . . ACP bananas were, generally speaking, 1.5 to 2 times more expensive than Latin American bananas. ACP bananas, therefore, were only able to penetrate markets where they were protected against unlimited competition from Latin American bananas. (GATT 1993: 56)

Consequently, while arguing that it did not violate the GATT rules regarding discriminatory policies, the EU held that differential policies were in some instances justified.

Such a position was upheld by Jamaica, which gave witness within responses from "third countries." These responses included comments from nations not associated formally with either the complainants or the EU but that nonetheless had interests in banana trade. Jamaica was the sole Caribbean nation arguing before the panel, although in their assertions Jamaican representatives referenced Windward Islands producers a few times as if the total group of Caribbean banana-producer nations needed to be understood together. Like the EU, Jamaica focused on the legislation and the import regimes that predated the GATT and that, for the purposes of anglophone Caribbean nations, were mandated by UK law. And, like the EU, Jamaica justified upholding EU policy because, under the Lomé agreement, the ACP-EU trade arrangement constituted a free trade area, something over which the GATT had no jurisdiction and could not undo. Jamaica further contended that the GATT had no legal authority over Lomé and thus could not annul arrangements under that agreement. Finally, Jamaica appealed to the developing country status of many of the Caribbean and even other ACP nations, arguing that preferential and differential treatment for such nations was permissible under specific GATT clauses.

Yet, despite Jamaica's position and that of the EU, Panel I ruled in favor of the Latin American complainants, contending in general that its importing systems involved quantitative restrictions, tariff preferences, and domestic production-importing disproportionality that disadvantaged various banana-producing nations and that did not comply with GATT. It disagreed that the importing regimes of individual EU member nations, including the Lomé agreement, were justifiable within GATT's clauses regarding "existing legislation." This was because, Panel I held, importing policies that allowed market preferences and had been adopted in France, Italy, Portugal, Spain, and the UK "were not based on mandatory legislation" (GATT 1993: 78). Thus, the panel contended that it was not required to consider whether legislation in individual EU nations preceded the formation of the GATT. As a result, the panel *recommended* that Latin American complainants request that the EU comply with the GATT, giving support to the Latin American position without requiring that the EU adopt any specific corrective measures. This allowed the EU to avoid adopting the panel's recommendations, although the EU did revise its importing regimes in ways that opened up trade to non-ACP nations and that reduced the extent of trade preferences to the EU's ACP suppliers.

GATT Panel II

In response to the conflicts that developed through the first GATT panel, the EU set up the New Banana Regime (NBR) in 1993. The NBR honored trade preferences with the ACP suppliers while placing quotas on their imports and requiring that ACP suppliers hold licenses to trade particular quantities of bananas with the EU (Nurse and Sandiford 1995). Still, the NBR did not satisfy complainants to Panel I. It addressed some of the conflicting interests between Lomé and the SEM by limiting ACP imports through quotas and a licensing system; however, because different importing regimes for non-ACP and ACP suppliers persisted (e.g., banana import quotas applied to ACP countries were relatively higher than those for non-ACP suppliers), it did not satisfy concerns from Latin America about discrimination (Nurse and Sandiford 1995; Josling 2003; Grossman 1998). Thus, dissatisfaction with the NBR as a broad policy led to the convening of Panel II before the GATT.

Latin American complainants requested that Panel II, find the EU policy inconsistent with the GATT's articles pertaining to fairness or discrimination in importing restrictions and allowances. Their major complaints referred to applying: tariff concessions in nonuniform ways across suppliers; preferential tariff treatment allowing one set of suppliers to export bananas duty free while others were assessed tariffs; subsidies to EU producers; and quantitative restrictions on imports that came in the way of quotas, licenses, or pricing mechanisms, especially in discriminatory ways.

As in Panel I, the EU defended its quantitative restrictions and differential pricing policies—its preferential treatment practices—by citing the Lomé agreement and Protocol 5 as "part of the EU's heritage" (GATT 1994: 3) and by appealing to its obligation to fulfill the terms of Lomé, on which ACP supplier countries relied. Such a set-up, the EU contended, was provided for by GATT, whose articles permitted preferential systems for member nation's dependencies. The EU also added that preferential treatment was:

> known to GATT contracting parties particularly because the granting of these preferences occupied a prominent place in the Treaty of

Rome by a GATT working party. The preferential treatment of ACP counties was essential for the EEC for political, economic, and legal reasons. The EEC market was for all practical purposes the only viable outlet for ACP-bananas, while Latin American bananas were exported to many other destinations. ACP bananas would be completely eliminated from the EEC market by the highly competitive Latin American bananas, if the EEC did not grant preferential treatment to ACP-bananas. This could also lead to a total collapse of the economy of certain ACP countries. (GATT 1994: 13–14)

Thus, in some of its argumentation on Panel II, the EU took more of a social and economic position in defense of its policies, something it had tempered in earlier deliberations. Yet, this position was met with resistance by Latin American producers, who held that GATT did not "account for any 'special historical, cultural, or socioeconomic circumstances' offered by [a] contracting party" (GATT 1994: 14)

Sounding the EU's emphasis, "third-country responses" from the Caribbean this time included not only Jamaica but also all four Windward Islands, Surinam, and Belize. Caribbean countries' statements at the panel focused in part on their own disadvantages, especially relative to Latin American producers. They began by referencing the same social and economic argument that had been raised by the EU. Underscoring Caribbean *producers'* "dependency on bananas for the survival of much or most of *the economy*" (GATT 1994: 36), they stressed the importance of the industry at both an individual and a national level. Like the EU, they also highlighted the historic trade relationship that they held with European importing nations through Lomé. The benefits accruing from that relationship were based on Caribbean nations' status as dependencies. Indeed, the GATT articles, they claimed, allowed for differential and favorable treatment of developing countries—a status held by many Caribbean banana-producing nations. Third-party respondents from the Caribbean followed up by underscoring their own dependency on bananas. They differentiated themselves from Latin American producers, who, they contended, held a significant share of the EU market for bananas and who were not faced with the special economic needs of Caribbean banana producers. Thus, the argument for trade preferences here addressed the dual dependency of Caribbean nations (dependency on Europe and dependency on bananas) and the absence of such vulnerability among competitor producers from Latin America.

These arguments notwithstanding, the panel ruled against the EU again, acknowledging social and economic considerations but stressing that its role was to interpret policy strictly within the legal parameters of the GATT. It concluded that tariff quota imports adopted by the EU, the duties levied on imports by the EU, preferential tariff rates on bananas afforded to ACP suppliers by the EU, and the differential allocation of import licenses by the EU to its suppliers were not compliant with GATT. And, while this conclusion came with a recommendation that the complainants request the EU "to bring its tariffs on bananas and the allocation of tariff quota licenses into conformity with its obligations under [GATT]" (GATT 1994: 55), it was clear that the final ruling privileged open markets over mitigating social and economic considerations.

Meanwhile, the Banana Framework Agreement (BFA) was established in 1994 as an agreement between the EU and four of the Latin American countries that had brought complaints before the GATT. It was a measure that the EU put forth in response to the issues raised during the GATT panel discussions. The agreement retained banana trade preferences in the EU for former ACP colonies of EU nations in France and the UK. However, it also allowed for higher quotas of bananas to be imported into the EU from the four signatories to the BFA. These four nations' quotas were greater than for those non-ACP nations to which the NBR still applied. However, objections to this plan arose when, for instance, Ecuador and Panama claimed that they were disadvantaged by the BFA, which excluded them, and when Venezuela and Nicaragua's quota levels were not set as high as Colombia's and Costa Rica's (Brenes and Madrigal 2003). The BFA also marked the formal involvement of the United States in the dispute over the EU banana trade policy, as well as claims regarding corporate rights. This occurred when the United States charged that the framework agreement's policy for import licenses discriminated against Chiquita Brands by allowing more licenses to European companies that traded bananas from ACP countries (see USEU 1996).

Taken together, the arguments described here show how the globalization of bananas within the context of EU integration raised questions about whether to privilege an integrated economy where all were subject to the same terms or whether national regimes built on individual circumstances could prevail. The arguments were, more simply, a wrangle over how far to extend neoliberalism and to whom. Indeed, focusing on their status as dependencies and their disadvantage as developing nations, the Caribbean countries held a position that neoliberal principles needed to be tempered, while the Latin American nations pushed for unfettered trade regardless of prior history and socio-economic standing.

BANANAS LOCALLY FIXED & GLOBALLY CONNECTED

The Caribbean often has been understood as an economically vulnerable area precisely due to its countries' tendencies to produce no more than two main exports as well as its open economies and high degree of trade dependence. Further support of this idea is that imports to individual countries tend to represent a greater proportion of exports (Deere et al. 1990). Jamaican economist George Beckford (1972) considered the Caribbean (and other plantation regions) to have been in "persistent poverty" or underdevelopment based on its historical plantation economy, which promoted trade dependency between Caribbean plantations and the European metropole. That relationship, Beckford contended, led to the underdevelopment of national economies, a scarcity of employment opportunities, and social and economic stratification. Others have contended that the Caribbean's economic and social vulnerability can be understood through the ways that, since colonialism, the North Atlantic has always approached the region with a view toward consuming its resources, inclusive of its material goods but also its people through tourism (Sheller 2003). Thus, in part, the Caribbean's economic and social vulnerability has been traced to the colonial legacy that imprinted an enduring focus on siphoning off local resources for external use.

In the 1990s, a similar pattern of economic dependency and social and economic vulnerability was in place in St. Lucia. The island's economy was centered in two primary sectors, tourism and agriculture, both of which brought in revenue through attachments to overseas consumer markets in Europe, the United States, and Canada. Banana exports sold to Europe were part of these attachments, as were export products such as cocoa, coconut (or its by-product, copra), and a variety of other vegetable and fruit products (Ministry of Finance, Statistics and Negotiating

1993). However, the banana industry represented St. Lucia's primary export product. Returns from international banana sales in 1990 contributed up to 13% of the country's gross domestic product (GDP) and served as an important employment source for agricultural producers, farm laborers, and others working in sectors (e.g., transportation) linked to the industry (Caribbean Development Bank, cited in Kairi Consultants and Agrocon Ltd. 1993: 17–18;[10] U.S. Department of State 1994: 1, 3).[11] Among banana producers, approximately eight to ten thousand were self-employed in the industry throughout the late 1980s to early 1990s (St. Lucia Banana Growers Association files, 1991–93; Yankey et al. 1990: 3, 159).

Based on its organization around export-oriented production and distribution in the twentieth century, the banana industry was part of a contemporary global arrangement. Yet, it also emerged out of colonial interests and political and economic objectives dating back to the eighteenth century. From the early part of the twentieth century, the banana industry was set up around two significant and seemingly divergent (yet connected) concepts: the global contextualization and the local fixity of production. Concerning the former, Britain especially inserted itself into the possibilities and practices for organizing the industry in two important ways. First, the industry was constructed around events and dynamics in Europe with a constant sense of industry uncertainty. In a popular sense, this notion of uncertainty was accentuated through an unseen and unpredictable entity: the British consumer, specifically, "the British housewife." Often signaled in official and popular discourse, "the British Housewife" was emblematic of distant tastes and preferences that shaped, perhaps dictated, the possibilities for long-term and short-range sale of West Indian bananas.[12] Her image circulated publicly and pervaded rural West Indian homes when banana growers were reminded by SLBGA and other state representatives about the importance of satisfying foreign consumers, in particular the person presumed to be most responsible for feeding British citizens. Second, industry officials relied on a British buyer, Geest Industries, whose role was not only to purchase St. Lucian bananas but also to supply St. Lucia and other Windward Islands with critical information regarding consumer demand and pricing for bananas. This meant that, when devising policy, institutional representatives within the local industry attended strongly to information and recommendations regarding European market shifts supplied by Geest, a transnational corporation (Trouillot 1988).[13]

But, banana producers and state officials working in the industry simultaneously operated around the notion of a "guaranteed market," an idea that banana production in St. Lucia was unstoppable due to a long-standing trade policy with Europe. Interestingly, the global context fueled this outlook. The presence of a steady British buyer (secured through a long-term contract) and the existing UK market officially set up for an unlimited supply of Windward Islands bananas, enhanced the sense of an unending outlet for bananas. Comparatively, local policy tended to downplay diversifying into other crops or economic sectors and instead promoted a very extensive institutional and state apparatus organized around regularly, quickly, and effectively producing St. Lucian bananas for Europe. Banana industry policies in the country, as we will see, tied banana production to the island's social and economic landscape in ways that rendered it integral and affixed to everyday life. Consequently, the industry was run under an assumption about banana trade as a fixed and long-term activity, but it also was set up to engage with and respond to admittedly unpredictable external institutions, individuals, and developments related to supply and demand. The very state actors who made the industry a transnational and global activity subject to constant transformation and uncertainty and who publicly conveyed a message about foreign market unpredictability also were invested heavily in shaping the industry as a locally unshakable fixture. This prompted tension around coordinating the two issues of local fixity and global uncertainty once the industry's long-range status was in jeopardy.

From its inception, the industry was charted through the intersection of foreign markets and foreign capital and the St. Lucian colonial government or (later) the independent St. Lucian state. Indeed, the first banana growers' association created on the island in 1926 was set up by the Imperial Economic Commission of the colonial government (Welch 1996). By the 1930s, small-scale farmers were growing bananas for Canadian and U.S. markets, as they held long- term contracts with various North American shipping companies (Biggs, Bennett, and Leach 1963; see also Trouillot 1988). Growers' work and contract terms were coordinated through the St. Lucian Banana Association (SLBA), a local statutory organization whose primary role was to work with banana dealers who purchased bananas from St. Lucian banana producers (Welch 1996).

Colonial administrators took on an even larger role and interest in coordinating banana production when the sugar industry experienced severe economic decline. Established in the late eighteenth century, sugar production had been St. Lucia's major export industry that predominated on the country's major estates and smaller estates as well. Thus, when world demand and prices for West Indian sugar dropped first in the late nineteenth century, St. Lucian planters began leaving plantation life behind (United Kingdom 1897).[14] Their withdrawal from production continued gradually for over four decades until the 1950s, when the sugar industry was in virtual collapse. At the same time, colonial administrators began looking to peasant farming to bolster the ailing colonial economy and absorb the large labor force previously applied to sugar plantations. The colonial state supplied peasants with funding and technical assistance for banana production and thereby became involved more directly in managing peasant production as well as organizing peasant associations such as the SLBA (Development and Welfare Organisation of the West Indies 1951).[15]

Yet, by the 1950s, private and foreign capital played a more direct role in the St. Lucian banana industry. The SLBA was turned into a private company in 1953 and became the St. Lucia Banana Growers' Association Ltd. (SLBGA Ltd.) (Biggs, Bennett, and Leach 1963),[16] a company operated by shareholders (Welch 1996). This turn toward privatization grew out of two events: a developing concern about government control of the industry among large growers, who dominated the association's board of directors, and the recommendations of a colonial "expert team" investigating ways to improve the island's economy amid a downturn in sugar production (Biggs, Bennett, and Leach 1963; Welch 1996). Because of this and the island's unstable economy, the team called for adopting an institutional model similar to a successful one in Jamaica that could be applied to managing banana exports in St. Lucia. The goal of the transformed association was also for it to work more directly with producers by supporting their economic interests, representing them in contract arrangements, and developing research on banana production (Welch 1996: 150).

Along with this development, in 1954 a British shipping company known as Geest Industries came along. Geest had long-standing ties to agricultural production and distribution in the region, and in St. Lucia the company entered into a ten-year contract with the SLBGA Ltd.[17] The agreement was for the SLBGA Ltd. to sell bananas to Geest on a weekly basis and for growers to receive monetary incentives for adhering to Geest's fruit packaging recommendations (Biggs, Bennett, and Leach 1963: 25–27).[18] Banana producers working under contract through the SLBGA Ltd. thus could sell their goods regularly, receive a steady income, and obtain other financial benefits for complying with the transnational's specifications (Haarer 1963: 35), marking a shift that brought new possibilities for sustained production. As shown in table 1, the economic and social incentives provided by Geest, as well as the prolonged arrangement for distributing St. Lucian bananas through the company, coincided with a staggering rise in small-scale producers' investment in banana exports, suggesting a link between Geest's presence and the sharp growth of the industry. The simultaneous decline in

TABLE 1.   St. Lucia Banana Exports, 1925–60

Year	Number of Stems (or equivalent)
1925	20,818
1935	40,000
1936	90,000
1937[a]	110,000
1938	140,000
1939	70,000
1940	65,000
1941	50,000
1942	5,000
1947	1,511
1948	1,853
1950	20,862
1951	10,000
1952	38,000
1953	130,000
1954	295,000
1955	445,687
1956	783,950
1957	953,000

Sources: "Rise of the banana industry . . ." 1955 (figures are approximate based on chart data); Geest Industries Ltd. 1959–60: 40; Development and Welfare Organization of the West Indies 1951; West Indies 1951–52.

[a]Two sources ("Rise of the banana industry. . ." 1955, and Development and Welfare Organization of the West Indies 1951) report conflicting data for 1937. The Development and Welfare Organization of the West Indies reported 127,000 stems of bananas.

the island's sugar industry also fed into this shift, as peasants cultivating and selling sugarcane to island plantations were making obvious turns toward small-scale banana production and away from sugar once returns from sugar sales dropped off significantly (GOSL 1960).[19] Along with this, Geest's role as a continual distribution link to the UK market provided an outlet for peasants' bananas and thus helped usher in the sharp and vast turn toward production of this crop as a mainstay of the local economy.

The growth in banana exports corresponded to a historic transition in the plantation-peasant dynamic in St. Lucia. During the peak of plantation sugar, production was led by estates operated with approximately three thousand core laborers (United Kingdom 1897: 116) and supplemented with input from peasants who were known as *contributors* because they grew sugarcane and contributed or sold it to plantations. In this historic and common arrangement, plantations were set up on the most fertile lands and produced the bulk of sugar exported from the islands while peasant contributors relied on plantations as an outlet for their product (sugarcane) and worked on marginal lands (Breen 1844; Adrien 1996; Acosta and Casimir 1985). Yet, ten to fifteen years after Geest arrived and purchased two of St. Lucia's ailing plantations, a major shift occurred. The bulk of cultivable land remained in the hands of large plantation owners on the island's three major estates, but the place of smallholders in the industry was also significant. For example, landholdings attest to the predominance of small growers once bananas took hold. According to the 1973–74 census data, 88% of holdings were under ten acres (Ministry of Agriculture 1973–74: 15), rising only slightly from 85% in 1946 (Central Bureau of Statistics 1946: 35). But, the total number of holdings had increased drastically from just over five thousand in 1946 to over ten thousand in 1973–74 (Ministry of Agriculture 1973–74: 15), reflecting the increase in small-scale producers over time. For peasant growers, however, the novelty was not that they outnumbered large-scale producers; it was that they were at the forefront of the industry and that they also could finally work independently of the estates (Acosta and Casimir 1985: 51).

As the role of large plantations was eroding during this period other dynamics were developing. By the 1960s, most plantation owners had converted their fields to bananas, and by the next decade they had moved out of direct production altogether. Owners of St. Lucia's three largest estates, including Geest, which owned two, sold part of their privately owned operations to the St. Lucian state and turned their plantations into ventures run both with state and private funds in the 1970s (National Development Corporation 1987; Severin 1989). This period marked an important transition in the island's agricultural industries: it moved them away from the plantation structure after which most West Indian economies were modeled for centuries, and it also moved them toward production coordinated by the state and foreign capital while led primarily by small-scale producers.

Further, in the 1960s, both plantation and peasant proprietors continued to work side by side, depending on the same primary crop and selling via the banana growers' association to the same international agent. Yet, of the 10,000 registered banana growers in place at this point (Biggs, Bennett, and Leach 1963: 11), small-scale producers contributed more bananas to the total output than did their large grower counterparts. Figures from the next decade show that of the approximately 6,300 growers registered in 1978, more than 89% were classified as "under small," a category designating those whose production level was below five hundred pounds per week and who, because of their low production level, did not hold rights within the SLBGA that "small," "medium," and "large" growers held (Yankey et al. 1990). By contrast, medium and large banana farmers, who grew no less than fourteen hundred pounds per weekly average, represented .6% of the farming population (GOSL 1980: 28).

Small-scale producers farmed on lands that they owned or rented or to which they had usufruct rights (e.g., through communal inheritance or "family land" arrangements or the *métayage* arrangement, which, like sharecropping, granted a tenant access to land in exchange for a portion of the returns from his or her crop sales).[20] However, also included among smallholders in the 1970s were those who farmed on former plantation lands owned by a company formed through state and private funds. The lands were subdivided into small plots and leased to individual producers, whose activities were steered by company representatives. This followed a popular Caribbean model of integrated land settlement schemes where production was led by smallholders after the companies leased lands to former plantation workers and independent farmers with the goal of "transforming worker/farmers into owners and operators of commercialized property" (Crichlow 1997: 4). In the western plantation town of Roseau, for instance, small farmers leased lands from St. Lucia Model Farms Ltd., a company formed in 1982 that was owned by Geest Industries, the St. Lucian government, and the Commonwealth Development Corporation. By 1987, over one hundred small farmers had entered into leasehold agreements with an option to purchase their parcels after fifteen years (National Development Corporation 1987: 2). A similar pattern also occurred in the Dennery Valley with the creation of Dennery Farmco, a state and private company that leased plots to small farmers in the Dennery district. Producers *for* Model Farms were required to cultivate pure-stands of bananas on the five-acre plots in the valley flats or diversified tree crop cultivation on ten-acre plots on hillside lands (National Development Corporation 1987: 3). Leaseholders with Model Farms or Farmco also were required to employ farm techniques and maintain specific crop mixtures specified and monitored by the company. In this way, production on large plantations was transformed into smaller operations that remained centralized, organized by foreign capital and overseen by state representatives attached to Model Farms or Farmco. Such a shift was important, for it signaled an emerging trend of linking peasant production to the state apparatus in more detailed, everyday ways than existed during the early work of the SLBA and the SLBGA Ltd.

In 1967, SLBGA Ltd. was succeeded by the SLBGA, marking a major institutional transition that legally engendered a role for the state in banana production. The immediate prelude to this shift was an official inquiry into the industry that was undertaken when, in 1958, discord among large and small grower representatives almost led to the overthrow of the board of directors (Biggs, Bennett, and Leach 1963; Welch 1996). This tension, occuring during St. Lucia's decolonization period when internal self-government over more direct colonial rule was on the rise, marked the beginning of overt political concerns within the association. A large grower-led SLBGA Ltd. had caused some to fear that a particular political orientation would dominate the organization given the common political affiliations of the businessmen and large-scale farmers who controlled the association's board of directors (Welch 1996). To stem these conflicts, the commission recommended that "[g]overnment should have powers to intervene in the affairs of the industry in certain circumstances." It also recommended that affiliates of political parties be barred from sitting on the board (Biggs, Bennett, and Leach 1963: 7). This laid the groundwork for more formal means of government intervention into the industry simultaneous with a push to separate activist party politics from industry organizing. Large-scale (plantation) growers had wanted such a change but small-scale growers, who were supported and often mobilized by trade unionist political representatives, did not. Indeed, the policy shift meant that there was an attempt to integrate (small) growers' work with the work of the colonial state while separating out the swelling political scene from the formalization of banana production structures.[21]

The emerging setup illustrated how independent producers were not truly independent because, like most contract *laborers*, the terms for their work were not of their own making.[22] This was true for those in integrated land settlement schemes such as Model Farms and for those who cultivated bananas, on their own, outside of the schemes. The work of both sets of producers was overseen by a state or quasi-state institution as a result of the formal structure of the industry. However, the contract between Geest Industries and the SLBGA also helped secure this arrangement whereby the state had a prominent role in production and producers were not independent. For it was in this contract that the responsibilities of the association and Geest were laid out, including the SLBGA's obligation to work with no other buyer and to provide Geest with bananas on the days, of the quality, and at the price that Geest designated. To fulfill its contractual obligations, the SLBGA had to ensure that an acceptable product was delivered to the company in a specified time frame, and the coordination of state legislation alongside SLBGA operations toward meeting this mandate rendered all producers pseudo independent. Put more directly, banana growers could not produce and sell their product by terms of their own choosing due to the contractual agreement (a point that Michel-Rolph Trouillot [1988] has emphasized) and the mobilization of certain state resources around that agreement. The contract clearly gave Geest greater leeway than the SLBGA for deciding how and when bananas would be grown and distributed, but SLBGA administrators who represented growers were part of the negotiation with Geest and they were instrumental in organizing producers' daily working lives to ensure that the contract terms were met.[23] It was the role of the SLBGA in advancing this schedule of daily production toward meeting the requirements of a "one transnational buyer" agreement that rendered banana production fixed specifically in the local, everyday economy but also set up for a global market context.

As the law that guided the important SLBGA, the 1967 Banana Growers' Association Act linked growers inextricably to the SLBGA and consequently to the contract with Geest. The act defined growers' major rights and responsibilities as well as the roles of the association's board of directors and managers. It declared that all producers in the country wishing to sell bananas *must* belong to the SLBGA, sell their bananas to that body, and follow the association's production guidelines, under penalty of law.

> No bananas shall be exported from the State [of St. Lucia] or bought for the purpose of being used in or for any manufactured product except by the Association [SLBGA] or some person who purchases from the Association under a contract on that behalf. . . If any person exports bananas from the State or in any way acts in contravention of this section, he shall be guilty of an offence and liable on summary conviction to a fine not exceeding three hundred dollars or to imprisonment for a term not exceeding six months. (St. Lucia Banana Growers' Association Act, 1967, clauses 7[2]; 7[4])

Thus, growers were severely restricted in how they could dispose of their own product and, for that purpose, were necessarily and legally tied to the association to unload their crop. The restrictions were due in part to the contracts one-buyer clause but also due to the structure of the SLBGA, which permitted only a limited role for banana growers to chart their own production. Indeed, the act was revised several times, especially during the late 1980s into the 1990s, and at each of these moments a larger role for government input into association planning and structuring was secured.[24]

For instance, following a formal investigation of the industry in the 1980s several recommendations were offered, including that government and government representatives hold greater power in the association (GOSL 1980). Thus, in 1988, the Minister of Agriculture was designated as the sole person able to dissolve and reassemble the board of directors at his discretion and to postpone the date of the Annual Conference of Delegates, a meeting for policy decisions led by farmer-members of the SLBGA who growers elected to represent their districts. The minister also was permitted to appoint a larger number of members to the board than those elected by growers. Persons appointed were those whom the *minister* considered qualified in "the subject of agriculture, banking, trade, finance, business management and accountancy and *other related subjects*" (GOSL 1967: 15, emphasis mine). Further, even though they were justified economically, changes to the act also can be seen as political maneuvers because with each amendment political representation within the association shifted. Before the 1988 amendments, the elected board was represented overwhelmingly by the then opposition party, the St. Lucian Labour Party (SLP), yet after amendments and a newfound role for the Minister of Agriculture the SLP's position was replaced by an interim board made up of supporters of the reigning United Workers' Party (UWP).

This late 1980s trend of reducing the grower's role in defining and steering production also emerged through the 1986 Banana Protection and Quality Control Act (popularly known as the "Banana Act"), another legal provision governing industry operations. The Banana Act was the domain of the Windward Island Banana Growers' Association (WINBAN), an institution that represented all of the Windward Islands and that was charged with conducting research and development for the region's banana industries. WINBAN was responsible for the terms outlined in the Banana Act, which itemized production methods that growers had to follow in order to produce and maintain quality bananas. In great detail, the act laid out the required methods for packing and transporting bananas (GOSL 1986).[25] In all instances, procedures were outlined to demonstrate the steps necessary to render a banana salable, and to reference the threat of rejection were procedures not followed. An example relates to the Banana Act's discussion of "rejectable cartons," which spelled out the steps a grower had to perform in order for his or her bananas to be eligible for purchase.

> A carton of bananas is rejectable after inspection at a boxing plant or at a reception depot: . . . b) if the lining packing material is absent, of the wrong type, dirty, discoloured, insufficient, excessive, or wrongly placed; c) if it is underweight, that is, if the contents of the standard carton weigh less than that prescribed by the Authority [WINBAN], . . . e) if it is crushed, badly mis-shapen, excessively bulging, wet, or with the divider badly placed. (GOSL 1986: 30)

This level of detail outlined in state legislation—beyond the act that guides the SLBGA—illustrates the extent to which the state apparatus served to affix banana production nationally and globally. For, here, the Banana Act prohibited conduct that would have jeopardized rendering bananas available to Geest. Moreover, by crafting the act and designating a local "Authority" to enforce it, the state was the monitor of growers' compliance with specific production and postharvest production methods deemed necessary to meet contractual terms. This was evident since WINBAN was appointed *by the state* as the "lawful Authority" to inspect farmers' practices. Of course, an important point here is that WINBAN was partially funded by Geest (Welch 1996) and operated off of market information supplied by Geest (Trouillot 1988). Thus, Geest could continue to shape the direction of the island's production through the contract but also through a regional institution—placed in direct contact with production activities—with which Geest had deep ties. The outcome of this setup was that the company, the state, and a regional quasi-state/quasi-corporate institution (WINBAN) were organized and interconnected to oversee and chart the production conducted by thousands of individual producers. However, the state and WINBAN had a more visible role and, in some ways a more physically powerful role, in the St. Lucian context than did Geest. For example, WINBAN inspectors were charged with devising the production methods that were required of growers; the state, as outlined in the Banana Act's clauses, assigned the national police to assist WINBAN in monitoring growers' farms to ensure compliance with the act.[26] As we will see in the next chapter, SLBGA representatives also were more readily recognizable in the day-to-day production activities occurring "on the ground."

As an accompaniment to the Banana Act, the Fruit Quality Task Force was created in 1989 with the stated purpose of "review[ing] and analyz[ing] quality performance data, . . . defin[ing] the factors associated with the decline of fruit quality in the industry chain from production . . . market[ing], and . . . mak[ing] recommendations pertinent to the attainment of required high quality levels" (WINBAN 1989: 3). To this end, monitoring farming practices for their conformity to quality standards was a subtext of these objectives. Established due to "current and foreseeable circumstances" such as inconsistent quality from year to year, the task force acknowledged its priority in devising methods to maintain compliance with "standardization measures and procedures . . . for agreed quality" (WINBAN 1989: 4).

But, the Fruit Quality Task Force and the Banana Act were indicative not only of a general concern with the market context or an effort to render St. Lucian bananas appropriate for shifts within that context; their creation and revitalization signaled anticipatory concern over the advent of a Single European Market and the implications of this market for St. Lucia's banana trade with Europe. For the task force and the Banana Act were both developed and/or resurrected in the late 1980s when European integration and its implications for market trade were on the minds of Caribbean policymakers, including those in St. Lucia. Indeed, the report that gave rise to the task force laid out the importance of bolstering the existing Banana Act to ensure fruit quality, all the while citing the need to meet "*changing* market demands" and "consumer preferences" (Fruit Quality Task Force 1989). Thus, the report highlighted market conditions and linked them to national production. Moreover, the St. Lucian state and the Windward Islands governments reinforced efforts to address fruit quality concerns due to a changing market context. In the late 1980s and early 1990s, they commissioned some studies (see Yankey et al. 1990; Atkinson et al. 1993; Kairi Consultants and Agrocon Ltd. 1993; Windward Island Banana Growers' Association 1989), designed to examine the status and future of Windward Islands banana industries in light of globalizing markets.[27] Here, the goal was to consider ways to maintain and strengthen the existing industries given market changes, rather than to consider economic alternatives.

Thus, the state worked to encourage and preserve banana production in St. Lucia through explicit, multiple, and intersecting policies and studies, but the state also promoted banana production through *nonpolicies*. That is, the absence of clear and detailed plans for organizing alternatives to bananas helped further entrench investment in the banana industry. Especially with the expectation of economic unification in Europe after 1992, politicians and policymakers frequently suggested that dependence on bananas needed to be avoided, yet the practical efforts supporting this claim remained weak. For instance, in the 1980s, St. Lucia had a Small Farmers' Agricultural Diversification program designed to enable farmers to pursue other, nonbanana crops; self-sufficiency in food items; substitution of imported food crops; and general improved nutrition of farm families (GOSL 1990: 26). Yet these initiatives were notoriously fragile and ill-supported. An audit report by the St. Lucian Ministry of Agriculture (GOSL 1990) found that inadequate measures existed for considering and ensuring the availability of markets for nonbanana crops such as vegetables, plantain, root crops, and citrus. Several impediments to the successful execution of these programs included insufficient extension staffing and funding for extension agents, inadequate market outlets for crops, competition due to continued importation of crops selected for diversification programs, and lack of integration of selected farmers into the goals and purpose of the diversification program (GOSL 1990: 26). Thus, this ineffective push for diversification occurred amid an unrelenting and heavy investment in the banana industry, fixing banana production firmly within the country no matter what.

CONCLUSION

The local, national, and global placement of Caribbean bananas has been at the heart of debates surrounding institutional policies within St. Lucia but that placement also relates to the larger issue of transnational corporate maneuvering and international accords. In their disputes with the EU, Latin American nations forcefully upheld a belief in market-oriented policies and argued vehemently against trade preferences understood as discriminatory trade practices. The EU's arguments, which hinged partially on the importance of honoring history and attending to the social and economic needs of ACP countries, countered claims about trade preferences as economically discriminatory or unfair. Thus, the debate between the two "sides" centered on whether liberalized markets were discriminatory and how discrimination was to be assessed. It centered on whether discrimination could be offset or justified by historical relations and factors of social and economic vulnerability. Here, the negotiation of neoliberalism was around the degree to which a neoliberalist agenda hinging on fully liberalized markets should be tempered.

While Caribbean banana-producing nations supported the Latin American position presented at the GATT panels, at the local and national levels St. Lucian state policy advocated that producers work within neoliberalist agendas. Through legal writ and a detailed state apparatus built around smallholder production, the industry was nationally set up for global markets. State representatives told St. Lucian banana growers that they had to work according to the dictates of foreign market pressures to ensure the island's competitiveness. State measures served to channel Caribbean bananas globally by detailing and requiring local measures for promoting production and grower compliance. While these measures came across in legal doctrine and formal policy, as we will see in the next chapter, the state's local position on global markets also was mobilized in more nuanced, everyday settings.

II. GLOBAL INTEGRATION & THE LOCAL/REGIONAL VALLEY

3. *Disciplining Local Farms for Global Markets*

O<small>N A TUESDAY AFTERNOON</small>, I took a break with Trevor, a banana grower on whose farm I was working for the day. We rested at the top of the hill, where his plot sat, and where we were able to look over the entire Morne Verte area, seeing the rooftops and expanse of banana farms stretching from every vantage point of our hilltop view. The day was not a harvest day—the peak day of a two-week banana production cycle. He was doing maintenance work: pruning and covering banana plants as part of the routine activities that producers performed between banana "cutting days" (harvest days). As we looked out over the area, Trevor noticed two people in the bottom of the valley, and he pointed them out to me. "See them?" he asked. "I could report them to the SLBGA." I looked carefully and saw two figures who, to me, were unrecognizable but clearly moving quickly as they walked up and down a pathway. "Why could you report them?" I asked.

Trevor explained that the people were harvesting their bananas, carrying the fruit closer to the road where they would leave it in preparation for tomorrow's official harvest. He went on to say that growers were not supposed to cut bananas on any day except the days designated by the SLBGA.

"I could go to my field officer right now and report them," he repeated.

Then, he explained further that, were he to do this, the growers would receive sanctions for failing to comply with the harvesting regulations. As we stood there for what seemed like a long time, watching the two people scurrying up and down the road with what Trevor said were trays of bananas, Trevor's friend came to join us. Curious as to what we were watching, Trevor pointed to the people and repeated what he had told me. The man nodded, agreeing with Trevor that the people were indeed harvesting early and that they could be subject to some sort of penalty from the SLBGA.

Daily farm life in the Mabouya Valley was beset by an ever presence of the SLBGA in ways that this story reflects. Until the mid-1990s, SLBGA staff was charged with visiting growers' farms to both monitor and advise on multiple dimensions of producers' farm practices. Usually, the visits were uninvited but understood as part of SLBGA field officers' regular work schedule. Beyond the farm visits, SLBGA employees and growers interfaced every two weeks when growers presented their fruit for sale to SLBGA staff, went to SLBGA buying depots to purchase cartons or to have their bananas inspected, and visited the main office in Castries to receive their pay for boxed bananas. They also interacted when SLBGA staff inspected growers' fields, monitored growers' harvest and postharvest practices, and distributed industry information to growers by radio and written materials. Moreover, as the incident with Trevor revealed, the SLBGA was present *through* growers: residents of farming communities could serve as secondary agents of the association in their ability to survey and report on work practices. In these ways, the SLBGA's *visible* presence in producers' routine was continual, ubiquitous, and more pronounced than that of other institutions attached to the industry.

Indeed, growers' daily routines did not require interaction with Geest Industries. Given the institutional and legal apparatus around which the industry was organized, the SLBGA—and not Geest—was charged with ensuring growers' compliance with the contract by the very routine surveillance of producers' activities that the association performed. While Geest was known to growers (and was indeed a household name), the company's power was diffused and obscured from St. Lucian producers due to the more regular and obvious presence of the SLBGA in producers' lives. Growers knew that Geest brought their bananas to Europe, and in the early 1990s even large-scale producers (the minority) had their fruit boxes inspected by Geest agents rather than SLBGA representatives. Yet, the company was not present in the majority of producers' daily lives. A bulk of its representatives was based in the UK, and those based in St. Lucia were most active in translating market expectations to WINBAN and SLBGA managers and executives. Geest representatives also were responsible for holding contract negotiations with St. Lucian state representatives and advisers. Thus, Geest worked more at those professional levels within the industry.

By contrast, the SLBGA was the evident agent in growers' daily lives since association staff made regular public appearances and announcements to growers regarding industry practice and policy. Indeed, the association was the day-to-day purveyor of global market demands, which were embodied in Geest's work "higher up" and overseas. In Morne Vertians' working lives, there were three intersecting features to the SLBGA's presence that stood out: surveillance, hierarchies, and sociality. That is, it was in local space that growers were surveyed continually by SLBGA representatives in ways that set the two simultaneously in unequal and socially connecting relationships. Moreover, the possibilities and contexts for this set up were spatialized. SLBGA staff members, whose roles were defined and created in the urban space of the SLBGA "head office" in Castries, transgressed the spatial distinction between the urban office and the rural valley farm in order to bring SLBGA (and by extension, WINBAN) policy directly to growers.[1]

This socio-spatial dimension became especially significant by the 1970s due to a shift in the organization of production. Between the 1960s and 1990s, St. Lucian banana producers worked in a set of prescribed weekly activities that included pruning banana trees, weeding, harvesting, and packaging fruit in preparation for shipment, yet the routine also included a series of regularized social interactions and relationships. Such relationships encompassed habitual encounters between growers and laborers who worked on their farms, but they also involved repeated interactions between growers and state representatives, who regularly monitored producers' on-farm tasks. For example, from the 1960s onward, a producer could not complete harvesting and postharvesting tasks in a given week without at least encountering an SLBGA representative, who evaluated the quality of a growers' fruit and then helped channel the product through a series of processing events. From the 1970s onward, during each week a grower could possibly receive a visit from an SLBGA field officer, who might measure the grower's production, forecast his or her yields, or assess the status of his or her field; a grower also could receive written or audio information from the SLBGA regarding specifications for proper production methods and SLBGA policy. For this reason, routine monitoring by SLBGA staff was inescapable and, importantly, occurred in local space (i.e., specific farming communities) as part of everyday valley life.

This contrasts with the plantation model of banana production so often cited in Latin America, where production tasks and interactions between plantation managers and workers have been more circumscribed within the space of the plantation (see Bourgois 1989; Purcell 1993; Euraque 2003; Striffler 2002; and Forster 1998). In the contract labor model of agriculture production at work in St. Lucia, surveillance of producers' work was more diffused, continual, and localized through the present and ubiquitous role of the SLBGA. The SLBGA's status as a statutory agency also meant that surveillance was enacted by the state. While foreign capital had an obvious and significant role in organizing agricultural production under contract labor in the late twentieth century (Little and Watts 1994; Watts 1994; Collins 1993; Carney 1988), the state also had a key place in production (Raynolds 1994a; Grossman 1998). For instance, policies and material support for domestic crop production may pale in comparison to that which is applied to production for foreign markets (see Andreatta 1997). In St. Lucia, the few SLBGA staff members who monitored and guided growers' work disciplined farm labor for global markets by inspecting growers' activities on a consistent and continual basis and by assuring that their practices and products were suited for foreign tastes and demands.

In this setup, the SLBGA's presence was justified by notions of expert knowledge that differentiated growers from SLBGA staff. Poststructuralist scholars (Escobar 1995; Crush 1995; Arce and Long 2000)[2] have shown how development efforts often are framed within a power-knowledge apparatus. Here "experts" with "development knowledge" are engaged in a set of controlling and surveillance tactics directed at specific populations deemed less knowledgeable by virtue of their socially marginal status (e.g., the impoverished, indigenous groups, women, and so on) (Cooper and Packard 2005). In the case of St. Lucia, growers were classified officially as self-employed producers or independent farmers,[3] but implicitly they were not considered sufficiently knowledgeable about their craft. State representatives existed as trained "agricultural experts" set in place to inform, instruct, and monitor producers' work. State power experienced through surveillance tactics boosted the process by which social divisions partially built on knowledge difference occurred. Through these intersections of power and knowledge, global integration policies (embodied in the work of SLBGA/state representatives) were communicated, enforced, and legitimated in Morne Verte across the more than 250 banana farms (GOSL 1990). Thus, as state/SLBGA representatives and monitors were inserted throughout Morne Verte, the state became part of the local power/knowledge apparatus that enacted globalization policies. It did so by working with information ultimately supplied by Geest (Trouillot 1988) and by integrating growers into the global economy. This mobilization of different dimensions of state apparatuses through connections with global institutions is not uncommon in the organization of contemporary global economies (Trouillot 2001).

Relations with the state are not always oppositional and fixed as Crichlow (2005) showed in Jamaica. Further, when state surveillance is embodied within families and local communities, the verticality of state-subject relationships often is nuanced (Ferguson and Gupta 2002). Thus, another dimension to SLBGA-grower relations was sociality, interactions characterized not merely by hierarchical monitoring but also by more horizontal social communications and exchanges. While serving an obvious surveillance role that promoted distance and differentiation from growers, state representatives also experienced the building of close ties with banana producers. Ironically, such interactions were shaped through the power/knowledge setup because close bonds were possible due to the localization, intensity, and quotidian inspections by the SLBGA. The thickness of the daily work schedule, as well as relations built around it, shaped the extent to which specific banana production hierarchies might have been established and yet simultaneously unsettled. The continual presence of the staff in Morne Verte and the resulting development of complicated state-grower divisions revealed how socially uneven and yet close relations between the two were crafted, nuanced, and negotiated on a continual basis. Below we look at these dynamics as they played out in Morne Verte after first considering the historical foundation for their possibility.

IMAGINING & DEVELOPING
A "VOLATILE VALLEY"

To situate how Morne Vertians intersected with state representatives, it is important to look both at the larger interface between valley residents and nonvalley/urban residents across time. My own sense of this dynamic emerged once I arrived in St. Lucia and witnessed the area through media and verbal imagery of the valley from my location "in town." Until I could secure accommodations at my research site, I was living temporarily at a guest house in Castries, where I observed television and newspaper coverage of the intense farmers' strikes in October 1993. Media coverage of the valley was extensive entailing a flood of television images depicting masses of people crowding into the streets and burning tires and downed trees in the roadways. Angry men (and references to "angry farmers") were shown yelling in the street as they were interviewed by television reporters. On television, I heard and saw the prime minister address the nation and tell of what he described as the sad but unavoidable shooting of two male valley protestors, who, he said, had provoked police gunfire. He referenced a "complete breakdown of civil order . . . in particular in the Mabouya Valley" and cited threats to his own personal safety there when driving through and encountering an "angry mob" (Rt. Hon. John Compton, October 11, 1993). Adding to this imagery were comments I heard when I met people in the northern, more urban part of the island, including Castries and surrounding areas. Most offered widespread empathy for valley people's financial troubles and thought that prices had indeed dipped too low, but some also expressed disdain for the forms of protest that had developed. At times, the people I encountered seemed to consider lawlessness as a long-standing feature of the area. "The valley?" one person asked about my choice of a research site. "Isn't that place kind of volatile?"

Seemingly concerned about my safety, some advised that I live in town and only go to the valley on occasional visits to gather necessary data. By others I was warned that I might want to change field sites entirely and, perhaps rightfully so, they quizzed me about my ability to reside in a rural area, particularly one in upheaval with which I had no familiarity. Undoubtedly, reactions such as these were as much indicative of Castries dwellers' perceptions of the valley as they were indicative of peoples perceptions of me and the context surrounding my visit.[4] However, broader notions of the valley as a site measured against me and identified through the strike events also spoke to the social divide between rural and urban St. Lucia. The expression of this divide through assessments of me likely related to, or at least was understandably heightened by, the timing of my research and its coincidence with the intensity following farmer strikes. Yet, representations of the valley as volatile and worlds apart from urban life run deeper than this moment. Indeed, the appearance of such images during the 1990s reflected the profound history of relations among valley residents of differing social status, as well as relations between valley people and St. Lucian and non-St. Lucian "outsiders."

Representing the Valley during the Early Colonial Era

In some accounts, the valley has long possessed an image of lawlessness and danger in need of correction. In his 1844 "historical, statistical, and descriptive" account of St. Lucia, Henry Breen (1970 [1844]), British secretary of the courts of justice in St. Lucia, paints the Mabouya Valley region as largely unimportant to the commercial and administrative foundation of the colony.[5] Breen, then a thirteen-year resident of St. Lucia, clearly saw urban sites as most significant to the island, evidenced by the comparative richness and approving ring to his description of the cities of Castries and Vieux Fort vis-à-vis that of other regions on the island. For the Mabouya Valley in particular, he described it as at once lush and sparsely inhabited, devoid of any commercial development and also comprised of African descendants of questionable moral character. This latter representation was revealed in a story he recounted in a chapter addressing "the absence of religious instruction in the St. Lucian negro" (Breen 1844: 255), where he focused partially on the case of a non-Mabouya Valley woman's unfortunate encounter with a Mabouya male aggressor and a practitioner of Obeah, considered by colonial administrators as an Afro–West Indian form of sorcery.

> In the *wild* and thinly inhabited district of Mabouya, there resided in 1841 a coloured female, named Eucharisse, who followed the business of a huckster. Being a stranger in that part of the island, which had long been noted for the *lawless* character of its inhabitants, Eucharisse placed herself under the protection of a Negro. . . . Soon after the arrival of Eucharisse in Mabouya, a young man of colour named Martelly . . . conceived a *violent* love for her and tried all arts of seduction to gain her over to his desires but his overtures were contemptuously rejected. He then had recourse to her protector, and with the assistance of another coloured man . . . a notorious professor of sorcery, he obtained consent . . . to be allowed access to [Eucharisse's room]. The night . . . was fixed for the execution of this nefarious scheme. . . . Martelly having thus taken the girl by surprise as she lay

fast asleep, succeeded after a *violent struggle* in effecting his purpose. He was then about to retire when Eucharisse stood up, and, upbraiding him in an accent of despair, threatened to denounce his brutal conduct to the public prosecutor. At this Martelly became exasperated, and to wreak his vengeance upon her, he repeated the assault with such *savage violence,* that the poor girl, struggling in the defense of her honor, was actually strangled in the ruffian's grasp and fell a corpse on the floor (Breen 1970: 251–52; emphasis mine).

This assessment of violence, lawlessness, and immorality among Afro-Mabouyan men came through a British interpretation of Afro-St. Lucian interpersonal, cross-color, and religious spheres. Thus, Breen offers an "outsider's" lens on valley life. And, while the view resonated with the sorts of representations of valley residents that emerged in the twentieth century, his perspective also revealed the deep history of outsider/nonresident characterizations of valley people as volatile—characterizations that clearly indexed race, color, and rural contrasts with urbanity. It also revealed how representations of the valley and specific social divides between and within it were produced through valley residents' relations with the colonial administration and must have fed into justifications for modes of colonial control in "lawless" and socially/morally "underdeveloped" areas such as the valley. Patterns of mid-twentieth-century to postcolonial agricultural development efforts in the area echoed some of the ideas about a socially "underdeveloped" valley that appeared in Breen's account.

The State, Private Capital, and Development in the Valley

The context for bringing development to the valley in the mid to late twentieth century concerned shifts in St. Lucia's agricultural economy and its political status as well. Indeed, the late 1950s to late 1970s was a period of rapid and intense economic and political change in St. Lucia, and the Mabouya Valley was in step with these transformations. In some ways, the valley was at the center of them. Banana production accelerated and, by the mid-1960s, became an entrenched part of the national economy, surpassing the economic significance of sugar. The Mabouya Valley was important to this transition since it was one of three locations where small-scale banana cultivation actively existed alongside plantation banana production—a defining and unique dynamic of agricultural production through the 1970s (Adrien 1996). Additionally, during this period, universal suffrage was passed in 1951 and in 1967 St. Lucia became an associated state of Britain. Associated Statehood gave the island full internal self-government and therefore moved it closer to independence, while universal suffrage enabled the emergence of an Afro-St. Lucian political leadership. Political parties, trade unions, and government positions led by Afro-St. Lucians revealed the transforming political and social possibilities engendered by a colony on the brink of nationhood and independence. Moreover, as Afro-Lucians' ascendance to these new political spaces unsettled Europeans' political dominance on the island, it also fueled the development of a politically-engaged Afro-Lucian middle class that garnered its support by organizing a laboring class to agitate for work on the plantations.[6] Such events were intense between the late 1950s and early 1960s, when the island was beginning a dual shift out of sugar into banana production and out of colonialism with a new political and racial power base (Slocum forthcoming). The intensity resurfaced in the mid-1970s, when again plantation laborers' complaints of falling wages and poor working conditions were supported by a revitalized trade union movement.

The pressure from these 1970s events led the owner of the Dennery Estate,[7] Denis Barnard,[8] who was the first large plantation owner to adopt banana production in the mid-1960s, to make a major change in his estate located in the Mabouya Valley. In 1978, like all other large estate owners in St. Lucia, Barnard relinquished sole hold on the Dennery Estate by selling it to the National Development Company (a state corporation), which then leased the lands to Dennery Farmco Ltd., a company formed and jointly owned by Barnard, the St. Lucian government and a private British company (Advisory Committee for Dennery Basin Development 1985; Severin 1989). But, the initial plan for Farmco, as it was called, was short-lived. By the early 1980s, extensive plans for diversification and extended production on the estate collapsed under continued economic decline and worker pressures (Advisory Committee for Dennery Basin Development 1985). Barnard and the British partner sold their shares, and Farmco became entirely a state operation. This, then, marked the firm transition of the Dennery plantation from private to state ownership, as well as a new brand of development in the region. Alongside foreign capital, the reorganization of the estate inserted the state squarely into economic development ventures within the Mabouya Valley.[9]

Yet, the state's role in the valley emerged in other ways. In 1982, the

Ministry of Agriculture devised a land-titling and registration scheme for St. Lucia that was designed to precede an agricultural diversification plan for the country; the pilot project for the scheme was in the Mabouya Valley, where the ministry cited land scarcity and an "antiquated" land tenure system (e.g., family land) as impeding access to land and thus possibilities for extended smallholder production (Organization of American States 1991). The pilot project was a massive effort involving a team of government employees and research consultants from the Organization of American States, who together surveyed three hundred farm households (100% of the households in the area) across 350 acres in one area of the Mabouya Valley (GOSL and OAS 1983: 3, 7; Organization of American States 1991). With only one staff member residing in the valley, a temporary office of a team of staff members was set up directly in the area during the project's seven months. After conducting a massive information campaign to announce the project, they notified landholders that lands would be surveyed and recorded to assess size and ownership. They also gathered extensive data on household size, educational level, age, occupation of residents, farm products raised, quantity and size of land parcels, form of land tenure on each plot, type, and land size.

The project stopped short of its goals to register lands due to land-titling obstacles. Indeed, the final report stated that, while residents' responses to the project were favorable, some were reluctant to submit claim forms. This, the report said, was due to "cultural obstacles" to land titling (e.g, an unwillingness to forego customary and communal land tenure systems for a legal one) and widespread mistrust and confusion regarding the project (Organization of American States 1991: 21; GOSL and OAS 1983). In this regard, the only project interviewer from the Mabouya Valley mentioned: "I found myself spending more time explaining the purpose of the questions. The people were always very enthusiastic in knowing all about the project so they came to my home at all hours . . . expressing their hopes and desires, others expressed their doubts about the success of the project" (GOSL and OAS 1983: app. 6, 2). Thus, when implanted in the area, the project was met with mixed reviews by valley residents, as the project's goals were not well understood by all involved.

Citing insufficient lands (and not "cultural obstacles") to redress land scarcity in this area of the valley, the Ministry of Agriculture annulled the diversification and resettlement portions of the project. Yet, the data gathered and lessons learned became a catalyst for the Mabouya Valley

Development Project (MVDP). Begun in 1984, also through the Ministry of Agriculture, and eventually gaining external funding from the European Union and other international sources, the MVDP was a state-integrated rural development project much like those throughout the Caribbean in the 1970s and 1980s (see Crichlow 1997). As it extended into the twenty-first century, the project encompassed an area of over eight hundred acres and a total of eight residential settlements out of the valley's thirteen communities. Its goal was to create housing settlements, develop infrastructure, organize and create community social groups, provide land for farming, and promote agricultural diversification (Advisory Committee for Dennery Basin Development 1985; Severin 1989; Organization of American States 1991). Farming was a key to the project's goals and, through a land-leasing component, valley producers rented lands (which over time they could purchase) on which they grew crops specified by the MVDP. To this end, the Dennery Estate was divided into different areas, each corresponding to specific cropping patterns that small-scale leaseholders had to adopt.

During the two years that it was in operation, the MVDP brought a variety of economic and material outcomes to the valley and has been considered a Caribbean rural development success story. Yet, the project also attested to the presence of the state in agricultural development within the Mabouya Valley. The MVDP was run by government staff and openly situated in the valley, where its office was located along the main road. As part of the project, MVDP staff members visited producers' fields, surveyed their work, and processed their applications and complaints. This reinforced a preexisting arrangement in which, through the category of development, the state emerged as coordinator of production in the valley. There is no doubt that several growers made gains from the MVDP due to their access to land and other critical productive resources (Severin 1989; Organization of American States 1991). However, because these outcomes resulted with the continual presence of the state in its capacity as development authority within the valley, the project built upon some of the dynamics and hierarchies formed through the Dennery Estate. It also continued to mold those dynamics in the valley, although there was a difference between the MVDP arrangement and that developed through the Dennery Estate. Under the MVDP, a distinction was created between valley residents as pseudo-laborers and state representatives as residentially external but professionally present agricultural development "authorities." Thus, the role of the state in its

capacity as purveyor of agricultural development models partially organized with private capital became fixed in the valley. This built on preexisting principles of agricultural practice that had shaped interactions
between producers and estate owners and that resonated with outsider-
insider imageries of the colonial era. It also would mark the arrangement
growers experienced in the banana industry through the SLBGA into the
1990s.

DAILY FARM LIFE IN THE 1990S &
THE BANANA GROWERS' ASSOCIATION

By the 1990s, the organization of the banana industry and its interface
within Morne Verte demonstrated a connection to the legacy of development in that area. Like growers who had occupied MVDP lands or had
been part of the land-titling project, those who belonged to the SLBGA
also had constant and direct interaction with the state, which organized
agricultural development efforts. The 1967 Banana Growers' Association Act ensured that this interaction took place for all those growing and
selling bananas. It linked growers to the state by legally requiring producers to conform to specific production practices outlined by the
SLBGA and WINBAN. These requirements pertained to all aspects of
the banana production schedule: harvesting, postharvest processing,
product quality inspection, sales, and transportation. And, because all
growers cut and sold their bananas to the SLBGA every other week, the
routinized organization of production mandated continual contact
between growers and state representatives. This was because each stage
involved obtaining required materials from SLBGA offices, being monitored by SLBGA staff either at SLBGA sites or on farmers' fields, possibly being inspected by WINBAN or state representatives, and/or
receiving directives from the SLBGA about the setup of production.
Growers thus worked within a biweekly routine of production activities
and understood the organization of production through their relationship with the SLBGA.

Barbara Welch (1996) argues that the institutional role of the SLBGA
and other Windward Islands banana growers' associations in producers'
lives helped ensure that quality and expected quantities of bananas were
able to make it into foreign markets. Comparing the Windward Islands
associations with their neighbors in Martinique and Guadeloupe, where

institutional interventions on growers' behalf were far less pronounced, she contends that marketing support was particularly critical for St. Lucian and Dominican small-scale growers. Without assistance and intervention by the associations, she predicts, producers' ability to find outlets for their products might not have been economically feasible. Further, other interventions by the associations, such as fertilizer support, fruit disease control support, and buying depots, Welch claims promoted the "success" of banana production in areas of the eastern Caribbean. Thus, for her, like others who have heralded the industry's impact on small-scale producers' lives, the SLBGA should not be overlooked for its role in supporting the economic pursuits and advances of an otherwise marginal farming population. Yet, along with forms of resource support and economic benefits, other aspects of the SLBGA's activities can be considered in order to provide a rounded understanding of the political and social implications of the association's work.

The increasingly heavy labor input required by growers, for instance, was strongly shaped by the SLBGA's regulation of the production process. Of all production and crop maintenance activities, postharvest activities (i.e., all of the tasks following the cutting of bananas from banana plants) were the most laborious and time consuming. They included the point from which bananas were cut from banana plants, the application of a fungicidal treatment to cut bananas, labeling and boxing the fruit, and transporting it to point of sale. Through WINBAN, the SLBGA defined the organization of these tasks. Importantly, WINBAN's recommendations for postharvest techniques were constantly evolving and changing, which had implications for how growers worked.[10] The steady shifts in harvesting and postharvesting requirements meant that growers had to stay on top of new production specifications as communicated to them. This was especially the case after the 1970s, when transformations in production methods unfolded rapidly.

Before the 1970s, production and postharvest banana processing were centralized events conducted at SLBGA centers. Producers grew banana plants and cut stems (large bunches on a stalk) of bananas from the plants on their fields. They then transported the stems to SLBGA depots, where the fruit was washed, packed, and transported to the docks by SLBGA staff. But, by the early 1970s, a major shift emerged when WINBAN recommended that postharvest activities be carried out on individual growers' fields rather than at SLBGA centers. Producers went from unloading their harvested banana stems at an SLBGA site, where the fruit was further processed, to cutting the fruit from banana plants and then conducting all subsequent activities on or from their own fields with their own labor.[11] The new system thus shifted the responsibility and labor required for key tasks from the SLBGA to growers (ULG Consultants 1975).

This shift became more intense in the early 1990s. After minor changes in the forms of postharvest processing and after the adoption of different styles of boxes for packing bananas, yet another new and major postharvest innovation was introduced. This occurred after researchers and market analysts stated that existing techniques left bananas unsightly and negatively impacted consumer demand for the fruit (Malins and St. Rose 1994). Known as Mini Wet Pack, the method entailed new practices for fungicidal treatment, more labor intensity and costs for producers, and more spatially dispersed stages of postharvest banana processing

TABLE 2.   Postharvest System Changes in the Windward Islands Banana Industry, 1970s–90s

Postharvest System	Year Introduced	Description
Stemming	Pre-1970	Farmers wrap stems of bananas, and female "headers" bring them directly to the ship.
Centralized boxing	1970	Farmers deliver bananas on stems to boxing plant, where fruit is washed, dipped in fungicide, and boxed by BGA staff.
Field packing	1977	Farmers cut stems into bunches, place fungicide pad on crown, box bunches directly on fields, and transport boxed bananas to BGA boxing depot.
Centralized packing[a]	Approximately 1984	Farmers cut stems into bunches, place fungicide pad on crown, carry bunches (on heads) to nearby shed, box bananas, and transport boxed bananas to BGA boxing depot.
Mini Wet Pack	1990	Farmers cut stems into bunches, carry on trays to field shed, wash in fungicide bath, label and box bunches, and transport to BGA boxing depot.

Source: Adapted from Malins and St. Rose 1994.

[a]It was not compulsory that farmers adopt centralized packing. According to Malins and St. Rose (1994), only a minority of growers adopted it due to the need for a large number of field-packing laborers.

Fig. 3. Banana stem before it is cut from a banana plant. (Photo by the author.)

(Slocum 1996).[12] Much like the picture of a mini "factory in the fields," under Mini Wet Pack, growers worked more in assembly-line fashion: one male to cut banana stems, up to three males to pack and carry trays of smaller banana clusters to roadside sheds, up to three (typically) females to unpack the trays and apply the fungicide, and another female or two to label and box the fruit.

This segmentation and decentralization of the production process set in motion a new arrangement. First, compared to the pre-1970s setup, production was broken into a series of segmented and spatially diverse steps. These were structured according to gender and expanded from farm fields to roadsides, which could be as much as a quarter mile away. Second, while the work remained routinized due to the maintenance of a regular harvest and sale schedule, interactions between growers and SLBGA staff members became more extensive. They pervaded the interstices of daily life as surveillance efforts were stepped up and spread out to cover multiple farms and the expanse of activities on individual plots. Thus, as growers' work was extended and divided across activities, so, too, was the monitoring work of the SLBGA. And, while the pervasiveness of the SLBGA's surveillance tactics dovetailed with the changing organization of production, other forms of the association's work guided production but in different ways.

Continual Communication with the SLBGA

One of these ways concerned modes of communication between growers and the SLBGA with respect to appropriate production practices. The SLBGA Act defined work practices and parameters in legal doctrine while communication between the SLBGA and growers ensured that work was carried out according to the legal expectations. Through different forms, including face-to-face encounters and the uses of diverse media, a communication flow occurred seemingly at every stage of production. For growers to begin or proceed from one set of weekly tasks to the next, they required information, feedback, and sometimes approval from the SLBGA. Communication from the SLBGA, then, became one of the most important ways in which production strategies were defined, enforced, and overseen. Indeed, it was one reason why the SLBGA *appeared* to growers to be the institution that initiated and set the production process in motion each week.

Radio and television were critical to this information flow. Scheduling for the week was launched by radio when the SLBGA announced the

Fig. 4. Man "selecting" bananas, cutting a stem of bananas into smaller segments. Selecting was a male task. (Photo by the author.)

two days for that week that Geest's boat would call in St. Lucia. Throughout the day, listeners would hear radio announcers repeat the days when Geest's boats would arrive, followed up with information about the days that each district was to prepare to harvest its bananas. This informed producers across the country of the window in which they were expected to organize production from harvest to transport. Required to cut bananas on one of the two days designated for their specific district, growers had to ensure that all of their activities from harvest to postharvest would be completed so that all fruit could be on

Fig. 5. Banana clusters segmented and arranged on banana leaves
after having been cut from stems. (Photo by the author.)

the boats during the specified time. Although Wednesday and Thursday
were the usual days that the Geest boat loaded Morne Verte bananas in
the early 1990s, these days changed from time to time with only a few
days' notice. Geest could notify the SLBGA that the boat would arrive
on another day of the week, and, upon receiving this information from
the association, growers had to organize their activities accordingly.
This was especially the case for the 1993–94 period, when there was
tremendous precariousness in the SLBGA leadership and structure as
well as relations with Geest. Banana growers' strikes starting in 1993
influenced a change in the composition of the SLBGA board of directors,
debates about undoing or reworking some of the clauses in the SLBGA
Act, withholding of banana sales by many growers, and uncertainty in
the longevity and terms of the contract with Geest. As a result, from
week to week, there was marked uncertainty as to whether and when
harvesting would be scheduled. In Morne Verte, growers often asked
one another whether they had heard which days would be harvest days
in a given week, revealing the breakdown in communication during
these periods but also the extent to which growers relied on radio directives from the SLBGA in order to plan their weekly production activi-

Fig. 6. Roadside shed for washing and boxing bananas. (Photo by
the author.)

ties. Thus, while it often appeared that harvesting days were set and
repeated from week to week, the early to mid-1990s was a case example
of how the contract clause, which provided for the production schedule
to be flexible and based on directives from Geest, played out. Growers
had to continually stay abreast of SLBGA radio announcements regarding the designated harvest days and be prepared to shift plans on a
week's notice. Radio and word-of-mouth communications from others
who had heard this information were the primary means by which growers knew the production schedule.

Beyond the weekly schedule, radio and television were key for other
areas of production, in particular for updates on new production methods and also changes in market conditions. The association employed
media to inform or demonstrate recommended postharvesting techniques and available resources, as well as occasionally to announce
specific developments or changes in the local industry. Demonstrations,
such as methods for showing new techniques for packing bananas, were
performed on television. Announcements regarding industry develop-

Fig. 7. Bananas being boxed after washing and labeling. (Photo by the author.)

ments or market shifts also took place when the prime minister or the minister of agriculture addressed the nation about changes in the industry's structure. They occurred, too, when programs were aired about issues such as changes in market rates for bananas, developing trade policies, and so on. Addresses by government representatives were frequent, especially in the early 1990s, when the prime minister spoke to the nation concerning threats and outcomes of the banana strikes as well as decisions to restructure the SLBGA.

However, two regular radio programs hosted by the SLBGA dealt with questions of production techniques and industry policy, informing growers of how they should organize production with the new information in mind. Conducted primarily as a talk show, *Spotlight* tended to focus on interviews held in English (St. Lucia's official language) with senior staff and board members of the SLBGA and WINBAN while *Bon Kalité* (Good Quality) was an SLBGA-sponsored program conducted primarily in Kwéyòl (Creole, a language spoken widely in St. Lucia's rural areas). When interviewed, most growers in Morne Verte said that they listened to *Bon Kalité* most often, and, indeed, it seemed that during the 7:00 PM hour, when the show aired, it could be heard from many homes in the area. The announcer spoke in a lighthearted, often humorous manner but offered clear instructions and advice on how to operate on one's farm to ensure effective yields and, as the title suggests, to achieve the best-quality product. Thus, topics included fertilizer use, application of chemical and nonchemical products on the field, and techniques for postharvest and harvest tasks.

Spotlight, by contrast, was focused more on information such as detailed market developments and local industry policy. It appeared to be less popular in Morne Verte than was *Bon Kalité,* which may be explained by its subject matter and format, as well as its airing in English, while Kwéyòl was more commonly spoken among producers in the area. On the air, senior industry "talking heads" focused on the purpose and execution of specific industry policies. They were asked by the radio interviewer to comment on the adoption of specific policies in the industry such as pricing policies and fruit quality assessment policies, as well as broader economic trends in the global banana industry, specifically changes in market demand or competition deemed to impact price and shape local policy. Topics in the early 1990s included how WINBAN addressed market liberalization policies, analysis and explanation of the New Banana Regime, the purpose and benefits of the Mini Wet Pack system, the role of the SLBGA in developing the banana industry, objectives of a new pricing system in St. Lucia, and assessments of St. Lucian growers' performance. Through these, grower-listeners sometimes were introduced to the global market context and local policy development through radio discussions and analyses that linked both European market shifts (e.g., the New Banana Regime) with St. Lucian policy development (e.g., local pricing policies and mechanisms and the Mini Wet Pack system). The topics often were integrated as well, since discussion of the Mini Wet Pack system included mention of competition from Latin American producers or information about British market demands as justification for instituting new, more rigorous postharvest practices in St. Lucia.

During the early to mid-1990s, the program had extensive focus on the industry's restructuring and quality issues and sometimes connected these to grower behavior. Interviewees explained in detail about new structures such as the implementation of the Quality Assurance system (a setup of SLBGA monitoring methods to assess and predict the quality of individual growers' fruit) and the three-tiered pricing system (a pricing structure graded by specific quality levels) and then emphasized the importance of grower discipline and compliance with these policies due to market pressures. For example, in the early 1990s a senior staff member addressed the importance of quality and the institutional machinery that the SLBGA had devised to ensure it. After outlining the role of the SLBGA extension officer, the interviewer asked him "how important [it is] for farmers to exhibit strict discipline in the adoption of practices recommended by WINBAN." To this he replied:

> I want to welcome this question because one of the main problems in the industry is indiscipline in terms of [farmers] being contentious in doing practices that are recommended by the [SL]BGA and WINBAN. A lot of farmers . . . will pledge to do practices but as the field officer [extension agent] turns his back, the farmer goes back into the old way of operation. . . . [Production] methods will not bring about desired results if farmers do not discipline themselves. . . . Unless farmers are prepared to discipline themselves and do exactly what the authorities ask them to do, the recommendation will be a failure.[13]

Similarly, in another April 1992 interview, a member of the SLBGA board of directors cited one cause of the three-tiered pricing system as the tendency for growers to think they could avoid putting effort into their work because under the one-price system they would "get the same [price] as everyone else." Clearly, these statements that criticized producers' work behavior and advocated inducements for differentiating growers by work and product quality, were offered to justify and explain policy implementation in St. Lucia. But, as comments offered through the association that represented banana growers, the statements also added to the larger communication apparatus that steered growers into the fold of the industry. The radio interviewee's mention of the importance of grower discipline, as well as mention of the need for measures to ensure grower compliance with industry policy, built on the other forms of communication that both informed growers and drew them into industry standards. Announcing, justifying, and affirming the new practices and policies were effected through the public and habitual use of mass communication.

Mass communication, especially by radio, has had a particular resonance in St. Lucia. Paul Garrett (2000) refers to the expansion of forms of radio programming in postindependence St. Lucia, as well as the role that such programming has played in the process of nation building and mass consumption of popular culture.[14] But, in a broader sense, radio listening has been pervasive throughout St. Lucian society, and, in rural contexts, it has been a constant in daily life. In the early 1990s, in Morne Verte radios were tuned in and turned on frequently throughout the day in rural households, where people listened to one of the two or three stations that existed. Radios played typically within St. Lucia's minibuses, which were a common form of public transportation, and radios also were brought sometimes to Morne Verte farmers' fields as background music and discussion during farm work. Radios were sources of critical information, including announcements of hurricane updates and even daily obituary announcements, and they also were the forum for public political debate through regular call-in programs that typically addressed current events on the island.

Thus, programming for farmers broadcast on national radio stations was part of the larger use of radio in St. Lucia, revealing how the industry was nationally situated. Radio brought the "official" discourses of the banana industry into the households, farms, and minibuses of the wider society. Announcements on *Spotlight* profiled market considerations and simultaneously underscored that the terms and organization of production and banana sale transactions were non-negotiable and required grower discipline. By virtue of their place on widely accessible radio (and television), the announcements about industry policy and regulations came as broadcasts for all St. Lucians to hear.[15] At a broad level, this revealed one dimension to how the industry was situated nationally. At a more specific level, the widespread broadcasting of banana news meant that all St. Lucians were continually in touch with the setup and ideologies behind the industry, and, most significantly, they were also keenly aware of the power of the state and its role in disciplining and informing growers.

However, the SLBGA and WINBAN also communicated with growers in less public ways such as by disseminating written information only to growers. WINBAN provided St. Lucian and other Windward Islands growers with a banana growers' manual entitled "A Guide to Successful Banana Production in the Windward Islands." This detailed techniques for farm management and production, taking growers from preparation and maintenance of their fields and banana plants to methods for harvesting and postharvest handling of bananas. Yet, monthly meetings were a more common way of communicating specifically to growers. Organized by the SLBGA, these were held in all banana-growing districts across the country and were attended by the district branch chairperson, secretary, delegates, and general grower body. The field officer assigned to the region was the only SLBGA representative present. Each month, the Communications Office sent circulars to all district branches; circulars contained specific information about association policies and production procedures ranging from amendments to the SLBGA Act to new methods for harvest or postharvest stages of production. The office also sent replies to the questions and comments that had been posed by branch members during previous monthly meetings. Additionally, pending sufficient grower participation at the meetings, banana producers voted on resolutions on which the Communications Office requested input from districts. Meetings thus were organized around reading of circulars plus the development of questions related to topics discussed. Like the information distributed to growers from the SLBGA, growers' questions and comments were communicated in writing and sent back to the Communications Office. In this way, the SLBGA was distant and simultaneously implanted in local space. Communication here, then, occurred through disembodied and distanced interactions, although the site for receiving and sending communications was the local district branch, the farm communities where radio and television announcements also were broadcast.

Circulars distributed to growers from the early 1990s onward fell into three connected categories: policy changes, quality, and market developments. Announcements of policy changes frequently were justified with reference to quality concerns, while quality concerns and policy developments were contextualized within market shifts, including the impact of market integration in Europe. However, discussions of quality sometimes appeared without reference to the others. For policy questions, the circulars touched upon changes in pricing, amendments to existing parliamentary acts relating to the banana industry, and restructuring of various components of the industry, especially methods for processing bananas post-harvest. In 1994 alone, they addressed the shift from field pack to Mini Wet Pack, the introduction of a new field-based ribbon system to forecast production, European policy developments such as the NBR, changes in the price offered to growers, and institutional restructuring such as transformations in the composition of the board of directors. They also launched and explained new SLBGA systems to evaluate and ensure growers' fruit quality. In all of these, there was an appeal to the market context with an emphasis on the importance of complying with changed policies. Circulars often explained that if growers did not comply they would receive sanctions such as rejection of fruit, heightened inspection of their activities, and possible revocation of SLBGA membership.

The flow of information from the branch meetings to the Communications Office was important to the communication dynamic. Growers were permitted and encouraged to send back written questions to the SLBGA and also to vote on specific topics or agendas brought to their attention by the SLBGA. From Morne Verte, grower comments and questions sent to the SLBGA Communications Office addressed topics raised by the SLBGA circulars, but growers' comments also covered other areas. In fact, most often they took an almost opposite emphasis than that of the SLBGA and included inadequate inputs available to growers to assist them in complying with new production standards, input wastage, and improper handling of growers' fruit and resources by SLBGA staff, thus compromising the quality of growers' fruit and the prices they received. They also included complaints about fairness of the new pricing system, poor performance of SLBGA staff (including inspectors and field officers), improper practices and policies (at the SLBGA banana-buying stations as well as the general prices offered to growers across the country), insufficient grower participation and representation at branch meetings, and insufficient attendance by the branch chairman and delegates. Thus, Morne Verte growers, like the SLBGA Communications Office, focused on quality, yet implicitly (and at times explicitly) charged the association—not growers—with compromising fruit quality due to questionable SLBGA practices and non-adherence to set SLBGA standards and policies. This revealed a type of distant and implied disagreement between growers and the SLBGA as, remotely, they exchanged differing assessments of problems in the industry. The SLBGA blamed and warned growers while (at least Morne Verte) producers refused this stance, responding instead that the SLBGA had come up short. Put another way, circulars—perhaps like some aspects of radio programming—served as forms of labor discipline and reinforcement of a growing globalization discourse but were not easily received as such. In a sort of communications volley between the SLBGA and growers, the origins of fruit quality problems were debated between the two, as were suggestions about appropriate measures to solve them.

Wavering acceptance of SLBGA communications also was shown through the scant level of grower participation in branch meetings, where attendance in Morne Verte was notoriously low. Between 1988 and 1993, as many as one-third of all growers attended a given meeting. However, during this time an average of 15% attended per meeting, and it was not uncommon for no growers to show at all. Consequently, while the meetings were a space that the SLBGA designated for regularized important communication with growers, it was not necessarily the most effective forum for disseminating information widely or ensuring that growers received the latest directives about production requirements. Because growers did not frequent them and because growers often openly refused SLBGA meetings by not attending, the meetings were not fully effective in their goal. Indeed, to me, growers widely expressed skepticism that the meetings—and the association more generally— would respond to their concerns and foster change (Slocum 1996). Thus, growers' absence and the reasons given for it reflected a keen distrust of the SLBGA along with a willful disregard for the monthly space—like the disregard for *Spotlight*—where producers were organized primarily to receive communications regarding industry policy and practices.

Field Officers Enforcing Production

As growers questioned and avoided the SLBGA's interventions, the state continued to exert its influence, made possible, especially through the 1986 Banana Act.[16] Of all of the acts of Parliament related to the industry, it was the most clear in allowing for state surveillance and direction of production, as it spelled out how growers were to conduct their on-farm operations and proclaimed that failure to adhere to pre- scribed production formulas was a legal offense. Although the act desig- nated WINBAN as the creator of such production methods and as the inspection "authority," the key to effecting WINBAN policy was imple- mentation and enforcement. This role resided with SLBGA staff mem- bers directly involved in everyday farm life. WINBAN coordinated its continual and rapid development of new production practices, some of which were to address global market pressures, with SLBGA field officers, who were routinely on hand to inform growers about the new procedures, as well as to monitor growers' appropriate uses of them. Thus, field officers were important everyday conveyors of WINBAN policy—filtered through the SLBGA—as they visited farm communities on a regular basis, inspected farmers' fields, and attended and led community SLBGA meetings during day and night. Their presence was more pronounced and constant in banana-producing areas than that of any other SLBGA staff person or other extension agents such as those from the Ministry of Agriculture.[17] They were therefore a means by which producers "knew" the banana industry and gained firsthand comprehension of industry policy. Indeed, they were deemed more effective than the monthly meetings and radio programs, from which growers sometimes opted to disengage. Further, while SLBGA policies were written up in various legal documents and codified into laws that growers *could* see and read, field officers were more regular and steady translators and enforcers of such policies, particularly those surrounding production methods and techniques.

The six field officers working in the valley in the early 1990s were assigned to specific growers in their respective areas. According to their estimates, they were responsible for anywhere between 170 and 400 farmers total, visiting 80 to 180 farmers per week. Their formal working schedules were Monday through Friday for farm visits and one Sunday per month to lead and attend the district branch meetings. Yet, most of them pointed out that their schedules had to be very flexible and often extended outside of these specified dates and times. If a situation arose in which a farmer needed to see them on a Saturday, they would come to the area to work. All but two resided in "town" (Castries), and all but one held advanced educational degrees in agriculture. At the time that I met them in 1993, they had worked in extension with the SLBGA from two to six years and, beyond their studies at agricultural colleges, they had received training at the SLBGA before beginning their assignments. Their status as SLBGA agricultural "experts" was measured by their formal training rather than their personal experience. Their understanding of appropriate services for growers was based on a combination of the formal training, directives from the SLBGA, a routine schedule set by the association, and an assessment of individual banana growers' specific problems and needs. Thus, the daily, repeated, and most comprehensive interfacing between growers and the SLBGA came from field officers who were distinguished from the "average" grower based on formal agricultural training and thus "expert knowledge."[18]

Some of the viewpoints expressed by field officers revealed further degrees of social disconnect between themselves and growers. The labels for valley residents that I encountered during my initial stay in Castries appeared in conversation with field officers. While usually admitting that growers had extreme economic and material pressures, they also highlighted how banana producers sought shortcuts rather than following SLBGA guidelines completely. This, they claimed, led to a variety of other production problems. Thus, at times, field officers seriously acknowledged market constraints and the status of the SLBGA, yet often they linked the cause of growers' problems back to growers' own practices and approaches. As one field officer said (echoing comments from senior SLBGA staff interviewed on radio programs): "[T]hose who take an inept approach leads to low [fruit] quality and low production." Such comments imagined growers as exhibiting unproductive and unbusinesslike behavior that compromised the industry and had to be redressed.

And thus a solution was for field officers to survey and assess producers' work intensively. This occurred especially on harvest days, when field officers usually offered suggestions and reminders about how to properly perform postharvest activities. But also, by the early 1990s, one of field officers' major responsibilities was to assign field scores to banana growers and to assess grower performance in a variety of specified on-farm tasks. According to a SLBGA circular, the field score included "all agronomic practices" pertaining to maintenance and protection of banana trees from pests and weeds, removing from farm fields all "banana tree waste" such as fallen branches and dried leaves, weed control, drainage, and "general field appearance." Evaluating individual growers' performance in these areas and in this way introduced quantification and the application of a universal evaluation tool as a suitable way to assess the worth of growers' work. Because the method required that field officers make routine and repeated visits to farmers' fields and have detailed knowledge of how growers performed the specified tasks, it also launched the practice of regular monitoring and assessing growers' farm life at a much-heightened level.

In this process, field officers could attempt to shape farm activities without producers' involvement. Although field officers were expected to make appointments to visit growers' fields, scoring could occur in the growers' absence. A grower could receive a field score without knowing what that score was at the time it was assigned and without having an opportunity to discuss the evaluation process or refute the score with the officer. Further, field officers could write up growers who had not complied with SLBGA mandates, leaving the possibility that a grower could be fined or eventually have his or her license to grow bananas revoked. Thus, the possibility of field officers' appearance and the threat of their discipline (and its broader implications for growers' relation and place within the SLBGA) were ever present and outside of growers' control. Officers were the local eyes of the SLBGA. They were a critical conduit for gathering information about growers and also for disseminating information to them, while growers had little say in the SLBGA's assessment of producers' own work.

It must be noted that field officers did not always discipline growers but sometimes socialized with them. There was thus a mixture of surveillance and camaraderie. Indeed, when asked, all of the field representatives I spoke with offered that they dealt with the "social and personal" aspects of farmers' lives when farmers came to them for advice outside of farming. Yet, even beyond this dynamic of the SLBGA officer helping the grower (in any area of the grower's life), there were moments of mutual exchange and social proximity. For instance, the officer who lived in the valley was known widely and socially integrated into the community, while the nonresident officers sometimes befriended certain growers, spending time with them outside of a strict work relationship. One officer said that he had moved closer to the valley from his residence in the south, revealing a willingness to transcend expected spatial divides through residency and not to transgress those divides solely through employment.

My first on-farm visit illustrates the ways in which socio-spatial divides were sometimes transcended in field officer–grower relations. After meeting a field officer, he took me to meet a farmer in the valley. During the several hours that the three of us spent on the producers' farm, the field officer worked alongside the grower. Waiting to measure the grower's banana production level (the purpose of his visit), he spent more time helping the grower box and transport citrus (a nonbanana crop outside the domain of the SLBGA!) and listening to the producer talk about his own strategies for improving his farm. This differed from the more usual instance of field officers informing growers about farm work. In this particular case, the hours were passed in continuous conversation not merely about improvements for banana farming but also about producing other crops and about nonfarm issues such as family and politics. The exchange of ideas between the grower and the field officer broke down the more common setup based on hierarchies of knowledge. Consequently, while field officers' primary task was overseeing growers' daily work, the field officer role sometimes was complicated by a daily relationship through which close ties, friendships, and mutual exchange of information were spawned between the SLBGA "expert" and the banana producer. These ties were part of the process by which field officers' images of and interactions with growers were rendered complex, stretching across experiences from engaged sociality to modes of discipline. The social divides of education, residence, and employment between grower and field officer, which resonated with larger rural-urban gaps, were sometimes tempered by the social/friendship bonds ironically formed and made possible by the thickness of the everyday power/knowledge apparatus. It was because field officers were charged with continual and intensive farm monitoring that, ironically, they were able to build up ties with growers whose social and professional identities were, in most instances, considered less socially elevated than those of the field officers.

Inspecting Bananas, Determining Value

On harvest days, field officers' role ended at the stage when fruit was boxed and transported to point of sale. The next stage involved small growers bringing their fruit to banana-buying depots located in their districts, while large-scale growers brought bananas to the wharves either in Castries or Vieux Fort. In these locations, growers' fruit was passed through an inspection process wherein SLBGA and Geest staff evaluated bananas for their marketability—their "acceptable quality"—and ultimately it was where the value of the fruit was determined. Small growers went to SLBGA-staffed inland buying depots to sell their fruit while large-scale growers transported their boxes to the wharf, where they were inspected by Geest agents. To get to this point, growers queued in pickup trucks, the truck beds stacked high with boxes and the wait often taking hours, depending on the time of day and the season. By late afternoon in the peak production season, lines were stretched out of the district depots or extended far from the city wharves, and it was common to see growers waiting to have their fruit inspected long after dark.

Inspection procedures were mandatory but underwent significant reorganization in the 1990s along with other harvest and postharvest procedures. Before 1991, fruit was classified into two categories: acceptable quality and unacceptable quality. The latter meant that fruit was not salable to the SLBGA and thus had to be rejected (however, it could be sold at local supermarkets or to market traders, unlike acceptable quality fruit, which it was unlawful to sell to anyone except the SLBGA).[19] Fruit deemed acceptable was purchased by the SLBGA and received the predetermined price that the association had announced earlier in the week.[20] But, in 1991 the SLBGA introduced a three-tiered grading system in which banana quality was rated as either A, B, C, or unacceptable. Those classified as A grade received the highest price offered by the SLBGA, while those obtaining a C rating received the lowest. The process, known as quality determination, entailed inspectors selecting and inspecting a required sample of boxes per grower. The sample size varied according to the grower's annual production level.

To arrive at the rating, inspectors visually checked a farmer's banana boxes, assessing quality according to the presence and frequency of bruises, blemishes, and ripeness of the fruit. Blemishless fruit received an A. Blemished fruit's grade was determined by closer and a more complicated evaluation: a calculation of the fruit score *and* the farmer's field score entered earlier by the field officer. Like the field score, fruit evaluations and prices were non-negotiable; they were set by SLBGA staff without grower input, and growers were not able to observe inspectors' work. Inspectors operated off of a strict and fixed formula to make their assessments and had ultimate authority regarding fruit quality and the financial worth of bananas. Days later, growers learned of the price and exact sum they would receive when they went to the SLBGA main office to collect their weekly returns.

The post-1991 fruit quality ratings differentiated growers beyond production level and by more subjective standards, whereby producers were seemingly identified as "good" and "less good" producers. Fruit quality, as a measure of many factors about growers' work conduct, reflected how a grower maintained his or her work space, the extent of his or her fruit's visual appeal (e.g., presence of bruises), the fruit's fit with industry standards of size and grade, and the fruit's value. That there were consequences (other than simply not being able to sell one's product) for not ascending to the highest ratings also illustrated how fruit quality had multiple implications. Growers could be subject to more scrutiny from field officers after inspectors noted that fruit quality was substandard. Further, public shame was an unofficial consequence. Inspectors did not publicly announce ratings, but there sometimes were open squabbles over perceived inspection results. When producers questioned and argued over the grade into which their fruit fell, those waiting in line understood that a poor quality rating had been rendered. The scoring process, then, was a partial form of semi-public individual/professional assessment that allowed inspectors to engage individually and openly with growers and, in some respects, ultimately to define growers as "good" and "bad" farmers.

Although SLBGA banana inspection procedures reinforced a notion that growers' work and worth had to be carefully assessed by an SLBGA "expert," inspectors at the district buying depots (and not at the wharf inspection stations) sometimes were from the same communities as the farmers they inspected. This rendered the inspection process a deeply local experience since, for most, it not only was anchored in farming districts but also was performed through an interaction between local residents, who were differentiated only momentarily during the inspection event. Indeed, in Morne Verte, inspectors were not necessarily more educated or wealthier than banana growers who passed through the buying depots. Inspectors, too, could have had personal and ongoing experience in farming, working both as inspectors and as growers or residing in households where a family member grew bananas. This, then, was distinct from field officers, who were more apt to reside outside of the farming areas where they worked and whose competence in banana production was measured according to their formal training. Thus, as with field officers, growers were differentiated from inspectors by the "expert" position that inspectors held, but they also were simultaneously close to them. Ties were due to common experience of locality. In this way, surveillance and labor disciplining strategies were exacted through a space of both familiarity and difference as growers were evaluated and inspected by members of their own communities.[21] This meant that hierarchical modes of surveillance based on knowledge gaps and type were nuanced by relationships of familiarity and friendship. Forms of social disconnect were bridged by an affiliation and a familiarity with locality that both producer and inspector shared.

CONCLUSION

When Henry Breen spoke of an unruly Mabouya Valley in need of correction, he could not have forecast that aspects of his representation of the region would endure for over a century. Yet, the late-twentieth-century image of the "volatile valley" that emerged during my own visit to the area was meant to imply that the Mabouya Valley was given to violence and explosive events, presumably at the hands of its residents. One could argue that this imagery also was tied up in decades of twentieth-century development in the region. The long-standing relations that residents held with the Dennery Estate, the state, and the SLBGA, especially from the 1950s to the 1990s, had been fraught with uncertainty and hierarchical modes of interaction for decades. Estate managers, and later state representatives, exerted power through a variety of disciplinary practices that punctuated daily life and forms of social and economic organization in the valley. Such practices, founded on power/knowledge gaps between state/estate representatives and producers/laborers, were the basis for establishing social hierarchies.

The national context for these relations was especially the formalization of the banana industry. From the moment that banana production became the partial domain of the state through the 1967 SLBGA Act and the subsequent reorganization of the plantation system, it was organized around a hierarchy wherein the state had a *visibly* strong say in the daily activities of "self-employed" banana growers across St. Lucia. The terms securing that hierarchy intensified over time and, by the late 1980s, were set up around the overarching globalization discourse discussed in chapter 2. Such terms included the structuring of everyday farm tasks around ideas about market shift and the importance of ensuring adequate fruit quality and grower compliance with associated production methods. Inspection processes, postharvest tasks, and other weekly activities overseen by field officers regularly connected growers to the discourse. During the repeated weeks when they harvested and processed their fruit, growers were constrained by changing and intensifying methods that were officially designed to meet market demands. This process, which limited the range of possible farm tasks, helped strip growers of their official classification as "independent producers." Its legacy was fixtures such as the Dennery Estate and the Mabouya Valley Development Project, through which valley workers and producers came to see the estate as an economic development authority that contoured the organization of production.

Authority was also an important basis for promoting divisions in the valley, divisions that resonated with the politics of rural-urban spatialities. Often serving as SLBGA authorities, radio announcers and interviewees, field officers, and fruit inspectors served as types of "development" experts whose role was to instruct, inform, inspect, and *approve* all aspects of growers' work. They tended to be differentiated from growers by residence, education, and income, yet levels and understandings of expertise and agricultural knowledge seemed to hold more sway in the grower-SLBGA divide. The implication was that growers were in need of instruction and monitoring by urban, state-affiliated SLBGA representatives. Still, the regularity and closeness of grower and field officers' interactions meant that social divisions between the two were fluid rather than stark. Field officers who worked and in one case lived closely with growers developed friendships or extra-occupational bonds with banana producers. Inspectors, who often were valley residents, possessed authority and knowledge based on their status as SLBGA employees, but as valley residents (and sometimes growers themselves) they were experientially close to those they inspected. In these ways, the structure in which growers and the SLBGA representatives interacted was hierarchical and rigid on the one hand and flexible and incomplete on the other.

A key point here is that the location of grower-SLBGA interactions was important in defining how hierarchies operated, who fit within them, and how. Indeed, Geest was virtually and certainly visibly absent from hierarchies that played out through banana production in everyday valley life. Geest was a clear actor in the process of production and, arguably, was the strongest force setting production and distribution in motion.[22] Yet, in daily farm life in the Mabouya Valley, the company had more of a "behind-the-scenes" role in terms of growers' day-in and day-out activities.[23] As a mandatory and continual fixture in growers' daily lives, the state was the ever-present actor that appeared to arrange growers' work practices. Indeed, the micro-, place-based level of interaction rendered this setup and its appearance possible and also helped give the state the more obvious assignment of power. The "discursive space" (de Certeau 1984) of labor discipline was a mixture of legal, formal, and public policies—as well as the everyday and quasi-private activities—played out within the specific history and context of the valley.

4. *Freedom under Control in the Valley*

*O*N OCTOBER 11, 1993, St. Lucia's prime minister, the Rt. Honorable John Compton, gave a televised address to the nation following the first banana growers' strike organized by the Banana Salvation Committee. The strike's goal was to protest the decline in banana prices that farmers were receiving from the SLBGA. On television, Compton announced a government-subsidized increase in prices, but he also voiced outrage and dismay at the ways in which growers had conducted themselves during the strike. Publicly chastising growers and defending the government's approach to the industry, he claimed that:

> [c]ertain criminal elements of our society . . . took the opportunity to display the kind of lawless and criminal behaviour completely out of character of the majority of our people. They blocked roads, destroyed and burnt the sheds of farmers, attacked vehicles, molested tourists . . . and in general caused a complete breakdown of civil order in some parts of St. Lucia and in particular in the Mabouya Valley. . . . For myself, I have given my all to the banana industry and I have gained nothing for myself. . . . Why do I continue to sacrifice? Because men and women [farmers] who could not own a bicycle now have their [government-subsidized pickup truck] which they are able to purchase because of government concessions to farmers and the security of the income of the banana industry. . . . These are some of the things which sustained me on Wednesday when I faced alone the angry mob at [the Mabouya Valley], an area which has benefited so much from my work and personal sacrifice. (GOSL 1993: 1, 4–5)

Around the time of this speech, it was difficult to make it through a day in Morne Verte without hearing someone bemoan the state of the banana industry, or reference the prime minister's approach to it. Feeling insulted by statements in Compton's televised speech, some residents declared that the prime minister had gone too far in his pejorative characterization of farmers. For example, Mark, a banana grower from Morne Verte, spoke with vigor as he commented on this very issue.

> When farmers got to the street and [heard] the prime minister saying that farmers are greedy, these things got us sick because he knew what we were going through. His coming on national television made farmers feel very little and greedy whereas those in high ranks don't know what the farmer has to go through.

Mark referenced a sentiment that the prime minister was dismissive and disregarded farmers' hard work, while others in Morne Verte contended that the prime minister had actually taken over the industry. Because of this, people sometimes claimed that they were in fact working for the prime minister and therefore recouping very little for themselves. Morne Vertians publicly discussed how the government had actually controlled rather than boosted farmers (as the prime minister's speech implied) and how the SLBGA, not growers, was built on corruption and greed that disadvantaged most farmers. With vehemence, they complained that the price for bananas was too low, the costs of production too high, and the work increasingly harder and time intensive. Their assessments of the industry not only challenged the prime minister's take but also did not resonate with state-led discussions of the ways in which foreign market policies had destabilized producers' income potential and prompted a need for work intensification. Instead, their analyses focused on specific figures and institutions in St. Lucia and how these had shaped developments in the industry. They offered critiques of both the SLBGA and the government as agents of control, often seeing the two as working hand in hand.

Yet, alongside this complaint of control was the pronouncement that banana production engendered freedom. A less public but not a hidden discourse, discussions of work-freedom here were not heard in spontaneous street and farm conversation, but they also were not concealed. Rather, the complaint emerged openly in interviews and discussions, especially when I asked growers to tell me their thoughts on banana production or to explain why they had become banana growers. Some stated that they had taken up growing bananas because they lacked other options or because it was something with which they were familiar due to a long-standing family tradition of farming. Many, however, responded to my questions by characterizing banana production as a positive activity due to its status as a form of self-employment. For them, growing bananas was a means of achieving autonomy, a flexible work schedule, avoidance of an employer's overseeing, and individual security. Farming thus was pinned up as an individual endeavor, as were specific modes of organizing production that allowed one to pursue self-sufficiency. But, why would growers talk of being free in a production system so highly restricted and so shakily situated against competitor producers in other areas of the world? Why, in most cases, would they fail to cite the restrictions imposed by liberalizing global markets if they were continually exposed to information about the threat of competition and market loss?

It might be tempting to assume that ideas about freedom of work show growers' misguided understandings of their place in the global economy or of their role as subordinated quasi–contract laborers with Geest Industries. Indeed, I have been asked by social science researchers if Morne Verte producers' ideas about freedom of work do not reveal a classic case of "false consciousness," a failure to grasp one's disadvantaged position within a hierarchical structure. I also have been asked if their ideas about work freedom did not facilitate their own exploitation, since believing that they work freely would have created a disincentive to leave banana production, thus continuing their marginalization and oppression to the benefit of Geest.[1] These questions consider how, by their very placement within the banana industry, growers became or remained supporters of contemporary capitalist exploitation. Yet, while it is clear that producers' contract work facilitated Geest's profit making and the consolidation of power between the state and foreign capital, it is unlikely that growers were *unwitting* assistants to that process. To be sure, the juxtaposition of two concepts—freedom and control—negates the likelihood that growers suffered from false consciousness, since they expressed a pointed belief and understanding of their domination by "external" agents. Further, it is clear that ideas of work freedom did not *bind* Morne Verte growers to banana production, since, despite statements of freedom, there were obvious signs that some growers were moving out of banana production, partially or wholly, and that others had a desire to do so. Indeed, 15% of those I asked for an interview had already left banana farming, 38% recently had started to diversify into nonbanana crops, and over half of those who claimed to hold a secondary occupation had obtained it no more than five years before being interviewed by me (Slocum 1996). As such, it would be difficult to claim that the freedom of work narrative was an instance of growers' illusory understanding of their position within an unequally arranged industry. Considering themselves to be free did not preclude seeking out alternatives, especially when economic, political, and/or social circumstances seemed to call for change *and* when resources and options were available to make such a change.

The narrative constructed by growers presents an understanding of work outside of the ways it was conceptualized through the production practices mandated by the SLBGA and shaped by Geest and WINBAN policy. Talking about freedom of work, as well as organizing production around a concept of freedom, I argue, signaled growers' investment in the politics of defining production and work around meanings of place (i.e., meanings attached to Morne Verte) that were inflected with specific cultural and economic referents (Hastrup and Olwig 1997; Olwig 1997). As an alternative reading and political position on the definition of production, freedom of work represented a very *local* and *regional* discourse resonating with historical experiences around culture and economy in Morne Verte and the wider Caribbean. Uttered and expressed in Morne Verte by Morne Vertians, the discourse presented residents' 1990s' experiences of work, land use, and forms of social interaction through models similar to the historical experiences of Afro- and Indo-Morne Vertians as well as Afro- and Indo-Caribbeans. Those historical experiences included prioritizing flexible productive pursuits, with social implications, within a context of land scarcity and uncertain labor options (Besson 1987b, 1992; Carnegie 1983). In its 1990s' version, this was a flexibility that contrasted sharply with the more rigid and structured nature of banana production promoted by state policies. It also contrasted with the flexibility associated with contract work where corporations benefit by fragmenting and decentralizing work across numerous producers and thereby passing on the costs and risks of production to contract laborers (Harvey 1989; Lash and Urry 1987). Instead, growers' ideas about freedom of work conceived of flexibility as work autonomy, the ability to work for oneself, chart one's own productive activities, and pursue employment options as they arose. The meaning and cultural politics of work in a particular place were important to this conceptualization and its role as an alternative to the interconnected theses of economic globalization and work discipline. This is so because the freedom of work concept tied into Morne Vertian political and cultural experiences and histories.

FREEDOM & FARMING

Early morning. I rose at 6:30 to meet Susan,[2] a banana grower whose farm I frequently visited on harvest days. By 7:30, I was standing at "the Morne Verte gap," an intersection of the main road and the smaller feeder roads that led up into residential communities and further up onto farms high atop the steep hillsides. I often met growers at this gap. Her male friend, who had a pickup truck, would meet us, sometimes later than planned but always without fail. Along with others who would work on the farm for the day, I would climb into the truck bed and ride fifteen minutes upward (seemingly *straight* upward). On early harvest mornings, the activity both on the roads intersecting at the gap and on the farm feeder roads was lively. After hours of a sequential and routinized process of cutting stems of bananas, loading smaller clusters of bananas onto trays, carrying trays to roadside sheds, washing banana clusters in fungicidal solutions, labeling bananas, and boxing bananas, we took a break almost squarely at midday. By then, we had finished more than half of the day's work but still had, on average, three more hours to go. I usually returned home by 3:00 PM, sometimes leaving before Susan and her friends/workers had finished their work. After completing harvesting and boxing tasks, they took the boxes to the banana-buying depots, waiting in line to have the boxes weighed and evaluated for quality before the day's work was over.

These days were long and structured, but it was common to hear banana growers claim that they were free to work as desired and that they enjoyed a flexible and self-directed work environment and schedule. Stressing their ability to start a workday late, as opposed to making an early morning start, they argued that a grower set his or her own hours and left for and returned from the farm when she or he pleased in the absence of someone else's dictates. Freedom was the ability to organize a self-imposed workday.

This was a perspective that Tony espoused. An older grower who had been producing bananas for decades, he told me: "[As a farmer] I can leave here [from my house to go to work] anytime. . . . I don't have to wake up early. [I can] prepare myself and go in the garden [farm] and I am satisfied." Many growers like Tony underscored time and space as key parameters and dividing lines between wage work and "independent" banana production. Other growers cited set hours that they would have to follow if working for an employer compared to the ability to leave at a self-directed time if working for themselves as banana farmers. Wage time and sometimes even "self-employed time" within nonfarm occupations were conceived of and described as more rigid and outside of a worker's control. The alternative description of "banana farming time" showed that growers not only had more freedom of scheduling but also freedom of operating, moving, and organizing activities in a space outside of someone else's (an employer's) sphere of influence. The absence of an employer-overseer who would determine how one could work enabled freer spatial and temporal movement.

Added to this conclusion was the notion of limitless employment and income possibilities afforded by the nature of agricultural production, and banana production in particular, also due to individual effort. Growers described their work as guaranteed because they could sell bananas each week to a constant and regular buyer (the SLBGA) and because, as self-employed persons, the threat of losing one's job or being laid off did not exist. Further, income was considered to be steady given the weekly cycle of harvests and banana sales, as well as the perception of a guaranteed market for St. Lucian bananas. Employment, too, was seen as assured as long as a grower applied herself or himself to the work: a banana producer could always work for himself or herself even when other work opportunities did not exist. Indeed, growers argued that working harder could even bring greater financial benefits because work intensification and expansion could mean higher banana yields and thus higher incomes. Growers had the freedom to work harder and get more, the argument went, as opposed to working harder and receiving the same salary, as when one was an employee.

An obstacle to achieving freedom as a wage worker also was the character of the employer, who Morne Verte growers described as overbearing, demanding, and unyielding. Growers talked hypothetically of employers being strict and constraining of their time. For instance, Mark, a talkative, medium-scale producer in his late thirties said that previously he had worked independently and as an employee in masonry, carpentry, and construction. Yet, he was adamant that he preferred growing bananas precisely because he could avoid the heavy hand of an employer. Telling this to me in detail, he exclaimed:

> [W]hen I feel like going on my farm, I'll go. No boss will ask me where I was and why am I so late. . . . For instance, if I'm working for . . . [supermarkets and department stores in the city], when it's 7 or 8 o'clock I have to find myself at work. Before the door opens I really have to stand there waiting on the boss. And if I arrive two minutes late, he will ask me: "you don't want to work?" or why . . . [is] this [the] time I'm reporting for work. [So,] when [people say] they like to be their own boss, it's like they can go on their farm any time. They feel more free.

As did other growers, Mark cited specific urban department stores in Castries when he imagined the overbearing and restrictive employer, as if these places (places where he never said he had worked) were the quintessential sites of an anti-free work environment. These were stores owned by and named after some of the long-established fixtures and families of St. Lucia's social, political, and economic urban elite. Thus, in this instance of the freedom of work narrative, employers were cast as owners of specific and oftentimes well-off owners of urban businesses. By contrast, employers were *not* depicted as large-scale banana growers who employed landless or land poor workers from the valley—a common feature of Morne Verte's local economy. When growers spoke of work freedom, there was at times an assumption, like Mark's, that social hierarchies and unequal power relations underlay employer-employee relations *outside* of farming and *in the city*. Images of controlling employers, therefore, were marked by power, class, and region—as if the three were intertwined.

Interestingly, wage work was not foreign to Morne Verte households. Approximately half of producers, males and females, in the area had worked for wages outside of the farm sector at some point in their lives; the remainder always had worked as farmers or as laborers on other people's farms. In the early 1990s, there was evidence that some growers were beginning to seek alternative employment, even wage work. During this time, most (74%) of Morne Verte banana-farming households I visited were multi-occupational; in addition to banana production, household residents—including possibly the banana grower—held jobs in other areas (Slocum 1996: 122). Within this occupational mix, half of the nonbanana occupations held by producers simultaneously with their

work in bananas were waged jobs. Work in trades such as masonry, carpentry, and construction were most common, although clerical work,
factory work, and positions with the SLBGA were also part of Morne
Verte growers' occupational experiences. Moreover, there was a distinct
gender pattern to the occurrence of multi-occupationality: more than
40% of active male growers worked off of the farm either in manual wage
or self-employment jobs, while only one out of ten female farm heads
did. Thus, growers had firsthand knowledge of wage work, knowledge
from which their notions of freedom and farming may have sprung,
however, none were personally familiar with the wage work in urban
businesses that some claimed to deplore.

Beyond conceptualizing freedom *against* the restrictive scheduling of
work within urban businesses, growers understood freedom *with* its
potential for social and economic security and advancement. They
emphasized how, as banana growers, they had improved their social and
economic lives by obtaining land on which to grow their fruit and then
by working for themselves. Progressing as a banana producer was possible for anyone because, many held, education and special skills were not
required to pursue the profession. Further, many farmers who had scant
or no access to land equated attaining land and growing bananas with a
rise in social status and a decline in economic and social vulnerability.
This especially included those who acquired land ("on loan") from family members who had migrated out of St. Lucia or who had taken other
work. It also included those who were in landholding arrangements
known as *share*, a land tenure form in which use of someone else's land
was granted in exchange for a portion of the monetary returns from
bananas produced on that land.[3] In these latter cases, which were akin to
sharecropping systems, banana production was seen as an opening created in the lives of people for whom specific economic opportunities had
been closed off. The opening was the process toward achieving freedom.
Growers thus revealed the connection between reaching an ideal of
abandoning manual wage work, undoing a state of landlessness, cultivating bananas, increasing one's social prestige, and becoming free.

For example, John, a young farmer in his early twenties who had
grown bananas for what he estimated to be six to nine years, said to me
that he had been given "a break" when he gained access to land. As a
child, he had worked as a laborer on other people's farms, and when he
left school in his teenage years he continued this type of work. Consid-

ering himself to have limited options due to his family background and education, he sat at the kitchen table in the modest home that he shared with his godmother near the top of Morne Verte and told me:

> I have no choice. I do not really have a sound education [other than farming]—I can only work as a construction laborer. . . .When I left school my parents were too poor to allow me to further my education. So I decided to become a farmer. I started working with a man [as a laborer on his farm] and he just gave me a piece of land to work [on my own].

The land John worked was through *share* rather than leased or "on loan." Still, he credited the landowner for part of his employment gains. Unlike Mark's characterization of the department store employers in Castries, who would constrain his time and advancement, John portrayed the landowner-employer he knew in Morne Verte as someone who had helped him achieve freedom. He went on to explain that, as a laborer, the relationship he developed with the landowner was important in allowing him to gain access to land on which he could grow bananas for himself and not for someone else (i.e., the landowner). He went further to couple land acquisition with self-employed banana production, seeing them as a source of self-determination and an opportunity for professional and financial expansion:

> It's better to work for yourself in bananas because when you work for others you don't get access to other people's money. But when you have your own field you can extend the work time and try to get more money. [You can] squeeze more money. . . . Bananas never leave you with no work. Once you have bananas you are always capable of getting money. If I work for JQ [a large urban supermarket], I know my arrangement—$40/day. I know for sure if I do two weeks [work] I know what I will get. But, for yourself, if you push it a little harder— like if you have a shop and you [can] add things to sell . . . you can do something more to get more out of it. But with JQ you can't do it. You have access to your day's pay [only].

It may seem contradictory for John to equate *share* with being professionally autonomous, since he was required to give the landowner a portion of the fruits of his work. However, John's remarks point to a perceived importance of gaining access to land as a way to work for oneself, even if that land is not owned or is acquired through an imbalanced setup. The importance lay in the possibility of expanding one's work and potential profit margin.

John's sentiments were like those of Ellie, a woman in her thirties who lived in a section of Morne Verte where land had been especially scarce and who also gained land through *share* when her domestic partner's aunt gave her a small plot. Having acquired this land for the first time only three months before I met her, she claimed that she saw "no progress in it" when she worked for others in waged employment. Like John, she expressed the conclusion that working for someone else was akin to financial, professional, and social stagnation. Equally important to John's and Ellie's view was the idea that banana production could enable someone to overcome and offset particular limitations of social status because it did not require formal skills training while still allowing someone with few skills and scant formal education to progress. Thus, it was not simply land access, bananas, and financial possibilities that mattered. What also mattered was how these combined with the prospects of certain forms of wage work and bypassing an urban employer-employee relationship to define the possibilities for work independence, status attainment, and personal freedom.

FREEDOM IN PRACTICE & IN THEORY

Integral to the notion of freedom was flexibility, an aspect of work freedom achieved through the organization of farm practice, especially forms of labor and land use. While on its own farming was considered to engender open scheduling and independence, particular ways of setting up farm activities were seen as promoting flexibility, from which work independence could be further secured. Concretely, this meant working and enabling others (especially family members) to work independently by using land and labor in ways that facilitated both economic independence and the pursuit of a variety of employment options within and beyond farming. Land tended to be used individually rather than collectively among family members. Labor tended to be paid, relatively generously, rather than compensated in kind, and regardless of the relation between farm owner and worker. This arrangement allowed workers who were kin to earn an individual income and those without land of their own to gain access to this important productive resource rather than working as part of a collective unit and pooling resources. Flexibility, especially within families, occurred through this formation, which allowed people the room to pursue productive options of their own.

To many observers, including staff from the land-titling project and some SLBGA field officers, such practices often were seen as counterproductive. This was because the level of flexibility and the nature of the practices meant additional time and expenses than presumably would have been necessary with other available means of organizing production, such as noncommunal landholding systems. Indeed, the ways in which small-scale producers organized their farm activities (in the spaces not dictated by the SLBGA) drew much attention and consternation among several nonproducers, including academics, estate managers, government or industry officials, and development planners (Bruce 1983; GOSL 1977, cited in Barrow 1992; Development and Welfare Organisation of the West Indies 1951; Organization of American States 1991).[4] Consider, for example, the views of an upper level employee on one of St. Lucia's large estates. He once complained to me that high labor expenses were at the base of St. Lucia's problems in the banana industry. He told me of his knowledge of farms in Latin America, where he learned that farm laborers were paid $17.00 for eleven hours of work. He compared this with St. Lucian estate workers, who, he said, were paid $27.00 dollars for four hours of work. "St. Lucian workers," he went on, "go for actual wage rather than time. . . . They don't want to work long hours . . . [and] this has an adverse affect." "You can't have quality fruit if you don't have quality workers," he concluded. To him, the Latin American model of less pay for more work was something St. Lucia should emulate to save on farm expenses and to make the country more competitive globally.

While few farmers I met talked in the global terms that this person did, many farmers mentioned high labor costs and complained of "lazy workers," who had to be fed and paid handsomely for few hours of work. Yet, in the early 1990s, banana producers relied on hired labor at a relatively high rate (an average of $40.00 E.C. a day)[5] for performing the bulk of their work. Of those I queried, paid laborers accounted for 74% of all the labor used by Morne Verte growers (Slocum 1996: 114). Consequently, growers' labor expenses were relatively high and represented a large proportion of total farm expenses. Yet growers did not often complain about this fact as did the upper level estate employee. As some growers explained, any laborer (including kin) deserved the right to be paid, so that, as an adult, he or she could be self-supporting. With the exclusion of head of farm's domestic partner (e.g., common law or legal spouse) latitude was extended especially to household residents and/or family members who could pursue independent work options rather than be tied to a family farm.

While it was not unheard of for growers to use and pay family labor, growers also were known, and more apt, to make a conscious choice to finance labor where other less expensive options for meeting farm labor needs were available. In this way growers' farm practices diverged from conventional definitions of the "family farm." Indeed, on her two relatively small farms of two acres each, Ellie worked with four laborers. Two of these workers were her sisters, both of whom did not live with her and both of whom she paid. Two others were friends, one of which she paid and one of which she compensated in kind. John worked with three laborers, two of whom were non-family and paid. He also exchanged labor services with his brother who had his own farm. Mark operated a relatively larger farm of seven acres and also worked with four laborers, half of whom were paid non-family members. His girlfriend, with whom he lived and who worked for no pay, worked alongside him and his male cousin, who had his own farm and helped Mark one week while Mark returned the favor the next. Tony, on his two farms of one-half and three-quarters of an acre, worked completely alone, not expecting his daughter or son-in-law to help out except once when his daughter temporarily lost her job and had free time. Ellie and John's cases thus show compensation for all laborers, no matter the relation. Mark's case demonstrates the use of uncompensated family labor only for his live-in girlfriend, while Tony's case reveals an almost complete absence of drawing on help, non-family or family.

In most cases, farms were not operated by extended families who divided labor tasks and responsibilities among them or who pooled farm income and land resources for collective family needs. Whether or not they resided in their parents' homes, many adult children—especially young males—worked separately from their parents' farms and only assisted when their individual employment schedule allowed. Moving in and out of other options when such options existed, they would work, usually for pay, on a family member's or parents' farm when or if alternatives became scarce.

Ironically, and in contrast to ideas about freedom of work, household members' alternative forms of work usually did not involve self-employment. Their work included office jobs in Castries, factory work, house-keeping positions in tourist hotels, and even working on someone else's farm. Thus, "freedom as flexibility" referred to the possibility of improving one's status with family members working in urban businesses (the same ones that Mark and others critiqued) or local industries as well as working on one's own farm. But, it was the farm owner's privileging of flexibility for his or her family, even being accepting of household members' work in seemingly inflexible work settings, which reveals how notions of freedom achieved in banana production tied into the discourse on flexibility. Engendering freedom for children was important and made possible by a farm-parent being flexible enough to allow his or her sons and daughters to work independently and in occupations where they could achieve steady income. If a producer's adult children were securing work for themselves as individuals (as in the case of Tony), this rendered the decision to work separately from one's banana-farming parents acceptable and preferable.

Spouses or domestic partners (such as Mark's), resident children, and workers who labored in exchange for the friend's help on an alternate week were least likely to receive remuneration. This latter arrangement was known as *society*, or (in Kwéyòl) *associyé*, and was the most frequent form of unpaid labor in Morne Verte. *Associyé* entailed producers forming alliances with friends or family members with whom they could exchange farm work on alternate harvesting weeks. Another and rarer form of labor use in Morne Verte, *koudeman*, appeared as a less regular form of exchange and unpaid labor that tended to involve non-harvest-day tasks. Ellie participated in *associyé* with her female friend while John participated in it with his brother. Both had other paid workers on their farms, and thus *associyé* was part of a mix of labor uses rather than a sole basis of laboring resources. In these and other cases, instances of nonpaid labor use, such as participation in *associyé*, probably occurred out of economic necessity since growers producing the smallest volume of bananas were more likely to draw on unpaid labor. Women who represented the smallest farm operators in Morne Verte were three times more likely to use unpaid labor than were men (Slocum 1996: 114). Thus, when freedom of work was put into practice through labor-use arrangements, it was mediated by growers' production levels and resources, which were also intertwined with patterns of gender and income.

Land use practices reflected similar approaches to labor use and payment. On average, land parcels among Morne Verte banana growers were seven acres, yet a majority of people I encountered worked on farms that were between one and four acres (Slocum 1996: 81) (see table 3). Banana growers who owned or rented land tended not to share and work the land with family members, and even growers cultivating the smallest parcels of land (one to three acres) were known to divide the land into smaller plots. Most Morne Vertians reported to me that, while they had "family land," land they owned communally with multiple family members, they tended not to use the land if someone else in their family operated it. This supports research on the institution of family land in the Caribbean, which shows that heirs to family land frequently rotate or shift their use of the land rather than use it collectively all at once (Barrow 1992; Besson and Momsen 1987; Besson 1979, 1987b). This is true even if access to the land is considered unrestricted and serves as a symbolic value to all who hold legal rights to it (Besson 1979, 1992). In St. Lucia, family land use practices have also included coordination among multiple (but not all) co-owners (Crichlow 1994). For example, Tony said he still had family land in the area outside of Morne Verte where he was born but that his daughter used it and he did not, as if one person's use of the land precluded another's. Thus, it is possible

TABLE 3.   Land Size of Sampled Heads of Farm in Morne Verte

Acreage	Number of Farmers[a]	Percentage of Total
1	9	17.7
2	10	19.6
3	6	11.8
4	3	5.9
5	9	17.7
6	2	4.0
7	3	5.9
9	3	5.9
14	1	1.9
17	1	1.9
18	1	1.9
28	1	1.9
30	1	1.9
56	1	1.9
Total	51	100.00

Source: Slocum 1996: 83.

Note: Data are missing for five cases in which the size of land parcels was unknown.

[a]Numbers can include more than one parcel per banana grower.

that Morne Vertians' scant use of family land reflected this tendency to bypass working the land for the sake of other family members' use of it, as has been evidenced more widely in St. Lucia and the British West Indies. Such patterns in Morne Verte also spoke to the elasticity of land use patterns where people reported shifting their use of land. These shifts occurred either according to growers' employment status (e.g., if another job pulled them away from farming temporarily) or according to the circumstances of their family members, who might request or require that the grower look after land in their absence. Movement in land use along with noncommunal land use permitted adult family members to have access to land for their own use and, in the case of young adult children, access to land on which they could establish themselves as independent income earners.

The major exception to using land individually was spouses or cohabiting partners who considered themselves joint heads of farms. Spouses and partners might have worked a single (highest yielding) piece of farmland together as a family farming unit, but still it was possible for each partner also to possess additional and multiple parcels of land that he or she held and worked separately. Thus, even in cases of collaborative farming, producers still could maintain land that they worked individually.

Further, land use patterns were continually shifting. Brandon, a farmer who was barely thirty, maintained two farms: a seven-acre plot of his own and a smaller piece of land that he operated for his mother, who was unable to manage the farm. He managed both pieces with the help of six laborers, all of whom he paid except his domestic partner, who helped on harvesting days. In the past, he had participated in *associyé* with his cousin, but he said he stopped it in 1994 because, he suggested, the arrangement was not working out. The seven acres he worked came from his grandmother, who left the land to Brandon and his brother. However, his brother had migrated to neighboring Martinique in the early 1980s, leading Brandon to take over the entire plot with an understanding that he was working the land in his brother's temporary absence, *for* his brother. When his brother returned a few years after that, Brandon gave his brother back that piece of land to work on his own. Yet, once his brother migrated out again, this time to St. Croix, Brandon stepped back in. And, while it appeared that Brandon was expected to give his brother part of the returns from the banana sales from his brother's plot, Brandon mentioned that there was a time when he had to tell his brother that he needed to keep the money for himself since prices for bananas had gone so low. The apparent understanding between them privileged flexibility both in land use and in terms of farm financing. It allowed the two family members to adjust to ever-shifting dynamics of place, assisting one another to make such adjustments.

As mentioned, the ebb and flow of land use and land responsibilities among multiple family members reflects aspects of family land, a land-tenuring system in which multiple heirs gain rights to land parcels of a relative who dies intestate. Here, inheritance is unrestricted to kin, who are entitled to land through their parents, grandparents, and extended kin. Legally and theoretically, the land may not be partitioned and heirs do not gain rights to a specific portion of the land; all heirs are co-owners, and all are entitled to use the land (Besson 1979, 1984; Bruce 1983; Barrow 1992; Crichlow 1994). There has been much debate and critique of family land as a system of wasteful land fragmentation and subdivision across multiple heirs (Bruce 1983; Mathurin 1967; St. Lucia 1977, cited in Barrow 1992). Yet, some researchers describe it as originally and contemporarily designed to make land accessible to as many persons as possible (Besson 1979, 1987a, 1992; Barrow 1992; Crichlow 1994), perhaps as a response to land consolidation and domination problems that occurred under the plantation system and/or as a mark of symbolic value (Besson 1979, 1987b).[6] More recently, social scientists have argued that family land shields producers against contemporary global market uncertainty, as communal access to land offers a revolving safety net, especially for marginal populations (Dujon 1995: 21). In these ways, family land and the concomitant widespread extension of freehold rights across family members have been viewed as a form of social organization, especially among Afro-West Indians, which offsets systems of material and social inequality that are both external and internal to communities where family land use is practiced (Besson 1979, 1987b; Dujon 1995). Or, as Michaeline Crichlow (1994: 81) aptly puts it, family land has been more than resistance. It has been a means by which Afro-West Indians "established themselves as dignified citizens in a hostile socio-economic and political environment" (that included but was not limited to the plantation system).[7]

In practice, it has been noted that many people who possess family land in St. Lucia have informal ways of doling out use rights to specific heirs to the land rather than working land collectively (Barrow 1992;

Bruce 1983; Crichlow 1994). It is unlikely and rare that all heirs would work the land together and simultaneously. Instead, one person at a time would use it, according to an informal measure of economic and social necessity (Barrow 1992; Crichlow 1994). For instance, it was common for family members living abroad or in one of St. Lucia's cities to forego their use of family land (Bruce 1983). Indeed, in Morne Verte, this is similar to the pratices of people like Brandon who worked land (not necessarily family land) for family members living temporarily or indefinitely abroad and then gave the land back to those family members if or when they returned.

This practice of exchanging uses of farmland, and moving in and out of farming in general, signals people's attention to maintaining mobility and employment elasticity. More broadly, the practice reflects the high degree of flexibility that punctuates different aspects of social organization in Afro-Caribbean societies. Seen by some as a Caribbean cultural phenomenon (Carnegie 1983) and by others as shaped by economic change and historical patterns of social disparities, especially between Euro-Caribbean and Afro-Caribbean populations (Clarke 1966; Gonzalez 1969; Smith 1956),[8] different forms of flexibility have been noted to mark a variety of Afro-Caribbean social formations. This includes family patterns where the quality, number, and existence of partnerships that men and women hold with one another shift, grow, and recede over time (Gonzalez 1969; Smith 1956; Clarke 1966). It also includes households where the composition and responsibility of residents are frequently reconfigured (Safa 1974; Bolles 1996; Grasmuck and Pessar 1991) and where forms of guardianship for children cared for within immediate, extended, and fictive kin networks change at different moments (Barrow 1986; Bolles 1996).

Yet, flexibility also has been linked to work contexts. Perhaps the quintessential flexible Caribbean agent is the higgler who, like the Vincentian trafficker, has been known to move actively across territorial borders to purchase and sell goods. Often and historically a woman's role, higglering has been a feature of West Indian informal economies since slavery. It provides evidence of the Caribbean's regional trade networks as well as the development of consumer and producer linkages achieved through the active and mobile entrepreneurial work of women and, to a lesser degree men, throughout the region.[9] Carnegie (1983: 11) refers to St. Lucian women traders in the 1980s as engaging in "strategic flexibility." By this he means that their work strategies were guided by a principle of "adjusting to whatever comes along . . . and . . . building multiple options . . . to hedge against the future."

By the 1980s, higglers' work had expanded to local urban areas and also outside of the immediate Caribbean region, and it thus fit within wider Caribbean patterns of late-twentieth-century rural-urban and transnational migration (LeFranc 1989; Freeman 1997, 2002). This period has been marked by the formation of residential and (trans)nationalist-oriented Caribbean communities overseas due to the vast migration of Caribbean peoples, especially to North America and Europe. These overseas communities have been forged by active symbolic and material exchanges among Caribbean migrants and the communities and countries that they temporarily had left. Situated in and dislocated by the contemporary global economy, Caribbean migrants living abroad have maintained connections with communities and nations "at home" through material and social ties that stretch and transmogrify across national and rural-urban borders (Basch, Glick Schiller, and Szanton Blanc 1994; Olwig 1993, 1997; Glick Schiller and Fouron 2001). Made possible by the active networking of Caribbean migrants, this pattern also reveals how flexibility and mobility inhere in migration since, as migrants, people make use of their dislocation from their country of citizenship by seizing and crafting social ties across national borders. But, no matter the time period or the context in which flexible social forms develop and sustain, they clearly profile embedded concepts about and practices around individual freedom and flexibility. Elastic social ties prioritize a changing and supple, rather than rigid, way of structuring relationships and economic and social pursuits. While the individual engages in such flexibility, his or her approach is upheld and promoted by larger families and communities. Such a promotion reflects the mobilization of cultural meanings around work and economy in the place of Morne Verte.

MULTIVOCAL VOICES OF FREEDOM

Narratives of places are multivocal, meaning that they bespeak the multiplicity of people's experiences, histories, practices, and relations (Rodman 1992; Appadurai 1988a). Men, women, and children of differing races, ethnicities, ages, family experiences, work experiences, daily routines, and so on speak differently of places and their lives within places, giving places their multiple and varied meanings. Of course, the Morne Verte discourse on freedom of work was not uttered by everyone I encountered, and it also was not upheld uniformly. Distinctions in how people thought of work freedom seemed tied to the different intersecting social identities of each person with whom I spoke. Specifically, race, occupational status/production size (or class), gender, and age intersected to make up a variety of perspectives on the ways that banana production promoted individual freedom and flexibility.

In Morne Verte, a plurality of voices was evident through growers' particular participation within discourses of freedom and control. The discourses revealed the overlap of various aspects of growers' identities and social locations in Morne Verte as well as within the structuring of the banana industry. Among those underscoring a belief that freedom was achieved through banana production, small-scale growers[10] tended to focus on freedom from the rigors and restrictions of wage work, while larger growers tended to emphasize banana production as an ability to connect with ("be free in") nature. Women were more likely to stress how banana production enabled them to raise their children's status, while men tended more to underscore how their own status improved by farming bananas. More than younger growers, older growers emphasized how they attained freedom incrementally by acquiring land and moving out of wage work over the years. Finally, when she claimed to achieve freedom in farming due to a love of the land, the narrative of one Indo-Morne Vertian grower (out of three) connected with the ideas expressed by other growers, like her, for whom banana production was not the primary income source.

While I do not claim to offer definitive trends in the freedom discourse according to the various social and economic factors of different growers, it is possible to see overlap in particular growers' experiences and freedom narratives. To illustrate this, below I present the voices of Tony, an Afro-St. Lucian, older, small-scale grower; Betty, an Afro-St. Lucian, older, and small-scale female grower; Ellie, an Afro-St. Lucian, younger small-scale grower; Lynette, an Indo-St. Lucian, middle-aged, and relatively small-scale female grower who relied on a second income source; and James, an Afro-St. Lucian, middle-aged, medium-scale male grower who also engaged in another primary, non-farming occupation. Together, their narratives provide a glimpse into the differing perspectives and voices on the freedom of farming.

Tony

A small-scale, male farmer in his seventies, Tony fit among the 5% of farm heads who were over the age of sixty-eight, the 67% who were male, and the more than 40% who produced fewer than fifty boxes of bananas every two weeks (Slocum 1996: 82, 108). Like many others in Morne Verte, he had worked in other areas besides growing bananas, and, like few, he was not *from* the valley. Yet, his move there was part of his life history as a banana grower who had built himself up by engaging in years of banana production on valley lands. Born in a small rural village in the north, he worked as a laborer producing charcoal and *farine* (flour) but began his path of upward social mobility when he left St. Lucia in 1947 to work as a laborer overseas. This was a migration experience like that of many West Indian males of his era, who were labor migrants within the Caribbean region and who afterward sometimes reestablished themselves back on the islands of their birth. Returning to St. Lucia in 1953, Tony said he saw the banana industry just beginning during that time. He returned to the valley, the place of his wife's birth, where he had moved in 1945, and began planting his own bananas while also keeping ties to family land in his hometown. Yet, Tony established himself as a banana producer gradually, settling as a squatter on government lands and at first combining farm labor two times per week with his daily work growing bananas on his own farm. Eventually, in the 1960s, he moved solely into farming for himself, primarily in bananas. Confidently, he stated that he *only* "worked for people" (through his laboring tasks overseas, in farming, and in construction) until he could support himself entirely on his own farm. Even with modest holdings (less than two acres), he stated that he was able to "raise himself up" by working on the farm.

Weekly, Tony made the trek to his farm up in the hills by foot, as did many producers in Morne Verte. As a single man with many children, he maintained the farm with the help of his daughter and sons when they were old enough to assist but not yet old enough to have independent work of their own. Once they pursued non-farm occupations, he hired a few workers to help him complete the farm work. His farm costs went up as his children moved on, establishing themselves as independent income earners rather than family farm contributors.

By the time I met him in 1994, and thus in the later years of his working life, Tony kept only a portion of his farm in operation. He lived with his daughter and son-in-law (as well as his minor grandchildren), whose work in other trades contributed more to the total household income than did his below average sale of five to ten boxes of bananas every other week. His son-in-law was self-employed as a joiner while, shortly before we met, his daughter had been laid off from her work in a sewing factory allowing her time to help Tony on the farm. Despite his small production level, the added production expenses, and the stress of carrying the work primarily on his own, Tony continued to grow bananas. He said that the work supplied his "daily food" and that he preferred to maintain the farm on his own so that he could keep something for himself. Of farm work as a self-employment task, he said:

> I [would] rather work for myself, I don't like to get 20 dollars/day [as a laborer]. If I give a person [employer] enough satisfaction [i.e., work hard for him or her], he still pays [me] by the hour. [But on my own farm,] I leave the garden [the farm] sometimes 1–2:30 PM. [Yet,] [i]f I work for someone the person tells me I have to work from 7–3. This is why I [would] rather . . . work for myself, and most people feel so.

Tony saw independent farming as desirable because of the autonomy he could acquire, and he credited banana production with his development as an independent person and with his ability to improve his economic and social status. To him, the alternative option of working for someone else was the antithesis of banana production because the former placed constraints on time, personal freedom, and security. (Higher monetary returns that he might obtain from wage work seemed secondary to his ability to be free and secure in his work.) This is so because, out loud, Tony did not assert that banana production brought higher income than wage work. Instead, to him, the primary value of growing bananas was avoiding the wage setup along with its impositions on his space and time.

In his frequent and positive assessments of banana production, Tony followed with what seemed to be contradictory statements. Asked his opinion about banana production, he said that "those [farmers] who have it keep it because there is hardly an alternative." Here, his words directly contrasted with what he said were his own motivations and reasons for staying in banana production, as he suggested that banana production was a fallback for people with no other options. Yet, Tony had other options. He had viable support from his daughter and son-in-law and thus did not have to remain a banana producer in order to subsist. Further, the added labor costs with the implementation of the Mini Wet Pack system, along with the additional work he had to expend himself, meant that growing bananas in the early to mid-1990s was both cost and labor intensive for this elderly man. But, since Tony continued to farm on a regular basis, his tenacity in holding onto bananas and land (especially at his age) brought meaning and fulfillment that superseded the possibilities and pitfalls of profit making from banana sales.

Tony went on to speak of problems in banana production, characterizing it as "difficult" and saying that it is "a lot of hard work and hardly any money." For this, he vocally placed the blame squarely on the SLBGA and the state, although at times he did not fault the former. "The association encouraged farmers to work harder but gives them no pay to encourage it," he argued at one point. Yet, later he stated that the government intervened too much in the industry and should instead leave things up to farmers *and* the association. For Tony, then, farmers and the association sometimes were linked and perhaps coterminous, especially in their domination by the state, while he sometimes viewed the SLBGA as exerting its own control over farmers. Mixed with his claims about the freedom that felt he had achieved as a banana grower, Tony therefore stressed that the banana industry—as an entity of the St. Lucian state—exacted a level of control over farmers. As with other growers, this idea revealed Tony's recognition of the incompleteness of freedom in an industry organized heavily by the intervention of the state (and less visible foreign capital). Growers like Tony asserted their freedom while simultaneously acknowledging the vulnerability of freedom given its encounter with modes of control.

Betty and Ellie

Highlighting how he was free from wage work even though operating a small and expensive banana farm, Tony's views and experiences encapsulated the perspective of small-scale growers. Associated with his early labor migration, from which he was able to expand into independent production, and associated with his later residence in his daughter's house, Tony's experiences that partially inform his views about freedom and control of work also were masculinized within a particular stage of West Indian male life. Given conventional suppositions about gender and society, we might even expect that ideas about connecting work to individual autonomy, financial security, and an avoidance of power imbalances would be strictly that of men. However, small-scale women farmers in Morne Verte participated in discourses like Tony's as well. They emphasized rising out of a state of powerlessness by gaining an independent livelihood through banana production, and they also spoke of job security achieved through growing bananas. But, women (most of whom fell into the category of small-scale producer as well) referred less frequently to the ability to avoid employer-employee relations through banana production than did their male counterparts. Instead, they focused on the extreme value of a steady income and the meaning of self-employment to the improvement of their family status.

Women's experiences as farmers also were distinct from men's in important ways. Women who single-handedly headed farms in Morne Verte almost always were single heads of their households as well, while males who headed farms were either heads of their households (usually with a female partner in residence) or residents in their parents' or their adult children's homes. Thus, as is common for rural women in developing countries, Morne Verte women producers held the double responsibility of heading their farms and their households while this was not the case for most men.[11] Further, although many women also lived in extended households with working adult children, their need for financial security was high since their children were not expected to pool income with the household. There was also a particular issue of near-class invariability among women banana growers. With the exception of those who farmed *with* their spouses or *for* their absentee husbands, all women headed their own farms and were small-scale growers with production levels similar to Tony's. Women's incomes from banana sales thus were approximately two and one-half times lower than men's due to the comparatively lower productive resources and returns from banana sales to which women had access (Slocum 1996).

Betty, an older woman in her seventies, for decades had juggled multiple forms of self-employment while mothering multiple children. By the time that we spoke, she considered herself a "former banana grower." However, like many other women who claimed this label, she still dabbled in banana production, a task she began only two years after it was introduced to St. Lucia. At the same time that she made this transition, she also gave up participating in *koudeman*[12] and thus suggested that, with bananas, she worked mostly on her own with the help of hired labor. As someone who managed her own banana farm, she declared to me: "I have never worked for people. If I did, the little I would get would not be much [money]. So I prefer to work for myself." Sounding pleased, she told how she built herself up economically and socially through two ventures: a sewing business, which she ran out of her home like a few other older women in Morne Verte; and farming bananas, which she performed on her land in the hills of Morne Verte. Estimating that she had sewn for fifty years and grown bananas for more than thirty, she described how she juggled (and continued to juggle) the two tasks.

> I usually start [off sewing], go for a while, leave off and go to my bananas. Take it up again and have [time] off. Sometimes when times are hard, I would just make [some clothing] to bring in an income. I try everything and never restrict myself to one source of income. From bananas to garden to [needle and thread].

The second time we spoke at her home, Betty talked while in her living room and working on a dress for a client, taking a pause when the sound of the sewing machine competed with her voice. It was then that she emphasized her challenging past, when, after being widowed, she was left to her own devices to raise her many children. Talking of the difficult times of food scarcity and poverty for people in the valley during her childhood, she suggested that these features were challenges that led some to migrate out of the area and others, like her, to seek local options for themselves. Bananas and sewing, tasks that required no formal education and that guaranteed her an income as long as she applied herself, helped her overcome the many challenges of the times. In vivid and vibrant description, she focused on her hardworking nature and how she strove to get ahead for herself and her children. She described her days as if she went from farm to house carrying her children, spread across many ages, farming and sewing to make ends meet. But, not complaining about the schedule's intensity, Betty said she liked being self-employed because she "was best able to manage her time, energy and money economically and effectively." As she expressed the sheer exhaustion from this work and talked of the varicose veins that challenged her from climbing the ladders required to prune banana plants, I watched her actively move back and forth from her cooking in the kitchen to sewing in her living room throughout our talk. Her resolve that the work was worth her investment and her commitment to continuing to place herself in it (through sewing and gardening) was evident in her active demeanor that I witnessed at her home.

However, as she tapped into another idea, Betty said that today's banana farmers could not even feed themselves on the income from banana sales. She admitted that times felt better than when she was growing up and that she did complain that the younger generation did not appreciate financial struggle as she had known it. Still, she was critical of how the SLBGA handled the industry. She complained that the association extracted so many fees that nothing remained in growers' pockets. And, when asked further about the biggest problem facing growers, she brought up the role of the government.

> [The problem is] the same person who has been there from the beginning who has not changed. It is the government, the prime minister. He is only there for himself and he cares about no one else. . . . In fact, it is as if people are working for the [prime minister]!

Her point was quite interesting given the contractual terms that the association held with Geest, which indeed boiled down to growers working for foreign capital and the state. But, mentioned here amid a discussion of what banana production had afforded a single mother and farmer, the point illustrated how she—like most—saw her position as an intersection of subordinate worker/producer and independent ("free") banana grower.

A similar understanding emerged when Ellie spoke with me, even though key parts of her working life history were somewhat different than Betty's. When I first approached Ellie's house and explained about my interest in talking with her about her life as a grower, she discouraged me from interviewing her because she felt her production was too low to be significant. It took the prompting of her daughter and her neighbor (who Ellie felt was a better candidate for my questions given the neighbor's larger land size) to lead Ellie to agree. Almost forty years younger than Betty and taking up banana production at a different stage in her life, Ellie had never been a landowner and she had always worked for people. During most of her adult life, she was a paid farm laborer on a medium estate in Morne Verte. Due to the estate's presence, landownership had been least possible in this section of Morne Verte, since the estate that endured there until 1986 occupied the bulk of the area's fertile land. Thus, according to some residents of this area, many like Ellie were plantation laborers and had fewer options for landownership for residence and farming.

Ellie herself only began growing her own bananas a couple of months before she met me. This became possible when she acquired *share* land (similar to John's setup), her first viable opportunity to gain access to land. Ellie explained that previously she had worked for another farmer, who paid her poorly or not at all. At the same time, she looked after her domestic partner's elderly cousin, who, upon seeing the bind Ellie was in, offered to give her land in exchange for a portion of her banana sales. Thus, Ellie was clear with me that the cousin "saved" her because she enabled Ellie to move forward. With fervor, she distinguished her *share* setup from working for people, showing the latter to be less desirable and to yield less independence. Expressing happiness at "being on her own" as a *share* landholder, she announced that

> anytime you didn't have something and now you have it, it's much better than nothing. I can say it's going well with me. I harvest [bananas on my own] and I sell [bananas on my own]. . . . Sometimes [as a paid farm worker], I [would] get $40/day but if the [landowner gives land] to me [to use as share], I will get a better satisfaction [because] I work for myself.

Because she was married to a man who was employed full time in government service and because she had teenaged children, Ellie did not have the immediate dependencies and family considerations as Betty had, especially in the early years. Her husband's employment and her material goods, such as a "wall [cement] house" compared to the lower status wooden houses, also suggested that she was not symbolically or materially poor. But she still emphasized the need to have an independent income not merely for her own self-worth but also for that of her family.

> My mother does not have her own bananas. . . . She works for people on their farms up to now. . . . [So] I took the bananas . . . because I see that nobody in my family has their own farm except my uncle . . . and I say everyday that it is not wise to have all of us working for people. [When you work for people] . . . perhaps when you wake up to go to work the person might say that there is no work today. So, when you know that the bananas are yours you must get up and go on the farm.

Although a female, small-scale grower, Ellie sounded much like small-scale male farmers such as Tony when she mentioned the scheduling differential between wage and farm self-employment, as well as problems of job security with the former. Yet, this was not the focus of her account, and it was not the salient criteria on which she based her assessment of land acquisition and banana production. By relating the meaning of work to family and income, Ellie—like Betty—showed the wider gender implications of banana production. Like Betty, Ellie valued freedom of work not only for what it afforded an independent worker but also for its ability to provide greater capacities for taking care of family and helping to raise family status. Attending to and augmenting family conditions were significant to one's identity as a mother, adult daughter, and extended family member.

However, in a counterstatement, Ellie questioned whether providing for one's family and fulfilling a role as mother were fully feasible and sufficient in banana production when she cited low income as a major problem before farmers and an obstacle to her own advance. Like others, in Morne Verte, she felt that the prime minister's greed was the obstacle before farmers. "[He] does not give us enough money, for our bananas, and the only thing that will help is to throw [him] out of power!" Thus, she profiled her own and her extended family's freedom as banana producers but admitted to constraints on the possibilities of freedom, especially due to the actions and inaction of the state.

Lynette and James

Ellie and Tony relied first and foremost on banana sales for their income and Betty depended on bananas and sewing equally until she retired from farming. Indeed, relying on nonbanana income sources more than banana returns was not common among those calling themselves banana growers in Morne Verte. Yet, for those who had another primary income source the view on how farming bananas engendered freedom differed from those who did not. For instance, those producers relying less on banana sales than on other sources of income were not as vocal about government control in the banana industry. They also did not tend to foreground elevating one's status, avoiding participation in power imbalances, or seeking financial stability as reasons for growing bananas. Yet, they did characterize banana production as an occupation marked by freedom and flexibility. Producers who had other primary forms of income (including, in some cases, a second, higher status, self-employment occupation) and who often did not have a personal history of wage work, mentioned deriving pleasure from cultivating bananas, being outdoors, and working the land. Their preference was for farming independently rather than escaping the heavy hand of an employer. Consider the words of Lynette, an Indo-Morne Vertian grower and the only non-African-descended farmer mentioned in this chapter, who at the time we met sold no more than eleven boxes of bananas per harvest period.[13]

> I love farming. Since my husband and I bought the land, I have worked nowhere else. I have my own independent farm. Although I have been to [the United States] and back on vacation, I always come back to the land because I love farming. . . . I like doing it. . . . There are some little things that sometimes cause frustrations but still I persevere, and would not leave it since this is what I like to do. It is good for anyone who believes in moving forward. . . . It gives the farmer a certain independence. . . . [A]t my age I would not think of working for [anyone else] but myself.

Lynette's farm was fairly small, and she gained access to it from her father when he became too ill to manage the land on his own. However, she assumed primary responsibility for the farm only once her husband migrated overseas to work in another primary, full-time, and more lucrative occupation. Farming bananas became her main role in her husband's absence, even though she employed workers, who maintained the farm for her on a daily basis. This became clear when, relating the specifics of farm operations to me, she deferred to her male cousin, the primary farm caretaker (but not head of the farm), who clearly knew more about everyday activities and crops on her farm than did she. During our talk, she repeatedly asked him to verify information she gave me about specific aspects of her farm, unlike most others who I interviewed.

Lynette's status as an employer of full-time farm laborers, her large home, and her family's migration experience were part of her "wealthy" farmer identity. Through her husband's work overseas, she had access to money from his remittances to her, and she was quite frank in explaining that these funds sustained her more than income from banana sales. Also, her Indian identity and placement within an extended family in which land was available (she stated that her sister had a large estate) reflected aspects of the history of Indian indentured servants from the nineteenth-century British West Indies. In this period, Indo-Caribbeans working in the British West Indies, especially in Guyana and Trinidad, gained access to land as part of their servitude contracts (Richardson 1992).[14] Indians thus tended to be landed, owning sizable plots much earlier and for longer than did Afro-West Indians. In the St. Lucian case, however, land was not made available to Indians in the same ways as in Guyana and Trinidad, since the colony did not have the resources to provide land. However, many Indians who did stay on St. Lucia opted to purchase lands abandoned by former small estate owners, which became a way for Indo-St. Lucians to establish themselves (Joseph 2004). The record suggests that, proportionately, such purchases may have been less common among Afro-St. Lucians (Meliczek 1975).

Access to land obviously means that there is less potential for economic hardship. Indeed, Lynette's story did not include Ellie's struggle to become free by acquiring land. As Lynette described it, freedom of work through banana production had nothing to do with land access and had little to do with avoiding employer-employee power imbalances or a rigorous and barely beneficial work schedule. Although she mentioned her preference for avoiding working for someone else, she did not offer a lengthy comparison between (manual) wage work and banana growing, as did small-scale growers. Instead, she described growing bananas as if it lacked drudgery, allowing her to be in nature and to enjoy a leisurely lifestyle. Here, the essence of being free in one's work had to do with a chance to enjoy one's love of the land—something Lynette was able to do given the complexities of her labor base along with her marital, ethnic, and household occupational status. Having laborers that worked the land, a husband who held a relatively high paying job, and perhaps a history of access to plots of land connected her to productive and social resources. From these, she also was able to remove herself from the intensity of direct farm work and still see farming as freedom but a particular type of freedom associated with leisure.

James, a man in his fifties, conceptualized work as freedom in similar ways. As a banana grower with another primary occupation, James's experience growing bananas was less significant for his total income than was his construction business, which he had operated for several years. Like Lynette, he did not perform the bulk of labor on his farm and he relied heavily on hired workers. Because of this, he even told me that he was no longer a banana grower, but throughout our interview it was also clear that his farm was still in operation and he also repeatedly and somewhat longingly referred to himself as a grower. Despite his financial success in construction, he still praised farming over his other work and said that were infrastructural conditions better he would go back to farming in a more concerted way. The reason for this, he said, was the absence of intense toil associated with banana production that he saw with other forms of self-employment. Clearly referencing ideas of freedom uttered by others in Morne Verte, he said:

> As a [self-employed] *business* person [not as a banana producer], you become a slave and a beggar to the public. You have to leave and serve the customers, [whereas] on a [farm] you stop at lunchtime and eat lunch. (My emphasis)

It is interesting how, here, James cited scheduling constraints of non-banana work, as did small growers, but his point did not concern the hierarchies of employer-employee relations that concerned smaller producers. Instead, he was more concerned with being "underneath" and constrained by customers, much in the ways that small-scale growers understood employers as having the upper hand and restricting a working person's possibilities. Freedom to arrange his work as he pleased, *as* a banana grower, clearly was a factor in James's own freedom of work narrative, as it was in the narratives of growers with occupational experience, status, and production size that differed from James's. Yet, the work context against which he measured his freedom as a banana grower differed from the context signalled by other growers, especially those whose operations were smaller.

What also separated James from small growers, however, was his scant critique of the government's role and control in the banana industry. Instead of viewing the prime minister or SLBGA officials as responsible for some of the problems plaguing the industry in the early 1990s, he cited unreliable labor (like the estate employee) and poor road conditions as his biggest obstacles on the farm. Concerning the roads, he placed partial blame on the government but pointed more to growers when he said that "government should have a 40% blame [for the road problem] and farmers have a 50% blame because they can help themselves if they get together. I believe, if you try to help yourself government will assist." Thus, James participated in the freedom of work discourse while not engaging the discourse against government control to the extent that most did.

As mentioned, a tempered critique of government was common among banana growers with other primary income sources, as was a tendency to point to growers' own practices as harmful to the industry. Still, Lynette did not agree entirely with James. Her critique of government control was not as outward as most, but she still cited farmers' biggest problem as too much work. For this, she blamed the SLBGA when she said she thought the thing responsible for increased work in bananas "is the Banana Association since it is for . . . [the association] that we work. Besides, they are the ones that give direction to us as to what kind of work to do."

Like Betty, Lynette said that growers were "working for the SLBGA" and for various government representatives. Thus, her overall position helped underscore the various layers in growers' overall discourses. One layer was the juxtaposition of two seemingly contradictory ideas: that banana production is a source of freedom and a site of control. Another layer concerned how growers' experiences according to gender, ethnicity, age, and income mix also shaped very specific ideas about *how* work represented freedom: work as freedom for oneself or for one's family, work as freedom from employer-employee inequalities or freedom to be in nature, and work as a means to social status attainment and improvement. And yet another layer concerned the depth to which a grower was overtly critical of issues of government/SLBGA control in the industry, specifically the notion that various industry actors were both restricting growers' activities and narrowly charting their income and scheduling. The various layers and their connection to experience and identity suggest that, like the economic globalization discourse emerging at the GATT, dialogues and action around specific overarching ideas were not wholly uniform or universal.

PAN-CARIBBEAN & MORNE VERTIAN MEANINGS OF FREEDOM

I was once asked by an academic researcher of international development if the freedom discourse, however varied, does not illustrate how Morne Vertian producers were atavistic, seemingly "backward" thinking and acting, especially in their heavy reliance on paid family labor, their practice of parceling up land across multiple family members, and their discussions about how they were free as banana producers. Does this not show, the person wondered, that they are working [and thinking] in an economically impractical way? One response to this question could draw on Michel-Rolph Trouillot's (1988) study of Dominican banana producers, in which he makes a case for a kind of practicality to growers' work. In Dominica, he argued, one key to the successful entrance of export banana production into the local economy was its fit with a "peasant labor process." In that process, what peasants produced could be integrated with what they consumed—income-earning activities became significant inasmuch as they could fulfill subsistence needs. Thus, because unripe green bananas could be consumed by Dominican producers and were an important part of their diet, bananas possessed an important "use-value." Dominican growers he studied saw themselves, therefore, as selling a surplus of their food products rather than as producing a commodity for Geest Industries' profit making. Supporting their view, he notes that

> commodities have no use-value for the one who produces them. Their use-value is realized when they are consumed by the buyer who acquires them. Yet, the peasant labor process[15] . . . usually stands as an exception to this rule. Peasants tend to produce commodities that have *some* use for them. . . . [B]ananas offered much higher consumption thresholds . . . [as] the crop could be integrated in the peasant work process as well as, say vanilla or coffee, but reach a degree of consumptive integration that few other exports could enjoy. (Trouillot 1988: 132–33, emphasis in original)

Thus, Dominican growers' practices, which organized production around use-value, were linked to a particular history—the peasant labor process that was founded significantly on consumption thresholds and was built under slavery. They were also linked to a specific regional location where this labor process had developed around specific crops.

While history, region, and place were significant to Morne Vertian discourses of freedom, utility was not the primary basis on which banana production was evaluated there. Green bananas were indeed part of the Morne Vertian diet, and thus there was a link between production and consumption; yet, those advancing the freedom or work discourse did not profile the use-value of their product. The alternative emphasis on achieving personal freedom revealed the premium placed on the *meaning* of the work to the self and the family. Banana production was considered to be intertwined with access to land and financial possibilities in ways that fostered individual achievement and individual work autonomy as well as personal and familial social advance and the ability to shift the established cultural politics of class that pervaded work contexts in St. Lucia. Flexible and lucrative forms of production that promoted independence were thus socially meaningful, and, in this instance, meaning superseded practicality.

Putting growers' ideas about freedom and their flexible work processes in a historical and social context reveals another aspect of meaning to the freedom discourse. The discourse and formations it promoted resonated with historical forms of Afro-Caribbean social organization at the center of social and cultural politics between freed Africans and European colonizers in the postemancipation period. Because the freedom of work discourse highlighted land and farming as sources of independence, it connected with the meaning underneath several nineteenth-century Afro-West Indian social practices (e.g., land use, labor use, community formation, and family formation). Further, just as Morne Verte growers' discourses implied an open yet subtle refusal of the ways in which banana production was officially organized, some of Afro-West Indians' practices after slavery were in direct contradistinction to the goals and structures of aspects of colonial policy that impacted freed Africans' lives directly. The practices often included ways in which Africans and their descendants could gain varying degrees of distance from many restrictions of postemancipation colonial life.

One example of this concerns various work endeavors among Afro-West Indians. As mentioned in Tony's account, in the postemancipation period labor migration was common as a means to pursue employment options (Richardson 1989). In the several decades following emancipation in the British and French colonies, Afro-Caribbean men and women migrated within the region and outside of it, going especially to Panama to work on the Panama Canal, to the Dominican Republic and Cuba to work as laborers in sugarcane production, to Curaçao and Aruba to work in oil refineries, and to the United States (New York especially) and Great Britain (Richardson 1989, 1992; Watkins-Owens 1996). Those who continued to work on plantations abroad or at home were more likely to sharecrop or engage in *metayage* or perform part-time, seasonal, or "shifting" work on agricultural estates throughout the midtwentieth century rather than work as full-time plantation laborers (Marshall 1969; Hall 1978; Scarano 1989). Many of the freed men and women established themselves as peasant producers on lands that they rented, gained through *metayage*, or owned, enabling this type of partial work setup; many who migrated sent remittances back home, enabling families to survive economically and sometimes invest in the land (Richardson 1989, 1992). Anthropologist Sidney Mintz (1989) contends that postemancipation peasant development was a clear sign of Afro-West Indians using their labor skills and resources purposefully to bypass full participation in the plantation structure. Others have argued that working abroad seasonally or at home as a partial plantation laborer, with an eye toward achieving status as an independent producer, showed resistance to planters' strategies and reflected the value of preserving some level of independent production (Marshall 1988; Bolland 1992). In a slightly different take, Guyanese historian Walter Rodney (1981) held that Afro-West Indians (Afro-Guyanese in particular) were asserting their bargaining power and establishing themselves not only as proletarians but also as partially separate from the plantation when they negotiated for part-time work on Caribbean estates. They also were creating a new alternative vision promoting their freedom.[16] For Rodney:

> African people continued to work . . . on the plantation. But they did so under conditions in which they now had, and began to put into place, an alternative vision about the organization of work, about their culture, about their politics, and about what they expected in society, and this was where they came into conflict with the plantation system. . . . The workers were saying that we will work, but we will not work under a bond that limits our freedom of action over a long period of time. (Rodney 1981: 647, 649)

Rodney also addressed the development of Afro-West Indian residential sites in the postemancipation period. Known as "free villages," these represent another example of the emerging forms of individual social organization by formerly enslaved Africans and African descendants. They were communities created by and for freed peoples, with assistance from the Baptist church and missionaries, expressly to give former slaves a separate space in which to live and work (Mintz 1989; Besson 1992). In these self-contained communities, the church bought and partitioned land that was used for farming and for setting up residential settlements to form religious communities of freed men and women. Through land and community, Afro-West Indians could achieve fuller independence by organizing life distinct from areas of colonial life (Besson 1992; Mintz 1989). For some, postemancipation villages organized by African descendants were those forms of Afro-West Indian opposition or alternatives to the plantation system from which, officially, they were freed but in which they continued to be enveloped

(Carnegie 1987b: vii). Taking it further, Rodney (1981: 653) contended: "Living off of the plantation was a qualitative aspect of freedom. . . . [I]n the villages . . . [Africans] also began to exercise what was totally impossible before, some political power. . . . Africans themselves had the power to decide how that space [the village] was to be policed."

This interplay of partial laboring, migration, and Afro-West Indian village formation placed colonizers and former slaves into a continual struggle that endured for decades. For instance, planters, who were supported by colonial policy, strategized to tie freed Africans to the plantations by setting attractive wages and imposing land use restrictions, taxation, vagrancy laws, a wage-rent system, forms of debt peonage, and binding labor contracts (Bolland 1981, 1992; Scarano 1989). That indentured servants were brought in to make up for lost labor from freed Africans demonstrates the thorny nature of labor relations in the postemancipation period. It further demonstrates how forms of social organization were also political maneuvers in their challenge to a particular postemancipation social and political order.[17] The literature on Indo-West Indians is less extensive but does illustrate that land acquisition and community formation were also part of the establishment of Indian settlements following the termination of indentured servitude contracts, especially in Jamaica, Trinidad, and Guyana (Shepherd 1993).

In St. Lucia, these dynamics of community formation existed as well (Marshall 1965; Louis 1981; Breen 1970). The increase in freeholders between the mid-1840s and the mid-1850s suggests that there was a substantial establishment of freed African landholders following slavery (Louis 1981). Similarly, as in Jamaica, two villages of former slaves were established on the island while some village sizes were increased (Acosta and Casimir 1985; Besson 1992). Many not living in separate Afro-Caribbean villages were dispersed on rented or owned lands or held land as squatters or *metayers* (Acosta and Casimir 1985; Meliczek 1975; Besson 1992; Marshall 1965; Adrien 1996). At the same time, according to Joseph (2004) the creation of an Indo-St. Lucian peasantry was part of the overall development of a peasant class on the island as the Indian peasantry eventually emerged alongside the establishment of an Afro-St. Lucian small-farming group. By the 1870s, during the "second phase" of importation of Indian indentured servants to St. Lucia, the Indian population was less apt to repatriate to India and instead established itself in the plantation valleys around the major estates. This establishment was evident through Indians acquiring land from available Crown Lands and also through their cultivation of provision grounds (Joseph 2004). It set them in a similar pattern as Afro-St. Lucians who also were developing as a peasantry (Louis 1981; Adrien 1996).

For uses of land and crop cultivation, *metayage* was widespread and important in the Mabouya Valley between the mid-nineteenth century (just following slavery) and the mid-twentieth century. Social scientist Peter Adrien (1996), who discusses the development and expansion of *metayage* on St. Lucia, does not delineate which ethnic populations participated in the system, although Joseph's (2004) discussion suggests that Afro- and Indo-St. Lucians were both likely to have been *metayers* given the similar peasantry paths that both followed. At the same time, it is possible that fewer Indians than Afro-St. Lucians participated in this system by virtue of the smaller size of the Indian population. There also appears to have been an overall scant purchase of Crown Lands (Meliczek 1975) but, among Indians, a relatively high rate of such land acquisitions (Joseph 2004).[18] According to Adrien (1996), after emancipation *metayage* was a key facet of valley life that developed rapidly between 1840 and 1865, and it continued through the 1950s. By 1848, one-fourth of the sugar on St. Lucia was produced under *metayage*, and one century later, in the 1940s, *metayage* was responsible for over 40% of sugar cultivated in the island's eastern districts (De Guiran 1986, cited in Adrien 1996: 27). Adrien argues that *metayers* preferred this arrangement to wage labor because it provided greater possibilities for accumulating wealth and moving on to more independent types of work. Undoubtedly, valley people preferred *metayage* also because it allowed them to distance themselves from the rigors of field work under the thumb of an overseer (Adrien 1996). Yet, beholden to a landowner, *metayers* in the area (and elsewhere) operated at a disadvantage. Planters preferred to engage in the *metayage* system because it gave them access to a labor force through contracts that typically supported planters', rather than *metayers'*, interests. As colonial subjects, *metayers* had little legal recourse to lobby for better terms or to seek reparations when contract terms were not honored (Adrien 1996). This helps explain why moving beyond *metayage* or using the system as a stepping stone to independent farming was common among *metayers* and is true of today's Morne Verte participants in *share*.

Although Morne Verte residents tended not to work for the Barnard plantation, they did have possibilities for laboring on large estates and/or sharecropping due to the presence of the estates falling between one hundred and two hundred acres in the Morne Verte subcommunity of the larger Mabouya Valley. Land deeds of sale show that all but two of these estates had collapsed by 1951, however. Owners of the fallen estates passed their lands on to multiple family members, who, individually, continued to own and work the land into the early 1990s. Or, they divided up the bulk of the estates into small parcels (most falling under eight acres) for sale to several land-poor and landless residents. My interviews with Morne Verte producers suggest that these sales were how several people gained access to land in two areas of Morne Verte, especially around the 1950s and the 1970s. Indeed, the breakup of one large estate enabled the creation of one residential and farming subdivision in Morne Verte.

Additionally, only two of the older people who I interviewed in Morne Verte had any affiliation with the Barnard plantation. One person younger than seventy years of age had worked for the estate, and only a few over seventy had worked for any large estate. Close to half of all fifty-four growers I interviewed had worked (and in some cases continued to work) as agricultural laborers for individual small or medium-sized landholders, yet the goal was to move beyond this status. As with Ellie, there was a sense of pride about having "graduated" or "escaped" from "working for others," a sense of having elevated one's collective family status. Her views, considered with the obvious goal and experience of avoiding farm work, shed light on the repetition of the freedom of work narrative in Morne Verte.

There had been a history of viewing wage work as a restrictive endeavor or one over which to bargain. Land acquisition and access were the contrasting forms from which work could be mobilized and which were considered a source of freedom. Producers regarded land and work on it as a desirable pursuit over wage work—an *escape* from wage work. The accentuation of ideas about freedom and bananas thus resonated with a historically meaningful way of understanding land and agricultural production as something to do and achieve for oneself. In this way, the discourse was "localized," spoken and *placed* within the historical and cultural politics of land use and labor in a given region and residential settlement. It also was anchored within the historical politics of production and land use in Morne Verte. The freedom of work narrative prioritized concepts and ideas that in earlier times had led to Morne Vertians' release from plantation production and the establishment of firmer modes of self-employment through peasant production on available lands. Moreover, the ways that producers regarded banana production as freedom (because it contrasted with forms of urban wage work), differed from how they viewed the demands of other forms of self-employment that also engendered a freer and more flexible existence. Conceptualizations of *banana production* as a form of freedom fit with the early- to mid-twentieth-century approaches to pursuing rural work and residential spaces away from the restrictive and limited work contexts within which African and Indian descendants in the valley had lived historically.

While we can look to freedom of work as a local discourse connected to a particular place, region, and history, we must also consider that discursive practices within Morne Verte were not bounded. Indeed, as Appadurai (1988b) cautions, we must be careful not to apply particular images and concepts as one-dimensional labels or metonyms for particular places, as if those images are confined to a specific locale and represent all that encompasses it. Like virtually all Caribbean residential sites, Morne Verte was deeply global and had been for some time. Indeed, from the time of their creation as a plantation region, Morne Verte and the larger valley were constructed from both without and within. During the twentieth century, the community continued to function this way, as we saw in chapter 3, through influences such as development schemes partially drawn up by the Organization of American States (OAS) and funded by European organizations. As we saw through Tony's work history, Morne Verte's residents were mobile as labor migrants working within the Caribbean region and also abroad; as we learned from Lynette's and Brandon's experiences with their spouses and siblings, the family members' migration led nonmigrating Morne Verte residents to assume primary responsibility for farms and land. Moreover, all Morne Verte growers' everyday farm activities were necessarily formed within influences from elsewhere, given the organization of the industry around foreign markets and foreign capital, brought into the valley especially through the presence of state representatives and programming.

But more than this, and however small the community, Morne Verte had all of the influences of other Caribbean locales. Media programming connected to the United States was an ever-present quotidian reality. Indeed, tourists and food from Europe and North America passed through the community on a daily basis; Morne Vertian diets were largely made up of imported foods (despite the local production of fruits, vegetables, and livestock); and most community members had either migrated or had close relatives who had done so, while there was the continual return of migrants who brought stories from their experiences living and working in Martinique, the Virgin Islands, the United Kingdom, and the United States. Thus, possibilities for land use and farming were shaped by the ebb and flow of relatives whose land became available when migration called and then became unavailable when returning to Morne Verte called back.

Events involving some place(s) other than Morne Verte and St. Lucia thus intersected with banana farming in different ways. One example is the way that they were attached to U.S. media. It was common to hear growers talking of various U.S. television programs or even U.S. news stories as they worked on their farms. While harvesting, banana growers sometimes talked of soap opera characters from the U.S. shows that they watched, shared views on events from U.S. talk shows, or, discussed the breaking news of current events in the United States that sometimes interrupted regular programming. Moreover, while working on their farms, growers sometimes listened to local radio stations that aired popular music from the Caribbean and North America and that also broadcast news of St. Lucian migrants residing in the United Kingdom.[19]

But, in addition to media, growers had other ways of connecting to "elsewhere." When they went to and returned from their farms via the main road, they were met by buses of tourists headed for resorts in the cities. They also might have sold nonbanana crops or bananas rejected by the SLBGA at the Castries open market, which tourists frequented. Finally, while rejected bananas made up an important part of the Morne Vertian diet, along with other locally grown crops, meals also included salt fish imported from Canada, powdered drinks imported from the United Kingdom, and a variety of canned and nonperishable goods imported from North America and Europe.

Meaning and practice around farming in Morne Verte thus were made not from experiences roped solely within the geographical boundaries of this residential and farming community and events within it from decades past. Rather, they were necessarily produced out of experiences that crossed national borders; that were made out of events, activities, peoples, and places far and wide; and that were simultaneously centered in Morne Verte. Global and regional movements and ties were essential to the various discourses of freedom, which were in turn given life, meaning, and affirmation *in* Morne Verte.

CONCLUSION

It may be tempting to view the manner in which Morne Verte producers organized and conceptualized their work as atavistic, economically nonsensical examples of false consciousness, and globally noncompetitive. Yet, growers' simultaneous reliance on two seemingly competing ideas (such as freedom and control) makes clear that their own concepts and practices did not represent an illusory understanding of their own oppression and subordination within a globally structured system of production. Indeed, since their discourse about state control often gave way to their discourse about work freedom, we can see that Morne Verte producers had freedom under control. They understood their existence through the intersection of both state power and the possibilities for crafting flexible and self-organized work.

Further, it may be tempting to wonder if Morne Verte discourses on freedom of work are not necessarily transnational given the placement of the Caribbean and Morne Verte in the wider world. Yet, the resonance of growers' ideas with long-standing practices in Morne Verte and the wider Caribbean complicated the possibility that the discourses were uniquely and strictly transnational. They fit within histories of land use and work practices familiar to Morne Verte while, of course, simultaneously existing in a globalized community. The discourses drew on the place of Morne Verte—Morne Verte the global and local place.

The linkages producers drew between banana production and freedom/flexibility spawned discourses reflective of social, historical, and cultural meanings of the Caribbean and Morne Verte. That is, their narratives built on cultural and historical concepts about work, land, and freedom that operated widely and historically in the West Indies and especially in their community. By reinforcing concepts about freedom and flexibility—especially in response to questions about why they participated in banana production and especially in the spaces not dominated by the SLBGA—growers were connected and *connecting* to culturally meaningful discourses in Morne Vertian history and people's experiences residing in the area. They also were connected and connecting to discourses more pervasive in the British West Indies. Indeed, they reformulated the flexibility of organizing production for free trade in favor of a flexibility built on freedom, that is work autonomy.

Although situated in global context, what they did not connect to strongly were the widespread and public arguments about the need to structure the local banana industry according to the dictates of powerful global markets. That is, growers' narratives did not affirm a belief in operating farms stringently and inflexibly. In fact, their discourses did not cite foreign markets. Consequently, their notions of freedom and their flexible forms of organizing labor and land use implicitly countered a broader discourse of economic globalization and the necessity for regimentation within the St. Lucian banana industry. Based on the discussions of work that growers privileged, for them, work autonomy drawn from the experiences of Morne Verte and St. Lucia superseded work rigidity. This was so even when they were working within the context of global market integration and liberalization and receiving continuous information about market dynamics and the vulnerability of their work.

It is important to note that concerns about autonomy and place under globalization are not unique to Morne Verte or the Caribbean. Twentieth-century movements against globalization have included such questions as territorial protection, indigenous land rights against foreign companies' exploitation of the environment for profit (Sawyer 2004), indigenous cultural identity (Nash 2001), and threats to peasants' autonomous decision making with processes of agro-industrialization (Kearney 1996). Moreover, with uprisings against the deleterious social impacts of structural adjustment programs in Africa, Latin America, and the Caribbean, there has also been a sense that, with these global forms of economic restructuring, people's lives have been constrained (see Bond 2001; Thomas-Emeagali 1995; Edelman 1990). The call here has been for relaxing the economic and social restrictions engendered by the policies of multilateral agencies. Thus, Morne Vertian arguments for freedom were indeed situated within both a historical pan-Caribbean discussion of freedom and a broader global concern about autonomy within a globalizing world. Still, what distinguishes Morne Vertian narratives and claims about freedom is their subtlety, their pursuit of freedom not through obvious and outward cries for change but rather through conceptualizations of land and labor that bespeak local histories and experiences of work. Thus, in this instance, the call for freedom was not organized as in Chiapas or Ecuadorian collective movements for change. It was mobilized instead as an affirmation of place that was rendered by appealing to and engaging with notions of everyday experiences of work. The narratives were assertions about the quality of a working person's life in a particular locale. As we will see, more active, vocal, and public claims about producers' rights to a particular (and different) kind of freedom emerged within collectively organized events in St. Lucia that were engaged at the national (rather than community) level.

III. THE RURAL NATION

5. *Building upon Politics & Movements*

*A*T THE END OF SEPTEMBER in 1993, five men stood on a platform at a public rally and spoke to a national gathering of banana growers in St. Lucia. Calling themselves the Banana Salvation Committee in public for the first time, they openly questioned the cost effectiveness of the SLBGA and linked the association's financial corruption to a significant decline in financial returns to farmers. They further underscored that producers in the nation could no longer accept the going rate of eighteen cents per pound of bananas. Stating that the SLBGA had failed to look into its financial operations as formally requested by farmer delegates to the association that summer, the BSC announced that it would lead all banana growers in a strike of stalled harvesting and withholding bananas for sale to the SLBGA. As the situation intensified and a strike appeared imminent, on October 4, Prime Minister John Compton addressed the nation by satellite broadcast from Washington, DC, where he was attending international meetings. He asked that before farmers acted they would remember that the association had an obligation to supply bananas to Geest and that the nation was in a precarious place, which could be further destabilized by farmers' strikes. Nevertheless, his efforts did not quell the call to action in St. Lucia.

Thus, on October 5, 1993, for the first time in the island's history, independent banana growers throughout St. Lucia participated in a strike, refusing to cut or sell bananas grown on their fields. After three days, the strike that began as a no-harvest effort, turned into a public protest. It moved farmers' discontent from the field to the street in the form of burning farm and road structures (e.g., farm sheds and bridges) and preventing vehicles from passing on the road to the city. The prime minister continued to address the nation, asking for a reversal of the action. However, the momentum among banana growers continued to build. Even after protesters were injured and two were killed in the Mabouya Valley by police gunfire one day following the prime minister's address, the five farmers who had initiated the strike idea continued holding rallies and making periodic strike calls for over two years. They spawned a movement that pressed for improved prices and productive resources for growers as well as transformations in the industry and larger national structure.

Yet, only a few months into their work, the BSC's activities began to be dismissed as "just politics." When I began interviewing Morne Vertians in January 1994, several people stated that they had initially been interested in and persuaded by the movement's cause but had become disillusioned with it because they felt that the BSC sought political gain rather than price reform. This resonated with critiques I heard "in town" as well, where people suggested that the BSC was out for political mobility for its leadership. Indeed, as the movement grew, its focus shifted noticeably from a change in the price paid to growers to a focus on the problematic role of the state and, relatedly, the problems of the SLBGA's role in the industry. The BSC organizers lobbied for a complete removal of the state from the association, calling instead for growers to have full rein over the agency that represented them. This shift prompted public and popular discrediting of the movement as purely political and, at least in Morne Verte, lost the BSC a portion of its active following.

Still, as many claimed and as older St. Lucians recalled, the BSC's political jockeying fit within the trajectories of earlier movements on the island. Pressing for labor rights by working through and against existing formal political sites was indeed not new to St. Lucia's agricultural movements throughout the twentieth century. At least twice during the century, agricultural workers and producers had agitated for transformations in the terms of their work on plantations, though this effort was often organized by movement leaders who simultaneously cultivated attempts to rework St. Lucia's formal political and social structures. Specifically, during the 1950s colonial period, agricultural movements and their leaders pushed the possibility of forging a new Afro-West Indian government out of a European-led colonial administration. During the 1970s anticolonialism period, agricultural movements also were inserted into St. Lucia's transition to independence and the installation of a socialist-leaning administration. Further, St. Lucia's more than twenty-year decolonization process, stretching from the 1950s to the late 1970s, was ushered in and shaped by the varieties of rural-based agitation led by plantation workers and trade unionists. In all of these movements, where transformations in decolonization, nation building, and the fixture of a European administrative apparatus were occurring, race, politics, and nation figured prominently. As the 1990s' BSC movement blatantly couched its insistence on industry change within critiques of the ruling Compton administration and eventually drew out the significance of social distinctions between producers and the state within the nation, its work resonated strongly with the paths of earlier movements that had made up St. Lucia's political culture.

Consciously or unconsciously, social movements such as that of the BSC are built from structures, ideas, and themes of previous movements (Starn 1992). Indeed, movements' efficacy can hinge on the ways in which or the extent to which they connect with a history of organizing in a particular place (Keck and Sikkink 1998). Thus, it is impossible to look at the BSC's work outside of St. Lucia's earlier organized protests, which were instrumental in the formation of the nation. Although the BSC appeared on the scene after the island had been an independent nation for fourteen years, aspects of the group's work accentuated and bolstered the established legacy of defining nationhood through political activism around export agriculture.

TWENTIETH-CENTURY AGRICULTURAL MOVEMENTS & TRADE UNIONS

As in the rest of the West Indies, labor strikes and worker agitation were common in St. Lucia during the reign of the sugar plantations. While plantation laborers were noted for protesting estate conditions immediately following emancipation (Louis 1981; Breen 1970), the BSC's activities are most easily understood in reference to the St. Lucian movements that occurred from the 1950s and were related to banana production. Two of these that are frequently noted took place in 1952 and 1957. Another occurred across several years during the mid- to late 1970s, a period during which the plantation structure was eroding and the country was moving toward political independence from Britain. All of these movements concerned banana production at different stages of its development on the island. All concerned the plantation setting through which independent producers worked alongside plantation laborers. All concerned the possibilities for crafting and defining major political shifts in St. Lucia and defining the path of nation-building.

The 1950s strikes took place against the backdrop of a crumbling sugar industry that left the sugar estates economically precarious but also compromised in terms of available resources. As we saw in chapter 2, across the Caribbean plantations collapsed and/or were abandoned as the region's sugar industry no longer held its competitive edge in international markets. Between the early 1950s and the mid-1960s, workers repeatedly withheld their labor and complained of low rates of pay and lack of employment alternatives for rural dwellers (Malone, Hagley, and Pearson 1952; Jackson, Pounder, and Leacock 1957; Biggs, Bennett, and Leach 1963). This was reflected in subtle action, with producers' shifts to alternative industries, and in more overt action such as workers' and producers' strikes in the 1950s. The latter grew in number and intensity with the development of a vibrant trade union movement. During this time, trade unionists and other political leaders throughout the British West Indies organized politically within their individual colonies. This rendered them integral both in the movement for regional nationhood and in the restructuring of each island's political structures toward self-government and elected legislatures (Proctor 1962).[1] Begun in 1939 in St. Lucia, trade unions' efforts led to such significant events as the installation of the island's first Afro-West Indian chief minister after universal suffrage was extended (Charles 1994). The elections marked a stage in the island's transition from more direct colonial rule, as they set in motion the establishment of a government structure made up of local Afro-St. Lucian representatives rather than a Euro-St. Lucian or European colonial administration. The emerging Afro-St. Lucian political figures were often simultaneously active in trade union leadership as well.

While they were integral to this changing political structure, trade unionists also worked in the "sugar valleys," where they supported the labor rights of plantation workers and where they were both revered and feared. Threatened by their growing political power and impacts on the already shaky plantation economy in the 1950s, plantation owners charged that trade unionists spurred workers' strikes and operated off of false claims that they represented workers.[2] The intensity of conflict between estate management, trade union leaders, and sugar and banana laborers during this period led to detailed British commissioned inquiries into the two lengthy and heated labor disputes that occurred on the colony's large estates (Malone, Hagley, and Pearson 1952; Jackson, Pounder, and Leacock 1957). The inquiries solicited input from Afro-St. Lucian trade unionists, government representatives, and economically elite Afro-St. Lucian and European estate managers and owners. This reflected the mix of social and political actors, who, amid thorny relations prompted by St. Lucia's shifting economy and social landscape, became embroiled in these events.

The 1952 event that revealed these dynamics and that sparked one of these inquiries was known popularly as the "Brown Strike." Led by Walton St. George Brown, founder and leader of the Roseau Peasants' and Workers' Union, it occurred among sugar workers who organized to receive higher wages and better working conditions on the major sugar estates (Malone, Hagley, and Pearson 1952). Yet, the strikes were discredited by representatives of the colonial government, estate owners, and even by some trade union leaders due to a sense that Brown's motive was personal political gain. Questions about Brown's legitimacy spoke also to larger issues around politics and nationhood on the island. As a Bermudian who had moved to St. Lucia nineteen years before the strike that became so attached to his name, Brown's identity as a non-St. Lucian was profiled as problematic. The commission and others suggested that, as a Bermudian, he did not belong in St. Lucia and that his labor-organizing tactics were self-serving and unbecoming to the island. The commission recommended his deportation and organized an attempt to quell worker mobilization under Brown's leadership by expelling him, thereby marking off the boundaries of an emerging nation.

Brown's role in trade unionism was accompanied by others who could trace their birth to St. Lucia but whose placement in local politics also was a source of consternation. One of the personalities who played an important role in the 1950s' events was none other than John Compton, then a young Afro-St. Lucian returned migrant who had spent considerable time studying in London, where he earned a law degree. In his memoir on labor struggles in St. Lucia, former trade unionist George Charles (1994) notes that upon his return to St. Lucia, Compton devoted his efforts to trade unionism. In the early 1950s, he joined both the St. Lucia Labour Party (SLP) and the St. Lucian Workers' Union (SLWU), placing himself firmly in the role of local politics and labor issues. The move was not uncommon for many socially elite men who were active and mobile in St. Lucia's public and political life. For instance, Charles notes, Compton shifted political parties three times in the course of a decade, each time with an attempt to ascend higher within the island's political structure. His popularity and ability to hold political office were fueled by his work in labor organizing.

Charles (1994) states that Compton actively agitated alongside workers. He was a key representative for workers during negotiations in the aforementioned commissions, he started discussions with estate owners to obtain higher wages for sugar and banana laborers, he protested publicly on behalf of or with laborers, and sometimes he was arrested for civil disobedience (Charles 1994). According to Morne Verte folklore, he also encouraged sugar producers and laborers to divert their activities toward bananas, putting him at the forefront of the shift out of sugar into banana production. The United Workers' Party (UWP), which he helped found in the 1960s after he left the SLP, proclaimed its firm support for banana producers (not laborers) and all efforts to allow producers to be "insulated against any clandestine government interference [in their work]" (United Workers' Party 1964: 2).

In contrast to Compton's position, George Charles, then St. Lucia's chief minister, had won his seat by helping sugar workers in their labor disputes and by encouraging them to stay in sugar (Charles 1994). This placed Compton and Charles at odds. Compton's efforts to organize producers around bananas, of course, were more possible and attractive given the colonial government's backing of peasant production and banana production as well as Geest Industries' own shift into bananas. Thus, the story ended in the 1964 elections with the UWP candidate, John Compton, unseating the SLP candidate, George Charles, as St. Lucian chief minister. That dissatisfied workers were turning more frequently to bananas and Compton had ascended to political power was no coincidence. Yet, twenty years later, John Compton remained in power as the colony's chief minister and he later became prime minister, but the promise of an improved climate for workers in agriculture did not materialize enough to quell future complaints from plantation workers. Charles notes that those who labored on St. Lucia's large estates still were concerned about working conditions on these plantations, and they began again agitating for change again in the 1970s.

The workers were helped by two new intellectuals with advanced degrees from abroad, Peter Josie and George Odlum. Like Compton and the labor organizers of the 1950s and 1960s, Josie and Odlum placed themselves in direct confrontation with estate managers by organizing laborers to rally for their rights in the 1970s. Unlike Compton, however, Josie and Odlum critiqued the persistence of the plantation structure. Acting within the anticolonial sentiment that was sweeping through the intellectual and activist circles of the decolonizing and newly postcolonial British West Indies, the socialist path pursued in neighboring Grenada and Guyana, and the Black Power and black nationalist movement that had rippled through the Caribbean, these two men circulated throughout the country, calling on St. Lucians to challenge Geest's hegemony and the country's colonial status.[3] According to DaBreo (1981)'s account of men and politics in St. Lucia, their speeches were infused with ideas about the plantation as a form of neoslavery, colonialism as a form of racism, and Geest as the handmaiden of both. Their critiques were especially directed toward the Compton regime, which, they argued, had supported the colonial structure as well as Geest's domination.[4] To protest these issues, the two men organized workers in strikes that frequently turned into acts against Geest such as burning the company's plantation fields (DaBreo 1981). Some of the former plantation managers and owners with whom I spoke cited Josie and Odlum's activities as ushering Geest and Denis Barnard out of plantation ownership and smallholders into the acquisition of land parcels.

Like Compton before them, Josie and Odlum infused party politics into their movement by organizing eventually under the banner of the SLP. In 1980, the SLP won the national elections, Josie and Odlum assumed roles within the winning government administration, and the party embarked on a path to create massive reform of the country's economy and social structure. Considered monumental in St. Lucia's political history, the movement to which Josie and Odlum were attached is one of the most noted and remembered, perhaps because of its association with the country's independence. Popularly in St. Lucia, many link it with the steady erosion of the plantation structure and with a massive (albeit brief) disruption of Compton's twenty-year reign.[5]

The work of trade union leaders such as Brown, Compton, Charles, Josie, and Odlum thus involved tensions among the leaders in the rush to claim political power for individual parties led by different Afro-St. Lucian and Afro-West Indian activists. Yet in this struggle there was a common investment in defining the social formation of the emerging nation. In all cases, agriculture was the linchpin around which politics and nationhood became central.

THE BSC'S FORMAL GRASSROOTS STRUCTURE

Obviously, the BSC organizers developed their movement through the question of agriculture, but they did not work as political party members in the ways that earlier movements had, nor did they adopt the trade unionist organizational format that had marked the movements of the 1950s and 1970s.[6] Yet, there were other ways that the group situated itself within formal and established St. Lucian structures, particularly within the channels of the SLBGA, which meant that the BSC necessarily worked through and simultaneously challenged national structures. For instance, the BSC was formed during a monthly SLBGA district meeting in one of St. Lucia's largest banana-growing areas when farmers there expressed concerns that the price for bananas had dropped to eighteen cents per pound. This price was considered especially low because, branch members and other farmers argued, a grower had to be paid a minimum of thirty cents per pound in order to break even. Regarding this matter, the district branch sent resolutions and questions from the meeting to the SLBGA but the branch's members were dissatisfied with the lack of response from the SLBGA Communications Office (Atkinson et al. 1993). Branch members therefore used their right within the SLBGA Act to call an Extra-ordinary Conference of Delegates for all district branches in the country. In that conference, delegates and board members heatedly discussed the price problem, with most delegates suggesting that the price paid to farmers had declined due to problems of cost efficiency at the SLBGA. Following this, a unanimous resolution was passed calling for action in two ways: (1) to provide growers with a guaranteed minimum price, and (2) to form a review committee that would report within sixty days on the status of SLBGA operations. The long-term objective of the report was to determine ways of streamlining the association's costs and increasing its efficiency (Atkinson et al. 1993).

Yet, in the weeks between the August conference and the October strike, the results from the review committee were not presented as promised. At the same time, the price paid to farmers went up by only one cent per pound. This led five delegates to break away from their role within the SLBGA, form a separate group, and find another way of addressing the issues they deemed pressing. The group, the BSC, found itself on the platform in Castries in September 1993 embarking on a campaign of mass mobilization, consciousness raising, and protest.

Although many BSC activities were informal and departed from the official structure of the banana industry, the group continued to maintain a formal structure among its grassroots following. Its formalization, perhaps, drew on the members' experiences working within the formal delegate structure of the SLBGA. After its initial months of "campaigning," the BSC was officially registered in St. Lucia as a farmers' group, just like the National Farmers' Association and the Coconut Growers' Association, which represented and supported producers in specific areas of their work. Additionally, the group possessed a formal leadership that in some respects resembled the structure of the SLBGA. It had an executive board with a president, secretary, and representatives from various banana-growing regions, especially the eastern area of the country. At weekly meetings with the executive body, BSC organizers made all final decisions concerning group activities and strategies for changing and challenging the banana industry. These decisions included, for example, ascertaining where their rallies would be held, which topics they would address, and how they would correspond with industry officials. Such decisions were made democratically among the BSC members as they discussed and voted among themselves on future group plans and action. Yet, this democratic approach did not transfer to the ways the group engaged with its broader "constituency."

Those who followed the group, appeared at their rallies, and joined their strikes did not have input into the kinds of organizing decisions made by the executive committee. Growers were mobilized by the BSC and the BSC claimed to represent them, but growers' involvement was restricted to the audience during rallies and to labor withdrawal during strikes. In interviews with me, the BSC organizers argued that their decisions *were* influenced by rally participants, and that they decided to lobby the government for specific policy changes after consulting banana growers *in the audience* at their rallies. Yet, rally goers were not presented with various and possible plans, nor were they polled (formally or informally) for ideas about how to proceed. Consulting banana growers instead meant announcing one potential course of action at rallies and asking the audience if it supported the idea. Within this, there was no method for incorporating mass feedback to ensure that banana growers' views were represented. Thus, rally participants were excluded from crafting action plans that purportedly were on their own behalf. Formalization of the BSC project, then, entailed vertical organizing, which, ironically, was much like what the BSC had critiqued when assessing problems with the state and the SLBGA.

Added to this, the BSC board was made up of persons of similar background whose experiences, status, and identities were not typical of most banana growers on the island. Put more simply, board members had more economic and social advantages than most banana producers in St. Lucia. All board members were men, the vast majority were returned migrants from Europe or North America, all were conversant in both English (the official and elite language of the country) and Kwéyòl (the unofficial and more common rural language of the country), and all had participated in some formal aspect of the banana industry. Most had served as delegates or presidents of their district branches, as SLBGA board members, and/or as board members of other agricultural institutions in St. Lucia. To qualify as SLBGA branch delegates or board members, they had to be classified at least as small growers, a classification that most St. Lucian farmers did not reach.

Still, it is important to draw a distinction between the BSC leadership and the state officials of the industry. As small or medium banana growers, all BSC leaders did not attain the social or economic status of top administrators in the industry who were salaried civil servants, more conversant in English than Kwéyòl, generally with higher levels of education, and no longer (or rarely) residing in a rural setting. The industry administrators were office employees who readily interfaced with or, indeed, were part of the government while BSC members occupied positions that brought them into government and other institutional spaces for particular and temporary purposes (e.g., board meetings). Thus, at times the BSC members and industry administrators moved in similar professional spaces where they held a different status and, at other times, they moved in entirely separate social and professional spaces.

The BSC, then, may not have been representative of most growers or have been able to speak with the same voice as a large segment of the banana-producing population, but the group's organizers did speak from a subordinate position within the overall structure of the industry. Their work, in fact, interrogated this gap between growers/themselves and the more elite and politically central industry and state officials. As persons on the middle rung of that structure, they attempted to go between both levels and to use their "in-between" position as an advantage. Yet, being partially connected to St. Lucia's formal organizational apparatus while simultaneously attempting to unsettle the country's political and social structures accounted for the tensions that the BSC represented in its modes of political organizing.

FOCUSING ON GOVERNMENT (NOT GEEST)

Because of their position in various agricultural organizations and their experiences holding seats on the SLBGA board, the BSC organizers were familiar with the details of the banana industry structure in ways that many growers were not. It is thus interesting to consider why the group may have focused its energies on some aspects and actors within that structure and not others. Specifically, the BSC organizers did not focus on Geest as an agent behind the organization of production and instead reserved its attention for the role of the state within the industry, linking the BSC to the history of engaging formal national political structures during agricultural movements. Such ideas about the salient role of the St. Lucian government in the banana industry pervaded the thoughts of the BSC's followers as well.

As in Morne Verte, there was indeed a pervasive thought among growers at the rallies that the government was the key player in the banana industry and that no other social actor was as important. To be sure, pointing to the government was an essential part of the framework for the BSC's public work. The BSC slogan for the second major rally held in Castries read: "Come to Castries and Help Put the Real 'G' Back in the SLBGA." (see fig. 8) "Real 'G'" obviously referred to the growers and was a play on the idea that *Grower* had been replaced with *Government*, the false G. Of course, the other false G could have been *Geest*, but when asked directly about the shipping company the BSC made it clear that its focus was not on the company. One leader portrayed the transnational as profiteering more than all actors in the industry when he stated that due to the contract "it doesn't matter if you make ten cents. You [still] owe Geest a dollar. . . . [F]or the association to pay the farmers they have to go to the banks and work their overdraft. So, basically what farmers are doing is working for Geest. So, Geest's role in all of that is to make sure [it doesn't] lose a cent." While he clearly acknowledged the unfairness of Geest's profiteering, this BSC organizer justified it with the follow-up comment that "Geest has a business [and] any business is for profit." Thus, there was an acknowledgment that Geest had an upper-hand but, due to the BSC's emphasis, more accountability was placed on the St. Lucian state.

A strong critique of Geest, indeed, was not profiled heavily at the rallies. Nor were critical analyses of the policies of the European Union, the GATT, or other institutions "external" to St. Lucia. On occasion, audi-

YOU ARE INVITED

TO A MASS RALLY AND BANANA MEETING

Organized by

The Banana Salvation Committee

Venue: Castries Market Steps

Time: 2:00 p.m.

Sunday, September 4th, 1994

Come and hear the developments in the industry.
Help us get our association back.
Help put the real "G" back in the St. Lucia Banana Growers Association.

Don't miss it and please be on time"

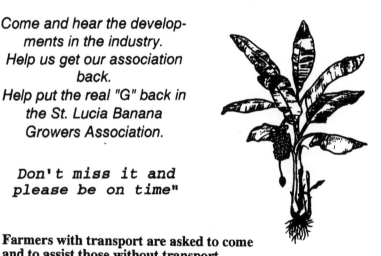

Farmers with transport are asked to come and to assist those without transport.

Fig. 8. Flyer inviting growers to attend a rally of the Banana Salvation Committee in Castries. (Photo by the author.)

ence members were told by the BSC that Geest's profit was too high, suggesting that the company's income was unfair. Yet, remarks like these represented one or two sentences within rallies lasting several hours. The comments were not backed up with detailed analyses of the company's actions or tallies of Geest's profits (as was done in critical assessments of government actions and policies). The BSC mentioned multinational corporations such as Chiquita Brands Corporation, yet it did not do so to critique the weight of multinationals on small developing countries. Instead, the BSC called for considering Chiquita's offer to replace Geest Industries as the buyer of Windward Islands bananas, claiming that Chiquita represented a better economic option for the islands' producers.[7] Consequently, for the most part, the BSC did not heavily critique the role of foreign capital in the St. Lucian banana industry or even attempt to explain low prices and other problems in the banana industry by reference to the power of transnational companies in the industry.

In addition to the structure of the industry, events in the national banana industry in the early 1990s help explain the BSC's positioning and perspective. As discussed in chapter 3, due to the ongoing organization of production, growers interacted remotely with Geest and in their daily lives they had the impression that the SLBGA was more behind organizing and enforcing production strategies than the company. But, developments surrounding the October 1993 strike also helped the St. Lucian state appear as an important player within the industry. Just after the strike, the prime minister dissolved the SLBGA board of directors and instituted a new board made up of 100% government appointees. In subsequent months, the prime minister prepared to place the association into receivership, giving further governmental control in the SLBGA and, by extension, in the industry. These developments were incorporated into BSC rallies, where the group presented and analyzed state maneuvers before rally participants. Repeatedly, the audience was told of BSC encounters with industry officials in a way that underscored government plans to edge out farmers' participation in the industry.

According to the BSC, the group's focus on the St. Lucian government, and not on global issues, was purposeful. At a presentation of my research at St. Lucia's Folk Research Centre (FRC) in 1998, I pointed out my observations that the BSC rallies rarely addressed the same factors of globalization that the St. Lucian government profiled when explaining imminent and existing changes in the banana industry. During a question and answer session, one of the BSC members responded to me by saying that the BSC understood fully the global context but felt that it was more important to address the national context before tackling "external" factors. Similarly, in an interview in 1994, when I asked BSC board members what the main problem before farmers was, their quick response was "government." Although at other times some members mentioned lack of information and "lack of foresight and fear [of mechanization]," their emphasis and a greater proportion of their comments focused on government control. This justified the focus of their rallies, as did reference to the need to fill a historical gap. To them, lack of information among growers, for example, resulted from an ongoing and purposeful power imbalance between the government and the growers. Therefore, they believed that a central benefit of the rallies was educating farmers about the growers' position within the national industry. A BSC member said the purpose of holding rallies across the country was

> to educate the farmer. It might appear that there are some areas [of St. Lucia] that we go to more often but . . . a goal is, number one, to educate the farmers, so we go to all the districts. . . . Now this thing [imbalance between government and growers] came about, I guess, from the beginning of bananas when farmers really [were] not educated. So they [farmers] had to turn to their educated few who actually [took] care of [farmers'] business for them, and [also] took care of *themselves* first. So it stayed there like this and I guess . . . [the educated few] didn't realize that farmers are getting educated and they can take care of their own business.[8]

News at the BSC rallies thus explicated and underlined how, according to the BSC, growers were not only exploited (especially with respect to income) but also grossly misled and misinformed particularly by government and SLBGA representatives. Rally information also corrected false and undisclosed information or reinterpreted the SLBGA's or government's perspectives on the industry. At the same time, it updated growers on national aspects of the industry, especially concerning developments in the leaders' interaction with government. Thus, as sites for the dissemination of information to growers, the public gatherings served to invert a setup between growers and the state that the BSC deemed to have been historically unequal.

The BSC's claims of government misdeeds also emerged through the way that the movement positioned itself politically. It aligned itself with the SLP, the opposition party to Prime Minister Compton's administration. At one point, the BSC stated that its members were open to working with any party that supported their cause, but eventually the group's leaders formally announced their affiliation with the opposition party. The leader of the SLP was invited to address the audience at several early rallies, and he also made statements in the newspaper heavily critiquing the ruling party for the way that it was handling the restructuring of the industry. His arguments underscored some of the key BSC positions. Thus, siding with the opposition in this way clearly demonstrated the BSC's belief in the national and political breadth of the growers' problems. It also proclaimed the BSC's formal engagement in politics. Amid much criticism for its alignment with the SLP, the BSC organizers justified their choice in a shrewd and bold maneuver: the group's organizers defended its political positioning by citing the legally sanctioned political nature of the industry. One BSC member argued that the placement of government representatives in the industry by law, due to the SLBGA Act, naturally politicized the industry. As one BSC leader said, "We are political because the industry, by its very structure, is political."

CONCLUSION

Members of the BSC were accurate when claiming that the industry structure was political. Their point was true due to the terms of the SLBGA Act of which they spoke but also due to the histories of organizing and agitating around conditions of banana production and laboring (a reference that the BSC did not make). Politics, then, *was* a defining feature of St. Lucia's agricultural industries, a feature upon which the BSC (like movements before it) seized in its own mobilization efforts. In addition to the formal ways in which the state was inserted into the industry through its role within the SLBGA, mobilizing banana and sugar producers and workers around formal and informal national politics was well established in St. Lucia. Indeed, the twenty-year period of decolonization and initial nation-building in St. Lucia was marked by the development of St. Lucia's first political parties, which accelerated in part due to the parties' investment in trade union activity focused on the island's plantations. From the 1950s onward, trade unions thus were featured in St. Lucia's emerging political parties, developing West Indian governmental structure, and accelerating political activism directed at plantation life. Agricultural movements during this period, therefore, were necessarily tied up in various dimensions of the island's emerging local politics, a combination that became the source of much consternation among St. Lucia's planters. This was so because planters found themselves economically vulnerable due to the declining sugar industry and cries for better wages for workers. They also found themselves less politically central once they lost their support from the previously European-led colonial administration on the island (see Jackson, Pounder, and Leacock 1957). Trade union activists, who mobilized within the plantation agriculture structure during the 1970s, also positioned themselves in formal political structures by combining their labor activism with their efforts to forge a socialist path through the SLP.

While the BSC did not get its start by aligning itself with a formal political party, as earlier movements had done, and while the group also did not affiliate with trade unions, BSC organizers still became embroiled in local politics based on their organizing tactics. Such tactics drew on those that occurred in earlier decades. This included aligning the movement with the SLP, the party that had long helped foster an intersection between agricultural movements and formal political organizing on the island. Less overtly, the BSC also actively defined the state as one of its principal targets and thereby inserted its work squarely within St. Lucia's formal political arena. By identifying St. Lucian state representatives as key actors against which they were organizing, the BSC organizers cited national politics as integral to the industry. Before them, Compton, Josie, and Odlum had similarly linked national politics to the industry, although, unlike the BSC organizers, these three activists *openly* vied for space within the government administration.

Not only did the way the BSC positioned itself vis-à-vis political parties contribute to the ways that the group was politically engaged. The BSC's forms of organizing and strategizing also were the basis through which the movement's work became largely national in its scope and orientation because the BSC's organizing tactics resonated with decidedly St. Lucian forms of organizing in agricultural movements of the past. By inserting itself into the history of activist organizing in the country, the BSC centered itself nationally. As we will see in the next chapter, the BSC movement also was national by virtue of its strategies for spatial organizing and also by virtue of the ways in which the movement's organizers interrogated cultural and social representations and relations within St. Lucia as these related to problems within the banana industry.

6. *Rethinking Space, Culture, & Nation*

The Banana Salvation Committee wasn't formed by Mon Repos [farming district] but by the whole nation—people from all over. It was a light for the eyes of the people.

    —comment by Banana Salvation Committee organizer at rally

THE FIRST TIME THAT I MET HER, Betty spoke openly about the strikes of October 1993. As we talked in her kitchen, she told me how on October 5 people protesting in the streets suddenly rushed into her road-side home when police gunfire began. Fearful, she cried out for them to leave, but she could not stop the flow of frightened bodies seeking refuge from the intensity on the road. She went on in detail about her panic during this moment and her view that farmers should have just stayed inside rather than protest. To further illustrate this, she uttered a phrase that I would hear from Morne Vertians again and again: "You can't fight guns with stones." As if following this motto, which warned against openly challenging power, people in Morne Verte never took to the streets during subsequent strikes called by the BSC, even when growers agreed to withhold banana sales. There was an obvious retreat from public agitation, especially during strikes.

There was also a shift in the BSC's approach. While the group maintained a relatively strong following in the immediate aftermath of the October 1993 events, not long after this its organizers shifted from a primary and almost sole focus on price reform and corruption in the SLBGA to one that included critiquing social and cultural dimensions of St. Lucian life. Clearly continuing to address material disparities experienced by banana growers, the movement also developed a pointed attempt to redefine and reshape dimensions of St. Lucian national culture through an analysis and restructuring of practices and conventions within the banana industry and St. Lucia. How the BSC achieved this relates to the group's mobilization of national symbols, ideas, concepts, and identities in the organization and content of its public rallies and strikes. The BSC built its movement around questions of social status, cultural identity, and citizenship *within* St. Lucia by analyzing and figuratively reworking individual representations, relations across social groups and categories, and political and social formations in the nation.

In relatively recent approaches to social movement studies, a debate emerged regarding whether class concerns or cultural issues motivate collective action (see especially Laclau and Mouffe 1985; Touraine 1988; and Melucci 1989, 1996).[1] By now many scholars have moved beyond this either-or discussion and instead have argued that for centuries movements we have lumped into one or the other have been organized around both (Edelman 2001). Some studies of class-based movements have admitted significance of cultural or social identity within the movements (Edelman 1999; Striffler 2002), while other studies of "new social movements," which emphasize how identity, subjectivity, cultural models, and symbolism motivate movements in a postindustrial society, have not denied that material and political dimensions form part of the context in which contemporary movements develop and accelerate (see Touraine 1988; Melucci 1989; Warren 1998). Thus, the question should rather be: where and how does class fit into movement activities and agendas organized around culture? Kay Warren (1998) reminds us that we must look at the ways in which "cultural issues . . . [are] infused in the construction of material politics as well as the [ways in which the] construction of materialist politics [is] infused in cultural framings of politics" (Warren 1998: 48). We should consider the salience and positioning of specific features (e.g., culture and class) that shape movements. Issues of class and culture might punctuate movements to differing degrees, and in different relationship to one another, not according to their newness or the time period in which the movements emerged but rather according to a variety of contextual factors in which movements are situated.

To be sure, the BSC *did* overtly rally around economic conditions, class disparities, and party politics. The movement targeted the state in a clear lobby for improved economic benefits for growers. However, the movement pursued these by accentuating and analyzing cultural representations and identities of growers while also the interrogating state representatives' constructions of subjectivity within the nation. This shift in emphasis from a firm and almost exclusive focus on increasing the price for bananas to a simultaneous and sometimes prioritized analysis of cultural and social definitions of St. Lucian social groups occurred over a short space of time. In pressing for reform, in a matter of months, the

BSC quickly began to make speeches and engage in action that assessed and symbolically reworked cultural images and definitions of people and relations within St. Lucia. In part, this was a way to push the movement's initial and seemingly unitary goals of changing prices, incomes, class inequalities (between growers and industry representatives), and political power. Rallies might have mobilized growers for better returns on banana sales; rallies also became the space for offering deep and lengthy analyses of cultural and social formations, which the BSC contended and suggested were tied up with growers' price problems.

Here, the symbol of the nation was key. It was the group's social uses of national space, its assertion of growers' rights to that space, and its interrogation of forms of social and cultural categorization and convention within that space that illustrated how the BSC analyzed and critiqued cultural and social conventions in St. Lucia. The BSC analyzed such conventions as national phenomena: contentious claims regarding who had which right were as much about political rights as they were about rights in the nation. The BSC's maneuvers thus revealed how the movement's work entailed engaging national cultural politics and issues of citizenship, sometimes accentuating income and always over profiling the power of global processes.

As the BSC used the nation as a site for collective cultural identity analysis, building, and reformulation, the nation took on qualities and meanings of place. Indeed, nations, as places, are sites of identity formation and construction (Radcliffe and Westwood 1996). Moreover, nations are made up of places in which people are invested. As Radcliffe and Westwood (1996: 107) note, locations such as neighborhoods and cities are national places and people have "clear ideas about how their nation is organized spatially and socially. . . ." Thus, in their dynamic relations with national places, people can wrestle and engage with official conceptualizations of national sites and the nation as a site if their own ideas about such places come into conflict with official ideas.

RECONFIGURING NATIONAL SPACE

The structure of the BSC movement was openly political, not merely by its alignment with representatives of political parties or its disagreement with state practices and policies. It also was political by the way that the movement played into the cultural politics of inclusion and exclusion within the organization of national space. As in many parts of the world, there is a pronounced separation of rural-urban spaces and peoples within certain activities and lifestyles in St. Lucia as the labels applied to Morne Vertians that were discussed in chapter 3 suggest. The separation set by residence was compounded by class and culture assignments that also shaped the politics of how and when people moved through and interacted within specific spaces. Thus, there was a decided, and in many cases stark, social and cultural positioning around national rural and urban spaces. Part of the BSC's efforts reworked these conventions; rallies and strikes were the two most important and intertwined ways that this occurred. Both rallies and strikes bridged and disrupted rural-urban divides but also helped growers claim the space of the nation as an important site for organizing. Further, there was a precedent for this, since claiming national space was a tactic employed by movements of the 1950s and 1970s.

As the BSC's signature public activity, rallies began in the former central plantation region of Cul-de-Sac, spread to other district areas in the north and southeast, and occurred repeatedly, especially in the final months of 1993. They served not simply as a way to render the problem of price and institutional management a public topic. They also served as a way to link farmers in a widespread discussion about the "banana problem" and to organize collective action. By January 1994, participation at BSC rallies had noticeably dwindled. The swell of crowds that had come to hear the movement leaders in October through December 1993 diminished, and, although some people still traveled to the events, participation tended to be by those who resided in the district where a given rally was being held. Still, in those first few months of heavy rally and strike activity and the continued BSC work, there was the creation of a public transdistrict connection. Through the repeated participation of farmers from across the country and the collaborative engagement of diverse rally participants in rally chants and rally cries and no-harvest strikes, there was a semblance of group action. Due to the public quality of these activities, the range of people that they drew in, and their geographic location, rallies and strikes attempted to forge a public collective identity that disrupted conventional understandings of social position and spatial organization.

Rallies

Despite their common membership in the SLBGA and their relatively small numbers, banana growers across the country never had the opportunity to meet as an entire group based on the way the industry was arranged. Rather, the approximately eight thousand growers in the country were assigned to one of forty-six different district branches according to the location of their farms. As we saw in chapter 3, growers conducted the bulk of their banana production activities within their individual districts and did not interact with growers of other districts while doing so. Only district delegates (one to five per community) met with growers from elsewhere at the annual Conference of Delegates, while the bulk of community members received and shared information either among those in their districts or with the head office of the SLBGA.

However, the rallies organized by the BSC transcended the district boundaries set by the banana industry. By organizing rallies advertised for all farmers to join, the BSC action shifted the established spatial arrangement and created a new transdistrict space in which farmers moved and interacted. The new space went beyond the constructed boundaries of their home districts and fomented a sense of collectivity. In repeated, widespread radio advertisements, public loudspeaker announcements within communities, and occasional fliers distributed throughout rural districts across the country, growers everywhere were called to attend the rallies. In the days before a given rally was scheduled, the events were billed as "public meetings" and announced as events for *all* farmers in the country to attend. Thus, they were collective events involving farmers from across the nation, who traveled to districts outside of their own. Rally goers carpooled in overcrowded pickup trucks or loaded into privately operated minibuses to attend the BSC rallies. Producers and nonproducers alike, all of whom congregated in banana-buying depots, participated in the rallies. Many men and noticeably fewer women, young people and adults from north, south, east, and west attended and joined in the activities.

Besides bringing people together from across the country, the rallies also possessed features that instilled this mood of national integration. Audience members, for example, listened to BSC organizers' speeches that were interactive with the entire crowd. Addressing rally participants by microphone, BSC speakers offered pointed and repeated critiques of the banana industry and its key organizers through methods of story-telling, which led the audience in en masse chants. Each rally was focused around several detailed stories told by individual BSC leaders, who recounted the latest interactions that they had had with specific SLBGA and other state representatives. As if participating in a "storytelling hour," the audience listened as different BSC speakers recited the series of events through which they went in their meetings and discussions with industry figures. The stories always included details of specific and named personages who typically were profiled as corrupt and who, in the stories, were pitted against farmers. Cheers and chants arising from the audience, as they responded with laughter, outrage, or groans to each descriptive event, gave the rallies a decided call and response theme. Further, the stories that outlined the more problematic figures and qualities of the industry typically were the preface to the BSC's call for organizing another strike. Thus, through the stories and the audience participation in them, the BSC was able to *rally* the crowd—as a group—to respond verbally if a strike was needed. Without fail, there was a resounding yes, which became that collective affirmation that a strike should occur.

Yet, what also generated a transdistrict connection and promoted the formation of a group identity was the location of rallies. Frequently, rallies were held in the SLBGA banana-buying depots, where banana growers typically convened weekly to sell their bananas, to purchase the boxes required for packaging the fruit, and to attend formal monthly meetings. These were key organizing sites for the SLBGA, the mandatory or expected spaces through which growers had to pass to fit into the strictures of the banana industry. Yet, by holding rallies in depots, the BSC designated the established SLBGA spaces as sites through which to perform a collective critique of the banana industry and the way that the association had organized it.

Holding rallies in buying depots played right into the pre-existing and everyday tensions between farmers and the SLBGA that erupted in these very locations. For, it was here that growers most often experienced the unequal relations that they held with the SLBGA, and it was in here where tensions over that relationship came out. As we have seen, the depots were locales where growers brought their fruit to be evaluated by SLBGA staff members who pushed growers through an evaluation process. In that process, banana assessments and sale prices were out of growers' hands. Yet, despite the formal means through which this process stripped growers of bargaining power, depots on harvest and sale days were the sites of much complaining between SLBGA employees and producers, and among growers. Week after week in Morne Verte, growers argued with SLBGA employees or complained to one another about the evaluation of their bananas and the prices they received. Selling days were known for heated disagreements between SLBGA staff members and farmers because, despite the primacy of the SLBGA determination, growers' dissatisfaction with the returns on their sales often was heard under the roofs of the depots and out in the streets, where other growers were lined up to wait their turn. Additionally, as mentioned in chapter 3, the monthly meetings held in Morne Verte depots were notorious for poor showings and revealed a lack of widespread support for or perhaps interest in regular SLBGA activities. Thus, as BSC rally speakers announced grievances by loudspeaker and microphone, as they organized the audience in group chants against the organization, and as numerous rally participants flowed out of the depots into the streets to join in an anti-SLBGA meeting, the events rendered preexisting farmer-SLBGA tensions louder, more visible, more accessible, and more collective. By their location in the depot buildings, which were open structures, the rallies not only reinforced these tensions but also made them available for public consumption in spaces not typically used for congregations of this subject matter and size.

Another way in which the BSC brought the issue to a larger arena and re-created conventional uses of space was by moving their rallies to the city. Although only a few were held here, these rallies were profiled as "big events," involving heavy pre-rally advertising compared to that put into other public BSC gatherings. An example was the mid-March 1994 rally held in Castries as the first major urban-located BSC rally since the group's strike in October 1993. While the rallies had been weekly events in the fall of 1993, by the start of 1994 they were less frequent, sometimes being held as seldom as once per month or less. Thus, the Castries rally, as a big event, was perhaps an attempt to revitalize the BSC effort by organizing a more public and visible national event. Furthermore, prior to the Castries rally, all of the BSC rallies were held in buying depots across the country; thus, this was the first time since gaining public momentum from the October event that the BSC had moved its activities out of the rural districts to the city. The timing of this was also significant, for it was from January to March of 1994 that the BSC was engaged in a heated debate with the Compton administration regarding whether the SLBGA should be put into receivership. The Compton administration had argued that the SLBGA was in such dire financial and political straits that it was best served by government intervention while the BSC countered that this would lead to deeper state control, a signature concern of the BSC leadership. Thus, rallying in Castries came at a time when tensions were quite high regarding the political future of the SLBGA.

The Castries rally brought growers from all over into the streets of Castries at a central location: the market steps. The market steps had a particular resonance in Castries and St. Lucia. First, they were the site of much commercial and tourist activity, since this was where people came to buy and sell produce and small consumer goods from market vendors. From Monday to Saturday, the market scene was always bustling, heightened by the presence of the informal bus depots that bordered the market area. People were continually boarding and descending from buses, and buses were continually coming and going. Second, the market steps were the site of political organizing for St. Lucia's earlier movements.[2] They were the location for mid-twentieth-century activists' public activities and speeches during their own rallies. Thus, the BSC played into the preexisting political uses of this space, although the BSC's uses were more occasional than repeated.

With the March 2004 rally, there was a sense that growers were coming to the city to announce their claims more publicly but also to claim the urban space as rightfully theirs. Indeed, my own presence at the event was questioned by someone in the crowd. As I took notes and tape-recorded the speeches, a man identified me as a nongrower and assumed that I was there to question the growers' rally. Angrily, he told me: "You can't stop this event. We have to share in this country." The remark, particularly the notion of people needing to "share in the country," signaled an idea that growers possessed as much right to use of the city space as did nongrowers/urban dwellers (which I was presumed to be). This man's assertion divulged the tensions around farmers' symbolic and actual presence and rights within the urban and public national space, a tension revealed also by the BSC speakers on that day. One of the BSC organizers opened the Castries rally by announcing that the farmers had

> come to Castries with a message. The message is the banana farmers of this country have suffered. They endured the suffering; they took it in stride. And they did not complain. They didn't make money but they still harvested their bananas because it was for the benefit of this *country*. It was *our country* and we was willing to satisfy it, and sacrifice

to satisfy . . . so, when you sit in Castries and you do not see the banana trucks coming down it doesn't mean we are not able or willing to sacrifice. It is that we are not willing to [sacrifice] no more.

In claiming the nation as their own, in "bringing" a message of farmers' hardships to Castries, and in linking those hardships to a sacrifice on behalf of the nation, the BSC profiled both producers' economic problems and their rightful social presence in the urban and national space. Indeed, by announcing farmers' suffering and saying that they needed to take the problem to the city *for* Castries, BSC speakers layered the two issues: economic hardship and the unfair social separation of urbanity and rurality in the nation. Such an exposé was new to the BSC's work, which had begun almost six months prior to this Castries rally. Never before were BSC meetings that were held in rural areas profiled as bearing a message for nongrowers or as needing to explain farmers' problems to an audience. Thus, there was an acknowledgment that the Castries meeting was to take and assert growers' experiences and their rights beyond the rural areas but also to reveal the tense linkages between the rural, urban, and national sites that resulted from growers' work for the nation. Mirroring the ideas of the man I encountered, rallying in the city was therefore an assertion of a need to *share* national space with growers and acknowledge a crossover of the uneven (social and economic) divides of the various geographic and sociospatial sites.

Moreover, moving the rallies from the banana-buying depots to Castries' market steps transgressed politicized norms for organizing rural-urban space in St. Lucia. People from the country's largest farming communities intersected with Castries on a regular basis; women of Morne Verte and other rural towns shopped for food in "town" on weekends, and some sold produce on Sundays at the central market; men and women shopped there for personal items as well and frequently attended to financial matters at one of the city's several banks; and young adult men and women might have worked in one of the office buildings or within any of the industries or service sectors. Many Morne Verte farmers had household residents who worked in town, and virtually none I interviewed could say that they never went to town. Thus, rural residents were familiar with Castries for employment, schooling, commercial, business, and social purposes.

But Castries was a place where rural dwellers went to perform a specific task or receive or give a service, not to organize a social event of rural people. Although rural and urban residents moved in the same geographical space (Castries), they moved in it for different purposes and not together. For instance, unless a family member had moved "to town," Morne Verte residents I encountered rarely had friends there who they visited regularly. And, while weekend social events such as music concerts, restaurants, or clubs brought people from Morne Verte into Castries on weekends, and children in secondary school could be assigned to schools in town, the repeated and intensive engagement with the lifeways of "town" in a social way occurred on a small level, and on an individual or small group level, rather than a mass public one.

Consequently, BSC rallies held in town represented a new form of farmer organizing, rural interaction with urban space, and rural encounter with public space. Rather than looking to Castries to provide a service, rural dwellers came to receive and provide information. While the mass of rally audience members "received" information from the BSC, the notion that their concerns were being profiled in Castries was a transformation of their everyday interactions with that place. Furthermore, because such concerns were announced by members from the rural districts (rather than by "outsiders" or nonfarming district members), farmers at the rallies experienced a temporary shift in the hierarchy between themselves and nondistrict members in ways that undermined everyday forms of sociospatial interaction. Through mass rallies, interactive stories, group chants, and themes that drew out the farmer-SLBGA/government division, the crowd also was constructed as a unified group, identified by its uniform relation to officials in the banana industry and its united opinion about the need for action.

Strikes

Strikes organized by the BSC were integral to rally formation. At rallies, the BSC first announced plans to organize farmers against selling bananas to the SLBGA during a given week and against cutting and bringing bananas to the buying depots. The first announcement to strike came at one of the earliest BSC rallies in September 1993, which was followed by the momentous October 1993 strike events. Another announcement came in February 1994 when the BSC organized almost as many farmers as in October to challenge government plans to place the SLBGA into receivership. In addition to these, several strikes were proposed and/or threatened over a three- to four-year period, many of them attracting less participation than the October and February strikes.

But, each strike and strike threat was attached to demands for a specific policy change such as higher prices, changing the pricing and fruit evaluation system, and reducing the extent of government intervention in the SLBGA. Indeed, the possibility of an increase in prices appears to be what enabled the BSC to galvanize growers to support the strike effort. According to figures of banana sales from farmers for the week in October 1993, only one-sixth of the usual volume of bananas was supplied to the SLBGA, suggesting that a majority of farmers across the country did not cut and sell fruit that week (SLBGA files 1993).

In Morne Verte, there was indeed support for the October 1993 strike. It is true that Betty, Ellie, and Lynette *said* they did not support the strike. Lynette said she objected to being asked not to cut bananas after working so hard, while Betty and Ellie considered the idea of striking simply a bad idea, especially given the violence and death that resulted from the event. However, Betty and Ellie agreed with not cutting bananas to protest prices, but not with the other activities that were part of the October 1993 strike experience. John, Mark, Tony, and Susan, by contrast, said openly that they were in favor of the October strike, even if some of the outcomes were unfortunate. Another grower, Alphonse, was adamant that the strike was good due to the pressure farmers succeeded in putting on the SLBGA. "We had them locked," he said, "as though it [the low price] was something they had to stop." Tony also showed his agreement with the event and linked this to its larger implications when he said: "I must support [the] strike. I didn't go outside but I encouraged people who were striking [outside] in it. It [was] good for our government because [it was] in a strike [the 1950s strikes] that Prime Minister [Compton] got his position. . . . Now he's afraid of the strike because he's afraid to lose his position."

Support for the strikes thus ranged from a decision to stay indoors while not cutting (harvesting) fruit (Betty and Ellie) but also support of congregating and protesting vocally in public streets (Mark, Alphonse, Tony, John, and Susan). Many I interviewed in Morne Verte were uncomfortable with the open protest aspect of the strikes and described their fears when the vandalism and street protests developed. Betty told in detail of her own concern and experience once she realized that the public activities might turn violent.

> During the course of the first strike, I was on my balcony and a lot of people were around. They asked for my radio and were listening to

the news. While listening myself, I heard the directive over the radio that they [the police] could do what they wanted with people who were disturbing the road. I ran out to get my [friend]. As I was entering my house I heard the sound of shots fired. People began to run for shelter. They flocked into my house, hiding everywhere. I begged them to leave, telling them that the police would come after me. I was frightened. While there . . . [my friend said that] two people had been shot dead. When the people inside my house heard that two were already dead they started running inside of their own homes.

But Betty went on to explain how the plan to withhold fruit was something growers should have followed. "When the people [the BSC] instructed the farmers not to cut bananas, they [growers] should have listened and obeyed. But they didn't. So what they get is what they want. They don't know how to suffer a little for better results." Thus, Betty was among the many in Morne Verte who backed the BSC's call to avoid cutting bananas. Yet, she was openly critical of those growers who went further than this call and, in her view, provoked the violent results.

The street activities of which Betty spoke were reflective of how the strike was not simply a "farmers' event." Indeed, Betty claimed that the violent behavior was not the work of banana growers. "Farmers would not have done that," she claimed. And, while it is likely that those who took to the streets were farmers and nonfarmers, it is also clear that people who did not self-identify as banana growers gathered to participate in the activities or to show their support by helping with some of the banana growers' protest activities. For example, some nonprotesters in Morne Verte stated that they provided food to those who congregated in the street or offered their homes as temporary shelter when the police gunfire began. Beyond this, mass participation in the strikes included public assembly because much of the strike activity took place in the major roadways of the island's eastern rural districts.

Locating political protests in primary roadways for this first strike event was significant because the roads were major avenues for connecting rural areas and rural people with "others." As a small place, St. Lucia had one primary highway that ran along the periphery of the island and, without construction delays, took no more than six hours to traverse. Despite the existence of secondary roads (less traveled), that primary highway was the main (sometimes only) means by which people in several rural villages (including Morne Verte) intersected everyday with people from outside the island (tourists) and with people from other places on the island. Running right through the center of Morne Verte, it was also how villagers connected to points far and wide. The presence of rural people standing by the roadside waiting for transportation to go to town and the sight of tourists passing through were daily, indeed hourly, events in roadside rural towns. To get to Castries in the north, or to get to the south of the island where the larger airport is located, all St. Lucians had to travel the highway, passing directly through several rural districts alongside the highway in a journey lasting anywhere from twenty minutes to two hours. Children in the south attended school in the north and made the passage each day; children in the central districts also went either south or north. Van loads of tourists arrived at the Vieux Fort airport in the south, which accommodated jumbo jets, and then traveled north on the main road. A daily sight in Morne Verte was the tourists in minibuses as they peered out, often snapping photos of local sights on the way to their all-inclusive hotels in the north. Women traveled to "town" on weekends to sell fruit and vegetables in the city market or to buy food in the city grocery stores, where selections of food were more diverse. On weekends, youth and young couples sometimes went to Gros Ilet on "special outings," traveling north on the road to enjoy nightlife in a dance club or to have a date at a restaurant in the exclusive tourist areas. Hotel cooks and domestics, construction workers, office workers, and other employees from rural areas working in urban industries went to Castries and points farther north in the wee hours of the morning, returning home each night.

Similarly, there was a continual flow of large-scale growers, or their hired workers, who transported bananas to the wharf in Castries or Vieux Fort for fruit inspection. The truckloads of bananas brought south or north each week represented a constant and significant presence of rural dwellers in the island's two largest cities, *for work purposes*. On banana-harvesting days, a common sight was pickup trucks with banana boxes piled in the truck beds as drivers waited in traffic jams of other banana-filled pickups. Thus, urban people saw banana activity on a weekly basis, and in this way they were familiar with the banana schedule. Yet, the engagement with that schedule and those who operated directly in it was distant and relatively noninteractive.

However noninteractive, the traffic flow impacted nongrowers and those who moved through Castries and Vieux Fort. It slowed down people's movements, but, given the regularity of the schedule, people planned for and expected this. But, they did not expect strikes. For those living in the north whose work required travel southward through or to rural areas, one had the sense of being holed up in the city, restricted from a routine during strike periods. Those unable to travel became aware of the strikes and the farmers' complaints largely due to this disruption of movement. Also, if nonrural residents did attempt travel during those times, they interacted with—or experienced the *threat* of interacting *directly* with—banana-producing communities rather than "just passing through." In this way, the banana protests were experienced firsthand by many St. Lucians largely due to the public location of strikes, the significance of movement on the highway, and the public's familiarity with the banana production routine.

Although the first strike meant greater disruption of travel and movement to and from rural areas, subsequent no-harvest calls and threats also had important impacts on the reorganization of local space. They promoted local forms of nonparticipation that reshaped growers' activities in the industry. In Morne Verte, although support for the BSC dwindled rapidly after October 1993, there remained extensive withdrawal from harvesting and selling bananas during strike calls. Some of the forms of vandalism such as the burning of private sheds for processing and boxing bananas also continued though on a reduced scale.[3] The vibrant street action of October 1993 never reappeared during the BSC's most active period, but most BSC-led strikes showed lower levels of harvesting and selling activities than in nonstrike weeks (see table 4), suggesting that growers had agreed to participate in withdrawing their products for sale to the SLBGA.

Accompanying the decline in banana sales, however, was an overwhelming calm and quiet on strike days and during strike threats, in

TABLE 4. Production Levels of Banana Sales to SLBGA (in tons) during Major Strike Periods in 1993 and 1994

1993 (October)	1994 (February)
Week 38: 2,405.25	Week 6: 2,137.25
Week 39: 2,852.19	Week 7: 2,636.25
Week 40: 393.38[a]	Week 8: 827.13[a]
Week 41: 4,017.20	Week 9: 2,934.52
Week 42: 2,245.55	Week 10: 2,048.49

Source: SLBGA files.
[a]Designates strike week.

sharp contrast to the hustle and bustle of harvest days in Morne Verte or the fervor of the street action during the first BSC-led strike. The banana-buying depots were completely deserted, few people or vehicles were in the streets, and those who were out sat quietly talking to one another, their words inaudible to passersby, unlike the bustle and vibrancy one usually witnessed on "banana days." At night, the calm was even stronger. People stayed in their houses, often with the power flickering on and off and with sounds of intermittent gunshots up in the hills into the early morning hours. (Some Morne Verte residents said they thought the gunshots and loss of electricity were orchestrated by the government to help keep people in their houses and to avoid the mêlée of the first strike.) There was a widespread, almost automatic, consensus to not cut bananas and to stay home. Similarly, because frequently strikes were called, and then called off with little notice, the deserted and calm nature of post–October 1993 strike days remained. On one of these calm days, I asked a friend if there was a strike called for that day. She replied that she did not know, but, signaling the deep memory and tragedy of the farmers' deaths that resulted from striking, she repeated the same words that Betty spoke: "You can't fight guns with stones." Indeed, after October 1993, most people in Morne Verte steered clear of involvement in any public activities that implied protest and instead engaged in quieter expressions of discontent, with a sense that protesting publicly prompted too much danger.

Here, the choice not to cut bananas on suspected or obvious strike days might appear to have been driven by fear and uncertainty and thus was not an indication of willful nonparticipation. Yet, government representatives repeatedly attempted to discredit the BSC by claiming there were signs of dwindling backing for the group. To make this point, the minister of agriculture publicly claimed that lower sales in the week of a strike call followed by above-average sales in weeks just before and after the strike suggested that most growers were frightened to sell in designated strike weeks and instead overcompensated for the loss in income by stepping up production and sales in weeks following (see table 4).

Yet, while a numbers analysis such as this might suggest overcompensation for one week over another, production and sales are not the sole measure of BSC efficacy, for they are not the only indication of the impact of the strikes and strike calls. Self-restricted movement and calm during strike calls within Morne Verte are other signs of a widespread shift in growers' compliance and interactions with the state in a less out-ward but equally significant manner. Some growers did cut their fruit within the calm and thus did not heed the BSC calls; they chose to follow the official banana production schedule, dispelling claims of fear-driven action. Yet, for the majority, who did not harvest and sell bananas, there appeared to be a *decision* to bypass the official schedule, even if tem-porarily. The decision and (in)action was revealed by producers not only withholding a product but also by their disruption of a routinized and expected schedule. The no-harvest decision further reordered the social uses (and nonuses) of local and broader public space that configured how the state and growers could interact because it took growers out of the weekly spaces where they encountered SLBGA staff and requirements.

REPRESENTATION & CULTURAL REPOSITIONING IN THE NATION

How the BSC attempted to restructure state-grower relations occurred not merely through the group's analysis of government corruption and domination of banana growers or through the organization of its public activities. It also occurred through the representations or images of "farmers" and "government" that the BSC critiqued and re-created in its public discussions of state representatives during rallies and interviews with the media. But, public image making of farmers and government also occurred when government and SLBGA officials spoke in televised addresses and radio interviews, where they discussed growers' and officials' behavior. Thus, in most cases, critical speeches from both BSC and state representatives drew out claims about the other's identity in an exchange of public remarks that came across as a game of cultural and social self-positioning and repositioning. Charges of social inauthentic-ity, along with claims of cultural superiority or inferiority and privileged citizenship, developed through each party's analyses of specific person-alities and behaviors in the banana industry.

In an attempt to discredit collective action, state representatives not only held that growers unwillingly struck but also argued that the BSC called strikes on weeks when its leadership did not need to harvest and thus would not have sacrificed income. Again, the claim was backed with figures showing that, in the weeks preceding and following the strikes,

Figs. 9 and 10. Monument built by the Banana Salvation Committee and unveiled at October 1994 rally to commemorate the one-year anniversary of two farmers killed during the October 1993 strike. (Photos by the author.)

an oversupply of bananas occurred in the areas where the BSC organizers lived. State representatives charged that the BSC

> plans strike action on dates convenient to them; that is they organize strike action during certain periods when their members [i.e., organizers] have been informed well in advance so that they can harvest their fruit. Therefore, their members never are affected by strike action and consequently suffer no financial loss. This gives them the added advantage of time and freedom to mobilize for the strike *against* those farmers who would wish to cut their bananas. . . . [T]his shows . . . that the *genuine* banana grower is being . . . made to lose money, time and effort while the [leaders of the group] march to disrupt the industry. . . . [B]anana growers have invested in the industry

and should and must be permitted to benefit from these investments in time, labour, and money. They depend on bananas for their livelihood, for the education of their children, to pay the mortgages on their homes, loans on their vehicles, installments on furniture and household appliances. . . . The majority of farmers would like to . . . be free to harvest their bananas. . . . It is their democratic and constitutional right to act as free people. (Minister of Agriculture, Lands, Forestry, Fisheries, February 1994 [my emphasis])

By stating that most growers "depend on banana sales for their livelihood" the minister of agriculture suggested that the BSC leadership was more financially able to withstand financial losses than "other" growers. But the portrayal here also described the BSC as *qualitatively* different from most growers, particularly in terms of growers' perspectives and professional motivations. Moreover, its irony notwithstanding, a statement about the BSC's impingement on growers' democratic rights also distinguished growers from the group by social status, by placing the BSC in a dominant social category. Thus, public means of differentiating the BSC from growers turned on material classifications but also drew significantly on ethical and social ones as well. State analyses of the BSC here also set up that differentiation as an unequal and contentious hierarchy since the BSC was portrayed not merely as belonging to a different social echelon than most producers but also as working *against* the "majority of banana growers." As a result, attempts to discredit the BSC pushed the idea of a hierarchy *among* growers, rather than *between* growers and a nongrower group, and therefore challenged propositions about a unified farmer identity.

Such propositions were critical to the BSC's public and cultural work. Although the BSC designed its platform based on issues of income and institutional corruption, the group's later rally speeches, public statements, and press releases crafted claims that institutional and economic problems were mere epiphenomena of a larger problem: cultural divisions between farmers and the state. Through uses of language and specific strategies for action, the movement organizers suggested that there was a collective and cultural farmer identity and social status that needed addressing to solve underlying problems in the industry. Public and staged performances helped assert, redefine, and reclaim this identity and status, which differed sharply from popular and pejorative images of growers—including those images shaped by state representatives' speeches. At the same time that it shifted common and popular images and imaginations of grower identities, the BSC also reassessed the cultural identity applied to state representatives. This image making and remaking of two broadly defined groups further developed into a critique of class and cultural divisions within St. Lucia and an attempt to redefine where each group could and should have stood within the nation.

Shifting Social Status

The start of this public repositioning can be traced to the prime minister's speech to the nation just following the first strike. In this address, he chastised farmers for the violence they displayed and for their decision to strike and do harm to the nation's economy. Boldly claiming personal responsibility for making the country's banana industry a success, while not yet singling out the BSC, the prime minister claimed that growers had benefited from his lifelong work, now compromised by farmers striking. He made this point days after the peak street action during the October 1993 strike.

> I have negotiated many a contract. I have not only led St. Lucia but the entire Commonwealth Caribbean in international negotiations. All to ensure that the industry survives. . . . All my work in this regard has been for the farmers and for St. Lucia. . . . I seek no honour, no glory, no financial reward. My only reward is the advancement and progress of this country. . . . [I]t is . . . with deep regret that I have seen some members of the SLBGA departed from this [straight and narrow] path and betrayed the public confidence placed in them. And here I deal specifically with some of the members of the Board *elected by the growers themselves*. . . . [Y]ou must remember that it is the Board that the delegates of the farmers themselves elected. . . . These very directors chosen by them [the farmers] have in two years bankrupted the association and brought the entire banana industry to the point of collapse. And now they turn to Government to clean up the mess. (Rt. Hon. John Compton, October 1993 [italicized emphasis mine, underlined emphases in original])

The speech was motivated not only by the strike activities but also by the sense of urgency surrounding the industry following the strikes. Nine single-spaced pages long, it contained repeated references to the prime minister as selfless and self-sacrificing, the altruism and heroics of "government" within the industry, and "farmers" who had led the industry astray through poor election choices that had placed corrupt representatives in the SLBGA. There was an obvious irony to this latter point since the majority of representatives on the SLBGA board were government appointees. Yet, through his focus on farmers' choices, Prime Minister Compton did not assign strong blame to his administration. Instead, he sharpened his attention on farmers' behaviors, referring to them as "gangs of hooligans" and "criminal elements" when he described the October street protest actions as "outbreaks of indiscipline." Referencing the BSC more directly, he claimed that the street protests were incited by those "quietly instigating, encouraging and even financing the criminal elements."

Unsurprisingly, the prime minister's words sparked a strong reaction from many farmers, who objected to the idea that they had been well taken care of by the banana industry yet behaved frivolously and thanklessly. Recall Mark's comment in chapter 4 about the insult Morne Vert-ian farmers felt due to the prime minister's public charges against grow-ers. The BSC leaders took up public responses to these and other such charges, emphasizing the insult growers had received through the prime minister's words. Launching a "counterimage campaign," the group characterized government and farmers in ways that diverged from those described in the prime minister's speech.

One way the BSC achieved this was by emphasizing that the farmers were hardworking and living modestly, while receiving undue criticism for their misunderstood lifestyles. In rally speeches and direct responses to government images of growers, the movement leaders talked of how growers toiled for long hours, especially on harvest days, pointing out that much of growers' hard work was to the benefit of nongrowers. The argument was often made to discount the counterimage of growers as living frivolously and carelessly. At a meeting to iron out tense post-strike relations between growers and various industry actors, a BSC member stated:

> There is this myth. . . .that the banana farmer builds a big house, buys a 4-wheel drive and now he can't pay for it. . . . I'm telling you: the 4-wheel drive is to take the wife to town to shop, to take [a farmer] where the banana is . . . to take the farmer to church on Sunday. Meanwhile, you people here [government, SLBGA officials, repre-sentatives of the Chamber of Commerce] have your Toyota Cressida, but because we have a 4-wheel drive to bring the banana to town so *you* can sell your goods, it is a crime! (Banana Salvation Committee speech, February 1994)

With use of terms such as "you people," the BSC member enunciated a sharp social division between the world of the growers and those at the helm of the SLBGA and other prominent institutions in St. Lucia. How-ever, in the broader comment, the movement organizer declared the extravagant lifestyle of the nongrower world that contrasted sharply with the practical, work-ethics of growers. This "took back" the claim that growers were the ones living elaborately and excessively. For the comment, spoken like an announcement, criticized nongrowers at the meeting for their own mischaracterization of farmers' worlds, and asserted that such characterizations were more accurate depictions of nongrowers' own worlds.

BSC-constructed images of growers' worlds also included reference to farmers doing slave work, often with a suggestion that growers were working *for* the government and being inadequately compensated and unfairly treated by the government. The references drew a picture of growers subordinated to and exploited by the government, and forced to do oppressive work for no money, so that the government could pursue its extravagant existence. Speaking at a rally of growers, a BSC organizer proclaimed:

> [Industry officials] think that the money will keep coming down to Castries and the stupid people in the country[side] will keep producing. . . . Even the smallest [lowest paid] people in the [SL]BGA make $2000/month and you [banana grower] can't even make $200/week. And you are the one who has to produce bananas for them to have all of their good times. Tell me what we have to do . . . to get what is ours in our own land. (Banana Salvation Committee speech, March 1994)

This notion of grower exploitation and unjust SLBGA officials was later transformed by the BSC into a tactic of painting government and SLBGA representatives in the very images that the BSC claimed the government was applying to growers. For example, at the rallies, stories of government action and encounters with BSC members referred to industry officials as dogs, while stories of farmers compared them to hardworking subordinates misunderstood as ignorant and living beyond their means. In this way, conventional and popular images of each group were transposed. Top level government employees were cast as untrustworthy, oppressing, and living well while growers were portrayed as invested yet oppressed workers. Arguments that growers were treated and viewed as peons led to claims that the government employees and other representatives of St. Lucia's prominent institutions were corrupt, unjust, deceitful, unconcerned with growers, and at times unintelligent. This was in sharp contrast to the minister of agriculture's and the prime minister's self-characterization in their national addresses. BSC organizers speaking at a rally pointed out:

> [The minister of agriculture] is always in a hurry, having a cabinet meeting he have to attend, so that you don't have any time to check something [with him]. He has to go quickly because cabinet is waiting for him. Meanwhile, he is lying to you [farmers]. He's lying to you and anything he tells you he will not hold to it. It's not only [him] lying but it is big men that are lying. Big men, those in the Chamber

[of Commerce], Banana Association [SLBGA]. . . . Big men just name a place. Full of liars. (Banana Salvation Committee speech, March 1994)

Stories such as these were recounted in chronological detail and provided the location of a given interaction, verbatim dialogue with specific government representatives, and a detailed assessment of that representative's demeanor. The stories underscored the questionable behavior, attitudes, or motives of the given representative and a contrasting demeanor on the part of the BSC. Listening to the BSC's detailed and repeated descriptions of its members' attempts to negotiate industry policies with government and SLBGA representatives, rally participants understood that lying, corruption, and unintelligence were manifest at levels "above" growers. Constant storytelling of interactions with unscrupulous representatives reinforced a point about unreliable and perhaps even *small*, "big men."

The term "big men" referenced a general category of St. Lucian elites (which ironically included some women) who sat at the upper echelons of the country's prominent institutions. Always a means of differentiating such elites from growers (presumably, the "little men"), the category was the signal for wealth, urbanity, and upper level professionals. Yet, through BSC analysis of "big men's" actions, it also denoted haughtiness and institutional immorality. These values and characterizations that the BSC applied to the country's upper middle classes and contrasted with the values of poorer classes calls up Peter Wilson's (1973) work on reputation and respectability in the Caribbean. Wilson argued that Caribbean "lower classes" (and men, for Wilson) are most concerned with their reputation, values of equality and the Afro-Creole traditions, while the middle classes (and women, for Wilson) are concerned with their respectability, the values of hierarchy and the colonial social order. Indeed, when the BSC members spoke of "big men," they spoke of a group more invested in maintaining hierarchies and its own social position, compared to its social opposite, growers who the BSC understood as an undifferentiated group most committed to its work.

The "big men" category emerged blatantly and subtly in various BSC public speeches including a March 1994 rally where the BSC organizers talked of an event known popularly as the Coubaril Summit. This event was organized in March 1994, amid the rising tensions between the BSC and representatives from the Compton administration due to the continuing question of government input into the SLBGA. It was a major episode in this chapter of the banana industry's development because it brought together a variety of "partners," representatives from different visible and recognized social organizations in St. Lucia such as the Chamber of Commerce and the Christian Council of Churches. Thus, the previous strategy of negotiations solely between the BSC and state representatives was supplemented with a wider group of interested parties that, collectively, attended the summit to discuss the impasse between the BSC and Compton's administration. More broadly, the summit's charge was to assess and steer discussions about the future policies of the banana industry and the SLBGA in particular. By extension, the meeting was also an effort to stem disagreements between the BSC and state officials attached to the banana industry. However, tensions between the two sides did not subside during the summit, and the BSC brought stories of the experience back to public rallies. Telling rally participants about the summit, the BSC critiqued government organizers as deceptive, pompous, and working against growers.

> First day last week we were at Coubaril [the location] and [you should have heard] the [formal] name [of the summit]: (words enunciated slowly) "Conclusion of Consultation Meeting for March 9th" [audience laughter]. By Friday, Compton himself who promised he will [not put the SLBGA into] receivership, . . . by Sunday, he said he would put [the SLBGA into receivership] for Tuesday. By Thursday, he say he will take . . . [receivership] out and not put it in. By Friday, he was already in DesRuisseaux [a town in the south] giving someone a contract to build a [banana] buying depot, without asking anyone anything. Ladies and Gentlemen, it is time to wake up and open your eyes to what is going on because if you don't wake up in St. Lucia, the day you wake up you will find wood ants [termites] have eaten all you had while you were sleeping. If you don't do that, it will cause you great pain. (Banana Salvation Committee speech, March 1994)

This wake-up call highlighted the prime minister's attempt to make decisions without farmer (BSC) input and perhaps to farmers' detriment despite Compton's self-constructed image of conciliation and consultation, the image in which the Coubaril Summit was proposed. It also aimed to signal a sharp contrast between the world of banana growers and that of industry officials by referencing the stilted title of the Coubaril Summit in jest. The BSC speaker showed skepticism about the summit's agenda and its organizers as he poked fun at the summit's title, its lofty ring due to its lengthy and multisyllabic words. Doing this, he reinforced ideas about "big men," their extravagant lifestyles, and their haughty ways. The retelling of the summit experience showed that substance and truth in the big words behind the meeting were lacking.

The BSC analysis thus demonstrated not only misdeeds and weakness on the part of the "big men" to the rally-attending public. It also revealed the savvy and astute ways of banana growers who could perceive the truth behind the "big men's" image and reinterpret that image to restore its proper meaning. Indeed, a continual BSC strategy was to symbolically and analytically subvert the social standing of industry officials and others from a middle-class, urban sector by publicly airing a "true" analysis of government ways. Yet, another approach was to illustrate how the social position popularly (mis)assigned to growers did not apply, particularly with respect to intelligence and competence. When discussing how "people in Castries" saw farmers as "stupid" and how government officials viewed growers as "slaves," the BSC also warned growers that: "the thing that have to happen have not even started yet." By this, the BSC organizers meant that people in Castries, who were generally unaware had not seen the extent of farmers' power that could result from the strikes. In another venue, one BSC member shamed industry officials by asking them how they could not have known more about the banana industry's shaky economic status when farmers, by virtue of their experience and perceptiveness, knew all along. Thus, while the BSC constructed banana growers as mistreated and oppressed, the group simultaneously showed that farmers possessed unacknowledged intelligence and awareness that industry representatives and Castries residents (understood as elite urban dwellers) did not.

This circulation of imagery and ideas about growers, state representatives, and urban elites, along with the re-creation of social identities through the retelling and interpreting of events, challenged conventional understandings of the social position between growers and government. In fact, the BSC built its work on reassessing and re-creating images about the social position of each group, however symbolically, theoretically, and momentarily. The movement thus exposed publicly unacknowledged divides along axes of rural/urban and working classes/middle professional classes. Yet, in their critique of class divisions, interestingly, the BSC fell right into ignoring divisions along other lines. For, in its effort to depict farmers as a downtrodden group and government as a mistrustful group, the BSC failed to admit openly the divisions of class, gender, landownership, and laboring status among growers, staking the movement's politics instead on other divisions and relationships. Thus, the BSC constructed its argument by juxtaposing and contrasting the social status and cultural characteristics of two or three disaggregated groups (growers, urban professionals, and state representatives) to suggest a new means of positioning between them.[4]

Crafting Kwéyòl and Cultural Identity

In addition to social status, cultural identity was another important category that the BSC redefined. This was done through reference to rural ways of life and through claims to a Kwéyòl identity and mastery of the Kwéyòl language. In St. Lucia, the former British colony, English is the official language yet, reflecting the French influence on the island, a French Kwéyòl (Creole) is spoken more widely due especially to the predominance of that language in rural areas.[5] Indeed, it is the language most often heard in daily life in Morne Verte and, in many ways, it is one of the features of life that distinguishes rural and urban St. Lucians. More than a language, Kwéyòl has become linked to specific people and lifestyles, as well as serving as an important symbol of cultural and social identity. Conventionally, within Caribbean Studies, it is conceived of as a culture forged out of the encounter of multiple cultural traditions—particularly European and African—due to specific types of relations formed between these two groups interacting in a new and specific setting, especially under the conditions of European power through colonialism and plantation slavery in the Americas (Braithwaite 1971; Mintz and Price 1992; Yelvington 2000). In recent times, the notion of a Kwéyòl identity and creolization has developed a changing definition from the idea of two blended cultures or cultures developed through contact and under specific material conditions. Newer definitions include the notion of creolization as part of a process of cultural development and transformation (Garrett 2000); the interfacing of multiple groups under various conditions and circumstances (Bernabé, Chamoiseau, and Confiant 1989); or the process of transformation for a culture made up of multiple elements (African, European, Asian) and where people have been alienated from their histories (Glissant 1989).[6]

While the BSC rally organizers never referenced a Kwéyòl identity directly, they did call up its key and conventional markers, particularly when they described farmers as possessing a mixture of cultural traditions (e.g., "high" European culture along with African "Creole" culture). They also made direct reference to the Kwéyòl language either by using it or by talking about its significance to farmers compared to non-farmers. Kwéyòl language, then, was in the middle of their public activities because they spoke it throughout their public speeches and reserved English, the country's official language, for secondary use—even though they were conversant in both and were used to speaking English in certain public settings.

Most BSC speeches were conducted primarily in Kwéyòl and sprinkled with English throughout. Yet there were different ways that En-glish appeared. The rally organizers either spoke in sentences in which Kwéyòl predominated and English was used for one or two words, such as below where the English word "resign," was mixed into a Kwéyòl sentence:

Kwéyòl	English Translation
I ka mande nu resign.	He asked us to resign.
Ki moun vle nu resign?	Who wants us to resign?

Or they shifted between Kwéyòl to English:

Kwéyòl/English mixture	English translation
Nu pa zen. We will respect him [the prime minister] when he respects us.	We are not dogs. We will respect him [the prime minister] when he respects us.

Or they shifted from English to Kwéyòl:

Kwéyòl/English mixture	English translation
BSC is alive and well. I want you to know . . . BSC connat pwoblemn fig.	The BSC is alive and well. I want you to know . . . the BSC understands the banana problem.

Such uses of both languages throughout dialogue are common for Kwéyòl speakers in St. Lucia (Garrett 2000). English words for which there is no strict Kwéyòl equivalent typically are left in English, such as the word *resign* in the first example. This is especially true for younger speakers of Kwéyòl, who are more apt to incorporate English words into their lexicon than older speakers, who, rather than employing any English, would use Kwéyòl terms to denote a similar meaning. Similarly, where English words make up half of a sentence, or where English sen-

tences make up half of a paragraph, this signals a shift in which pro-
nouncing one English word might lead a younger Kwéyòl speaker to
shift languages temporarily. Interestingly, English speakers who know
and practice speaking Kwéyòl only slightly do not make the shifts that
Kwéyòl speakers do. Their sentences are filled much more with English
content, and, by contrast, speaking Kwéyòl is a temporary shift for them
(Garrett 2000). Thus, the BSC speakers revealed themselves to be much
more Kwéyòl speakers than English speakers, centering themselves
firmly within ways of life and a cultural identity that carried specific
meanings in St. Lucia.

Kwéyòl has long been the most debased of the island's two languages,
Kwéyòl and English. Its low status dates back to the period of slavery,
when the language was first associated with illiterate, African-descended,
and poor rural dwellers, while French (under French colonialism) and
English (under British colonialism) were the languages of the colonial
powers.[7] Throughout most of the twentieth century, the negative value of
Kwéyòl vis-à-vis English was evident in many aspects of St. Lucian life
and processes of socialization. Urban dwellers rarely spoke the language
or admitted to knowing it. In rural areas, Kwéyòl-speaking parents often
punished their children for speaking Kwéyòl, even though they could not
understand English themselves (Garrett 2000).

Kwéyòl's status underwent changes in the 1970s, spurred particularly
by a national attempt to reevaluate the language's place and status in
society. The Folk Research Centre (FRC), a nongovernmental organization, and the Mouvmen Kweyol (Kwéyòl Movement), a cultural
group, advanced this process of language valorization during the country's immediate postindependence period (Garrett 2000; Charles 1985).
Their work took place concurrently with the late 1970s movement led by
Josie and Odlum and thus was entrenched in similar ideas critiquing the
pejorative legacy of colonialism. They also spun their work off of a
larger, international movement of Kwéyòl-speaking nations in the
African diaspora that sought to retrieve what it saw as a "lost" culture
and history of African peoples colonized by the French.

A belief in a lost tradition emerged in St. Lucia's own attempt to forge
a Kwéyòl identity within the nation. For, although English remains St.
Lucia's official language and predominated in many formal settings such
as classroom instruction, Kwéyòl was publicly heralded as a positive
symbol of late-twentieth-century St. Lucian culture. Due to efforts by
the FRC, an official Kwéyòl Day (Jounen Kwéyòl) was created, and,
here, St. Lucians are encouraged to speak only in Kwéyòl and observe

various food, dance, and dress practices. Additionally, Kwéyòl television and radio programming occur on a daily basis, even though its representation pales in comparison with English programming. Thus, the FRC made public inroads in rendering the language more widely accepted and removing its stigma. Moving Kwéyòl gradually into these new arenas meant that the language was partially adopted by middle-class urban folk who previously had rejected it. Indeed, Kwéyòl became an emerging important cultural symbol newly attached to St. Lucia's middle classes at the end of the twentieth century, but its cross over was not absolute (see Garrett 2000).

That the BSC leaders spoke Kwéyòl at their rallies, then, was highly significant and helped place their efforts within the work of the FRC and the uneasy crossover of the language. The move crossed Kwéyòl over into new places and spaces. This is so since rural people often conducted their meetings in Kwéyòl, yet such meetings almost never were held publicly. Similarly, leaders of previous movements did not speak Kwéyòl at public venues. During the heaviest years of BSC activity, political leaders, too, were not known to give public addresses significantly in Kwéyòl. All of the prime minister's addresses to the nation, for example, were in English; the Coubaril Summit was held in English (except for the speeches by one BSC leader); and even the 1993 leader of the SLP, who joined forces with the BSC, barely spoke Kwéyòl when he made brief speeches at BSC rallies in support of the group. Thus, what rendered the BSC's language tactics curious and unconventional was the public and political dimension of the meetings in which Kwéyòl was situated, the tying together of Kwéyòl, politics and public life.[8]

As farmers conversant in English and familiar with the social place of Kwéyòl in public and urban contexts, the BSC men were well attuned to the significance of bringing Kwéyòl outside of accepted spaces. As SLBGA delegates and/or board members, they knew that Kwéyòl was forbidden at official meetings of the banana industry. And, as former migrants to the United States, they not only had lived in places where Kwéyòl was not a part of everyday life, but they also were familiar with the ways in which returned migrants elevate themselves by denying their Kwéyòl fluency and revealing familiarity with English. Therefore, the BSC's decision to incorporate Kwéyòl into public rallies represented a strategy to subvert convention and make Kwéyòl uncharacteristically public.

But, what could this strategy afford them? A quote from one of their rallies held in the capital city gives us insight.

The reason why this evening, which is abnormal for us, that I am speaking English on this platform is because there are a lot of people in Castries that are not St. Lucians. Whether you were born here or not, the mere fact that you say to other people "I do not understand the Kwéyòl, I do not understand what is going on," is telling us that you are not St. Lucian. If you [were] you would have understood it. And yet still, we are going to accommodate you this evening by talking a majority of our meeting in English because it is not that we cannot speak English. We are St. Lucian and we conduct our meetings in Kwéyòl. . . . [W]e from the farming community can speak both and therefore we are going to give you both this evening. (Banana Salvation Committee speech, March 1994)

By highlighting that urban St. Lucians did not know Kwéyòl, the BSC leaders exposed the fallacy that Kwéyòl had crossed over widely into the urban sector; they showed that it remained a central facet and fixture of rural life, and *only* rural life, revealing the myth of Kwéyòl's widespread changing social status. This was, then, one way that the group attempted to shame industry officials, by revealing their lack of familiarity with national culture and the very sectors of society over which they sought to take charge.

To be sure, the movement organizers took it one step further to suggest that not knowing Kwéyòl was akin to not being St. Lucian, again implying that growers were more firmly planted in the nation than Castries folk. At the Coubaril Summit, one BSC leader made this exact connection by showing how an inability to converse in Kwéyòl meant being out of touch with banana growers. Addressing the "big men" at the summit he said:

You bring people [growers] here so that when you say raise your hand they do it. But, as usual, they don't understand a thing about what is going on. . . . [During a break,] I asked the farmers [here] how they like the consultation so far and they said: "si bos-la pwe pale Kwéyòl mwen sa compwann pli" [if the boss (prime minister) would speak Kwéyòl I would understand more]. (Banana Salvation Committee speech, February 1994)

Comments such as this implied that the BSC identified more closely with the lifestyles of banana growers than did representatives of other important national groups. Again, the translation and movement between the two languages here revealed the group's familiarity with both worlds. Interestingly, however, the BSC organizers' ease with the world of the "big men" was disproved to the extent that their command of English was not exact and far from that of others ("big men") at the meeting. Thus, the critique was a kind of awkward critique, layered with various levels of social identity. In many ways, as it openly sought to expose that industry officials were out of touch with growers' work and lives (and thus, out of touch with the nation and national culture), it also uncovered that the BSC organizers' fit in the social world of the "big men" was not tight. Even so, by suggesting that those who speak both English and Kwéyòl, are more St. Lucian than the urban/middle-class folk around the table at the Coubaril Summit, the BSC members played right into the contested and political nature of language and culture in St. Lucia's nation-building. Their critiques and insinuations became a means of proving that urban folk, and by association officials in the industry, were unfamiliar with an aspect of St. Lucian life that had gained popular recognition as a symbol of the nation—a symbol ironically redefined by the urban middle classes themselves.

In this way, the BSC symbolically subverted class and cultural hierarchies within St. Lucia. They painted farmers as nationally and culturally superior to industry officials because the former were revealed as more attached to significant symbols of St. Lucian culture than the latter. The reversal of position was a pointed comment on common beliefs about farmers as lower-class "subcitizens" compared to middle-class urban dwellers, who were perceived as possessing more "culture" and "class."

The ability to make this claim through Kwéyòl was due to the changing status of language in the nation, the growing national and international movement valorizing it, and the BSC leaders' own in-between position in the country. Because they were linked to two class worlds in St. Lucia, they not only knew both languages and the place of language within both worlds; they also understood how to *use* both.

Rethinking Citizenship

Attached to the idea of cultural identity and its place in the banana industry was the leaders' claim to farmers' rights, especially the right to a place in the nation. This was evident in the BSC claiming banana growers were more St. Lucian than industry officials on a cultural and social level. As seen in critiquing farmers' treatment by state/industry representatives, the BSC referenced St. Lucia as "*our* land" and stressed attempts by these representatives to exclude farmers from it. Thus, within BSC-state interactions, the nation was a contested site where claims of (greater) deserved and earned citizenship were at the center. Additionally, the BSC pointed out the dependence of other economic sectors on banana production, implying that banana growers have made nonfarmers a part of the nation. Going further, the movement also chastised nongrowers for not knowing more about the banana industry, a key sector in the survival of the country. Speaking to nongrowers at the Coubaril Summit, one BSC leader exclaimed:

> The average St. Lucian says they don't know [that there is a crisis in the banana industry]. My God! You rely on the banana industry to sell your lumber, your chicken, your whatever and you don't know what is going on in the industry? (Banana Salvation Committee Speech, February 1994)

By emphasizing that officials, who purportedly were more educated than farmers, did not know the status of the industry so vital to the country, the BSC underscored a crucial irony. But, the group also pointed to the fact that farmers knew all along. Thus, in arguing the shame of uninformed industry representatives and "big men," the BSC also suggested that farmers deemed to be inept were more perceptive, and ultimately knew more about their country. Again, addressing nongrowers at Coubaril, one BSC leader made the following comment in this regard.

> I want to make it clear to people here: you would not have been here if there was no [BSC] because [it is we] who [brought] to the attention of the nation that there is a problem in the banana industry. (Banana Salvation Committee Speech, February 1994)

This discourse concerning social identity and nation seemed to bring the banana growers' movement full circle. That is to say, asserting and redignifying a collective cultural identity while unraveling the social identity of industry officials was a way to stake a claim for one's rightful place in the nation and to return to issues of national exclusion and control—the dynamics underlying the need to make these claims. The BSC organizers contended that growers had not been permitted to participate in all aspects of the banana industry. Their public speeches illustrated that, for them, a desire to participate fully in the industry became synonymous with participation in the nation. The link was made not merely by showing that the nation depended on banana production and hence banana growers. More importantly, it was made by emphasizing that the state controlled the industry (a key sector in the nation), thereby excluding farmers from belonging in their country.

CONCLUSION

The events leading up to the point where the BSC declared its place in the nation show that, although issues of global market integration and multinational profiteering had become legitimized in the views and policies of the state, the actions of farmers such as the BSC members attempted to nullify such issues. For, the ways that the BSC organized around and against national conventions reinforced the nation as a site of analysis, an important place for understanding the context of dynamics and problems within the banana industry. Like movements before them, the BSC reinforced meanings associated with being St. Lucian and interacting in St. Lucia, and the group also attempted to shift some of those meanings in its explicit and implicit critiques of social conventions and cultural representations of particular groups in the country.

Price was the initial motivator for the BSC's work but this was not the only, or even, eventually, the most salient factor that the movement underscored as the major problem before banana growers. In organizing its activities, the BSC's focus on growers' economic hardships and on institutional corruption within the SLBGA metamorphosed into issues of cultural identity, social status, social interaction, and belonging in the nation. This occurred in the ways in which the BSC organized its movement through and against the conventions of social uses of space in St. Lucia; analyzed grower-state relations as founded on pejorative representations of the former by the latter; evaluated state representatives as culturally inferior and nationally insignificant; and drew on forms of language and cultural practice to make claims about and against social conventions in the banana industry, which, more broadly, also circulated in the nation. These approaches were a means of interrogating relations and conventions in the nation, but they were also a means of reorganizing roles and social positions symbolically. Indeed, by asserting that state representatives were culturally and socially inept concerning matters of national importance, and then by showing how growers were culturally and socially savvy in these same areas, the BSC symbolically reversed the social positioning of the two groups. This served to re-represent subjectivities and identities and to imagine a socially reordered nation.

Through these tactics, which targeted the state, the nation, and cultural and social dynamics, the BSC engaged formal political structures and cultural politics in St. Lucia. Thus, the BSC's work was indeed deeply political, as the charge was often made. Like movements before it, the BSC played right into the existing formal political organization of the country in its alignment with the SLP but also in its repeated critiques of the prime minister, the minister of agriculture, other members of the Compton administration, and also the SLBGA. Yet, the BSC also played directly into and interrogated St. Lucia's cultural politics of identity construction, representation, and sociospatial organization. The two forms of politics, however, should not be considered distinct. Cultural politics was layered onto the more formal politics if, as the BSC claimed, the state apparatus was part of the vehicle through which cultural and social assignments and conceptualizations were set in St. Lucia.

IV. PLACING THE GLOBAL

7. *Placing Globalization*

LOCALIZING ACTION

THERE IS A PERVASIVE IDEA that we should think of and theorize ourselves as existing within a global system, attend to the connections that reveal and foster global linkages, and move beyond the narrow (local) fields of our lives. As a concept of geographic isolation, "local" is considered to have no place in today's world. We are, popular perspectives hold, in a new time, when individual community organizing and existence are either no longer purely possible or no longer very productive. As such, we have slogans such as "Think Globally, Act Locally," which urge us to work from the ground up in order to effect change beyond our communities. And although their purpose differs from the ideas behind these slogans, U.S. universities and colleges are developing global studies initiatives in lieu of area studies foci to reorient regional studies and instead promote investigations of broad and globally interconnected patterns and processes.[1]

Indeed, Bill Maurer (2004) is right when he examines St. Lucia as a case from which we can complicate traditional forms of boundary-making and the concepts, politics, and imaginaries that fuel such forms. To be sure, St. Lucia and Morne Verte are not isolated from the world. Like the rest of the Caribbean, St. Lucia's history includes series and centuries of human migrations from around the globe; local formations constructed out of colonial projects built on models of political, social, cultural, and economic development learned in Europe, the Mediterranean, and Africa; and lifeways continually shaped by cultural and political patterns from Asia, Africa, Europe, and North America. Moreover, the contemporary circuits of tourism, media, migration, trade of manufactured and agricultural goods, and even political and economic links to North America, Europe, and parts of Asia (especially China and Taiwan) are glaring evidence that there are indeed global connections that make up social, economic, cultural, and political possibilities on the island.[2] Beyond this, we can even look more narrowly to protesters within the banana industry to see other global connections. As mentioned, the founders of the Banana Salvation Committee all had lived and worked abroad, some for extended periods. Many of the banana growers in Morne Verte had family members living overseas, were often operating farms for friends of family living abroad, and sometimes went abroad themselves for holidays to visit relatives in French Guyana, Martinique, St. Martin, and Texas. Banana production was organized as a "transnational" industry, linked directly and especially to Europe but also necessarily intersected with North America, Central America, and South America.

The point of this book, then, is not that St. Lucians and those attached to the banana industry were bound to local and national sites or that St. Lucia was not transnational at the transitional time of the 1993 trade policy shifts. Rather, it is that growers' efforts at analyzing and making sense of the shifting banana industry drew significantly on local and national resources, categories, meanings, and relations, illustrating that growers "thought locally." The local constructs they accentuated were indeed global, however, growers did not appeal to the range of global connections that made up Morne Verte and St. Lucia. Indeed, it is particularly interesting that, given how the island is connected with sites far and beyond, residents of Morne Verte and protesters in the BSC increasingly placed themselves more firmly in local sources than in transnational or global ones as they waged a campaign that bypassed, and consequently disrupted, full participation in the extensive discourse on global markets and free trade. Their focus was decidedly local, on life in the valley and life in the nation.

One way to understand this focus is as Leslie Sklair (2001) does when he writes that

> the only chance that people in social movements have to succeed is by disrupting the local agencies they come into direct contact within their daily lives rather than the more global institutions whose interests these agencies are serving directly, or, more often, indirectly while workers are often confused about who (which representation of capital) to oppose when their interests (conditions of labor, liveli-

hoods) are threatened. Increasingly, as capitalism globalizes, subordinate groups find difficulty in identifying their adversaries.

We may not agree with Sklair that we can somehow measure movements' "success"; however, he also raises a different point that is important: that local institutions, which often are partial fronts for global institutions, are accessible, identifiable, and historically and culturally meaningful in ways that lead people to work within and through them even in a globalizing world. When people work in these ways, it may not mean that they necessarily and outwardly reject globalizing projects or even that they exist entirely separately from such projects. Yet, it does mean that people make choices about the spaces, practices, and relations within which they opt to organize themselves, even if they simultaneously operate in other arenas as well. This point resonates with Stuart Hall's (1991) argument, raised in chapter 1, that, amid globalization, people sometimes search for a sense of place, tapping into what is knowable and locatable. Put another way, people can *place* that which is global through that which is available, comprehensible, and significant to their everyday lives—through the local.

Of course, there can be no singular sense of place because places are made up of multiple and uneven social relations (Massey 1993) and places are connected to other sites. Yet, places still have histories, cultures, and politics through which people have specific experiences and relationships that they know (Mintz 1998) and upon (and against) which they can readily act (Moore 1997). Examples of this in the Caribbean point to how workers in global industries appropriate mandatory facets of the industry structure as a way to remake their social and cultural identities that are locally significant (Freeman 2000), and how national subjects reject the onslaught of a "global culture" arriving through massive tourism and imported professionals to work in offshore industries by creating and emphasizing specific national institutions (Amit Talai 1997). These examples highlight how an alternative or companion to accentuating and engaging with globalizing projects is to redefine and reemphasize place and the politics of place.

CLASS VERSUS CULTURE

If the local can be significant to how people organize while confronting neoliberal and other globalizing projects, the question arises as to which aspects of the local people draw on in that effort. Classic Marxist analyses, of course, look to class consciousness as the linchpin for revolutionary social change. Yet, some have argued that it is no longer sufficient to talk strictly in terms of social class in order to grasp how people organize (Laclau and Mouffe 1985; Touraine 1988). Popular identities, which are more complex than class, diffuse class as a fixed and singular social position. Consequently, multiple forms of social differentiation, including social identity, are important to the creation of political action (Laclau and Mouffe 1985). Also, it becomes difficult to talk of peasants as possessing a singular class identity and as people who exist in bounded rural locales. Today's rural producers participate in multiple economic activities that extend beyond agricultural production (Edelman 1996; Kearney 1996), and they reside within households made up of multiple class relations since, when considered together, household residents participate in a variety of employment contexts (Deere 1990).

Should class as an identity for social and political action, then, be discarded? For Edelman (1996, 2001) and Kearney (1996), class must remain important and is not completely absent as an axis on which people organize. Both contend that material conditions still prompt resistance even if cultural issues do as well. As Kearney (1996: 153) says:

> Concern with complex differentiation need not and should not obviate the fundamental material bases of social differentiation. . . . Although the complex multivocality of internal and external differentiation suppresses class consciousness, social scientists should therefore not fail to attend to the very real class differentiation that underlies so many other forms of difference.

Yet, there is another way to explore this debate. Rather than considering political activism as built from a mixture of class and culture, or built from one or the other, we might investigate specific contexts to uncover the salience of class and/or culture within them. Kearney (1996:154) hints at this when he asks: "For what do internally differentiated subjects . . . struggle?" It is a question we can answer through research in particular places. Indeed, if we agree that place holds and generates meaning out of localized histories, then we might look to specificities of class and culture within given localities. We can then theorize the intersection of cultural identities and politics or class and politics to uncover when, how, and through which vehicles activists engage especially with local cultural politics or class dynamics.

While the St. Lucian case shows a coexistence of concerns around class and culture within growers' counterdiscourses, it also reveals growers' gradual de-emphasis of material conditions and a rising focus on cultural identities, concepts, and categories. This was especially true with the BSC, which initially emphasized price change, technology shift, and government control but shifted swiftly to exploring cultural and social assignments in St. Lucia. Class mattered, but culture became a pressing term within the BSC's public work *and* the means by which to interrogate class. For Morne Verte producers, class and culture—as identifiers of growers' condition—were discussed and conceptualized simultaneously, though under different contexts when subtly addressing the significance of farming and when organizing daily activities. Local culture and history became important conceptual tools for accentuating Morne Verte notions of work and not privileging the globalization discourse. Material claims were more open complaints that, for both the BSC and Morne Verte producers in particular venues softened. For both, material concerns and class identities did not dissolve entirely, but cultural concerns and identities came more firmly to the fore and were often the lens used to understand class categories and divisions. For the BSC, the nation was a place with social and cultural meaning worthy of picking apart in challenging the state's power and globalization discourse. Growers in Morne Verte, drew on the histories of work and specific forms of social organization in the valley as they were pushed into practices designed to fit them into global markets.

The eventual reinforcement of culture over class in specific contexts seems to have been shaped by three factors. First, due to the death of the two farmers, there was a growing sense that "you can't fight guns with stones." Following the farmers' deaths during the October strike, the power of the state was a stated reason for people's withdrawal from street protesting over more subtle means of asserting critiques. Second, the time frame for this study also needs to be taken into consideration. That the impacts of the NBR and other policy shifts were newly unfolding and not fully felt during the time of my research and the BSC's emergence and might play into the extent to which producers rallied around material concerns. Third, and perhaps most important, the nature of global processes such as discourses around free trade and labor discipline, which invaded St. Lucian localities, perhaps made the salience of culture more significant to growers' actions given the sense of dislocation from local practices around economy, work, and culture that such discourses prompted. The state was complicit in the dislocation process and thus became a "local" actor against which growers organized on political, economic, and cultural levels.

FREE TRADE, FREEDOM, & THE POLITICS OF THEORY

How do we understand the significance of these dynamics around place, culture, and politics for globalization? One way is through "development," which is sometimes seen as a discourse, an "official" constructed reality about the "third world" versus the "first world" that operates through language and practice (Escobar 1995; Crush 1995; Arce and Long 2000; Ferguson 1994). There are multiple discourses of global integration (including the neoliberalist model profiling market liberalization) that emphasize a way to organize and "develop" the economy and that are made real through a variety of practices and policies. Thus, to see globalization as a discourse is not to suggest that it is not real, that there are not discernible political and economic processes associated with it. Rather, it is to suggest that global economic integration measures are fueled and shaped at a conceptual and a political level. They are simultaneously played out in very real terms with tangible, material impacts. These real terms are due to the actions, policies, and projects that concretize concepts about specific forms of economic organization at a global level and shape people's practice.

In the case of the St. Lucian banana industry, official statements at the GATT and more subtle practices such as everyday interactions in St. Lucian farming communities set in motion a discourse around market liberalization and consumer demands. Latin America, Europe, and the Caribbean debated the value of free trade, with one camp lobbying for unrestricted market access and another defending social, political, and historical motivations for differentiating trade policies for importing countries. From the debate, trade policies and practices were continually reassessed and revised over the course of at least two years. At the same time and following from this debate, in St. Lucia there were numerous (and sometimes contradictory) state policies and actions that defined how banana growers could produce and act around banana production. A theme in the state's work was the need to produce for emerging policies that sought to relax trade preferences and open trade barriers. The

St. Lucian state, therefore, participated (albeit partially) in the globalization discourse because, in coordinating with foreign capital (Geest), state
representatives often referenced the weight and importance of the global
market for the possibilities of St. Lucian production. In this way, the St.
Lucian state represented the active enforcer of labor-disciplining strategies that rendered labor accessible to foreign capital and liberalizing
markets. State representatives also drew on patterns created during earlier times in St. Lucia, patterns that reinforced and resonated with preexisting class and racial hierarchies through labor-disciplining strategies.
All of these state-driven policies were local formations through which a
discourse on neoliberalism was not discounted.

A different discourse was also part of this context in which global
market integration processes were profiled and prioritized in St. Lucia.
Locally situated ideas, practices, and language from Morne Verte to the
BSC offered an alternative vision of economy and work but also of place.
That vision was concerned with promoting and guarding freedom (of
work) and also with affirming and redefining local cultural identities
while asserting and redesigning rights to citizenship and social status.
Growers presented their vision in everyday practice and collectively
organized movements set within local arenas, but they also put the vision
forward at a conceptual level. That is, growers' underscoring of freedom
over free trade and their accentuation of cultural identities over market
liberalization offered different analyses of the banana industry.

The emphasis on an *analysis* of the banana industry is important here.
I began this book by discussing my goal not to define St. Lucian growers' practices and forms of collective and community organizing as successful or unsuccessful in challenging market liberalization. Rather, my
purpose has been to explicate vision, imagination, and conceptualization
within a context of global market integration and a neoliberal project.
Freedom was at the heart of growers' vision and conceptualization. In
obvious ways, Morne Verte producers highlighted the significance of
defining local economies according to degrees of freedom. But, the BSC,
too, raised questions of worker/producer autonomy when the movement lobbied for the release of state control over producers' working
lives. By interrogating categorizations and representations of growers
and how these served to engender state control, the BSC also entered
into a theoretical discussion of how control occurred discursively and
how freedom could be obtained by the same measures. A concept of freedom therefore remains operative for Afro- and Indo-Caribbean groups,

even in the contemporary period, centuries after emancipation and the end of indentured servitude. As the literature shows, freedom is not solely an axis on which to build resistance, but it is also a concept that has fomented Caribbean community building and forms of social organization (Mintz 1989; Besson 1987b, 1992; Crichlow 1994; Rodney 1981). That is, how Afro- and Indo-Caribbeans have organized collectively and in everyday life points up a conceptualization of a self-determined and flexible existence.

Consequently, when Morne Verte growers were invested in defining their working existence differently than the SLBGA and other state representatives had done, they engaged in a politics of theory around the intersection of local societies and global economies. This is so because growers asserted an unpopular perspective on their own social and economic reality. The interplay and contradictions of these diverse and disputed discourses and theories—one appealing to the global context and another firmly planted in place and locality—make up the global system in which we live.

8. *Epilogue*

*L*IKE ALL ANTHROPOLOGISTS, I had always been cautioned against seeing societies, communities, and peoples as static. Yet, I was never more aware of this capacity for change than when I began my research in St. Lucia in 1993. Within the first several weeks of my arrival, institutions shifted hands and were reorganized—in some cases undone—seemingly overnight. The banana industry in the early 1990s then was exceptionally dynamic and has continued to be so, even after the period that this book addresses.

In September 1994, Tropical Storm Debby blazed through St. Lucia unexpectedly, and its floodwaters wiped out banana plants across the country. With only two months remaining to my work, many people told me that they could not recover what had been lost from their farms. Many forecast that the storm's effects would shatter an already shaky banana industry. In subsequent years, Hurricane Lenny (1999) and Tropical Storm Lilli (2002) also devastated the banana industry, with estimates that Lilli destroyed 40% to 50% of banana plants (Melville n.d.).

In 1997, the disagreements that were aired before the GATT were pursued further before the World Trade Organization (WTO). At this point, the United States entered into the discussions and a dispute ensued between the U.S./Latin American complainants and the EU/Caribbean parties (see, e.g., USEU 1996, also Josling 2003). The dispute went through several panels, each time with the WTO ruling in favor of the U.S./Latin American position, even though the United States continued to argue that the EU had not complied with the rulings. In 2001, the U.S./Latin American side reached a settlement through the WTO. The

Figs. 11 and 12. Tropical Storm Debby, which struck in September 1994, devastated farmers' crops. (Photos by the author.)

agreement was to extend greater trading licenses to non-ACP suppliers and to have a type of graduated trade preference policy for ACP banana-producing countries. It was further agreed that by 2006 all countries would trade in a "tariff only system," that is on an open market without any preferences or quotas. Unfettered free trade would replace the NBR and the adjustments made to it since 1993 (Josling 2003).

In the early 1990s, Geest Industries changed the exclusive buyer clause in its contract with the Windward Islands and began owning plantations and shipping bananas from Costa Rica, a rival to the Windward Islands in the "banana wars." In December 1995, Geest and the Windward governments began steps to dissolve their partnership. A new company, the Windward Island Banana Development and Exporting Company (WIBDECO), was formed to replace WINBAN and handle shipping and price negotiations for bananas. In 1997, WIBDECO teamed up with an Irish shipping company, Fyffes Ltd., to acquire Geest Public Liability Company, including its ripening and distributing business and its shipping business. In a jointly shared operation, WIBDECO and Fyffes oversaw shipping, distribution, and ripening activities. They

also acquired Geest's farms in Costa Rica. Under WIBDECO, a five-tiered pricing system was implemented to replace the three-tiered system and to promote improved product quality through the incentive of paying higher prices for higher quality bananas (Lewis 2000).

In 1997, the St. Lucian Labour Party—the party with which the BSC had aligned and which was so significant to St. Lucia's political activist history—won the national elections except for one seat in Parliament. The SLP led by Dr. Kenny Anthony, replaced the United Workers' Party, which had been in power for thirty years, led by John Compton, with only a two-year lapse in its reign. With Anthony's administration, laws were changed to permit Kwéyòl to be spoken during parliamentary meetings.

In 1998, the SLBGA Act was repealed, the SLBGA collapsed, and the St. Lucia Banana Company (SLBC) was created. The SLBC is a private corporation in which individual banana growers must purchase shares; growers who cannot afford to purchase shares cannot be part of the company. Other companies developed in the country as well, offering lower prices for bananas and marking the beginning of internal competition for banana sales on the island (Lewis 2000).

In 1997, one of the BSC leaders gained a seat in Parliament with the rise of the SLP; another BSC organizer lost by a small margin. Further, a BSC organizer became the president of the SLBC. The BSC's work mobilizing farmers for change appeared to have decreased significantly by the end of the decade, although the movement remained critical of changes in the industry, particularly the restructuring efforts (Lewis 2000). By the turn of the twentieth century, people tell me that the BSC splintered and disbanded amid discord among its members. Lewis (2000) notes the emergence of an off-shoot of the BSC known as the Concerned Farmers' Group.

In 1999, I bumped into John, who in 1994 had been proud to have access to land through *share* but who, five years later, was working as a security guard at a school. His experience reflects projections about the Windward Islands banana industries: that growers, especially small growers, would be pushed out of the industry in droves given the increased trade obstacles, the privatization of the local industry (from the SLBGA to the SLBC), and the rise in stiff requirements for producing and selling bananas in St. Lucia. John said he had given up growing bananas as prices stayed low and the expenses of production grew higher. Even with the *share* system he had found so useful and promising in 1994, he was not able to sustain work on his farm as full-time occupation. His shift away from banana production differed from those few I met in 1993–94 who were then making an effort to diversify their economic pursuits. These tended to be middle-scale producers, not small-scale ones like John, who pursued self- employment ventures rather than wage work such as the security guard position John had taken on. I am also told that young men and women, many of them former growers, now migrate temporarily to neighboring Martinique where they can benefit from the high value of the Euro dollar (Angelina Polius personal communication).

In 1997, Susan, alongside whom I had often worked on harvest days in 1993 and 1994, told me that she began taking sewing classes and later in the year started making clothes for people in her community. She was proud to show me the clothes she was making and to talk of the clientele she had built up. As for her farm, she told me that her children and she rarely tended bananas, an occupation they could no longer afford to keep up. However, while moving forward with her sewing projects, she had kept her land and continued to keep other crops growing on it. Like the flexibility that marked Morne Verte during my research, she worked full time in sewing and on her farm, for herself, a few times per month.

Notes

CHAPTER 1

1. My study (Slocum 1996) showed that women's management of their households and their trafficking tasks were interrelated and interdependent. Trafficking helped support domestic roles and needs while household residents and resources also were channeled into trading work.

2. Morne Verte is a pseudonym.

3. All banana growers' names are pseudonyms.

4. The argument concerning disruptions, asymmetries, and the nonhomogenizing effects of global integration processes has been central within anthropology, as Inda and Rosaldo (2002b) point out. Some defining anthropological works in this area include Hannerz 1989; Appadurai 1990; Ong 1999; and Friedman 1994. See also Inda and Rosaldo 2002a.

5. Although all are contextualized (at least in part) by political-economic trends in world banana trade, this body of literature is diverse in geographical and substantive focus. For instance, Nurse and Sandiford (1995) offer an extensive analysis of the history and economic standing of Windward Islands banana production, leading up to a full discussion of the shifting trade arrangement that the region has with Europe. Sutton (1997) looks at the formal trade policies that Europe has held with regard to the Caribbean region, examines the policies' intersection with those of multilateral agencies, and explores possible outcomes of the shift away from preferential trade both for Latin America and the Caribbean. Lewis (2000) looks at the restructuring of Windward Islands' banana industries and farmers' responses to it while Clegg (2002) explores the Caribbean banana industry over a thirty year period, considering the shifts in the role of various interest groups attached to the industry. Grossman (1998) is concerned with the environmental issues surrounding contemporary banana policy in St. Vincent, while Moberg (1997) is interested in how ethnicity and class are shaped under contract farm arrangements in Belize. Raynolds's (1994a) work focuses on the Dominican Republic and concerns different forms of flexible labor arrangements in banana production there. Raynolds's (1994b) and

Raynolds and Murray's (1998) research examines banana trade regulation practices; commodity chains that differentiate bananas produced in Latin America ("dollar bananas") from those produced in Africa, the Caribbean, and the Pacific (ACP bananas); and possibilities for an alternative "fair trade" system of producing bananas.

6. For a discussion of media analysts' perspectives, see Slocum 2003.

7. In this initial work, I was interested in literature by anthropologists, sociologists, and feminist economists concerning class and gender in the formulation of household relations. Such research includes Carmen Diana Deere's (1990) *Household and Class Relations*, where she argues that households are made up of multiple class relations based on the different occupational statuses of household residents. It also includes Daisy Dwyer and Judith Bruce's (1988) edited volume, *A Home Divided*, and Lourdes Beneria and Martha Roldán's (1987) *The Crossroads of Class and Gender*, which consider the various ways in which women's work in the household is reconfigured and utilized through work arrangements. Finally, the rich literature on Caribbean women's roles, responsibilities, and networks in the household also influenced my project's early development. This literature includes especially Joycelin Massiah's (1983) *Women as Heads of Households in the Caribbean*, Christine Barrow's (1986) "Finding the Support: A Study of Strategies for Survival," and Lynn Bolles's (1983) work on households in Jamaica, especially.

8. The 1970s and 1980s work on women, work, and households addressed questions of household rights, roles, and responsibilities and the way that these varied or were negotiated according to gender. It was often an extension of a larger body of work considering women and industrialization as well as the intersection of women's dual work in domestic and extra-domestic spheres. Key sources for this discussion include Leacock and Safa (1986); Beneria and Roldán (1987); and Dwyer and Bruce (1988).

9. Early literature on the Caribbean considered "the street" and the public sphere in general as domains for understanding social organization and culture among rural West Indians. For example, the long-standing, influential work of Peter Wilson (1973) held that it was here that we can find cultural values of "reputation" marked by strategies of resistance played out especially by men and members of the middle class. This work has been critiqued due to its assumptions about culturally driven gender distinctions and reassessed concerning its emphasis on cultural duality and opposition. See, for example, Besson (1993) for a critique of gender distinctions; and Munasinghe (2001) for a discussion of the possible place of Indo-Caribbeans with respect to cultural polarities.

10. In an orthodox sense, the notion of neoliberal states may seem contradictory since neoliberal agendas are usually defined by the absence of state input in economic organizing. However, with the role that states now play in bolstering the spread of private enterprise and market-oriented policies, some now consider states to be part of the neoliberal project. For cases in which neoliberal

states have been discussed, for example see Sawyer (2004) for Latin America; and Dupuy (2001) for the Caribbean.

11. Philip Kasinitz (1992) discusses three major streams of Caribbean migration to the United States. The first stream occurred especially between 1900–1930, and was characterized by middle and working class West Indians. The smallest stream, between 1930–65, was made up primarily of middle class professionals and those joining their families. The third and largest stream, made up of Caribbeans of diverse class backgrounds, took place after 1965 when U.S. immigration laws opened up the possibilities for increased migration from the region.

12. The work on Caribbean labor movements, trade unionism, and activism points to the ways in which movements were situated both nationally and regionally. For instance Reddock (2004) and Sutton (2004) discuss the organization of women's labor struggles in particular colonies (Trinidad, St. Vincent, Jamaica, Barbados) during the 1930s and 1950s. Sutton's discussion concerns a case of women agitators in a wild cat strike on Barbados, protesting the specific conditions of plantation work on that island. Reddock (2004: 22) makes clear that the 1930s movements in Trinidad, Jamaica, and St. Vincent were "part of a wider [early twentieth century] ferment taking place in the Caribbean region," but she also provides the specific issues on particular islands that gave rise to these movements and the ways the women organized themselves locally. Nigel Bolland (2001) also demonstrates that there were trends among labor movements throughout the British West Indies but he provides case examples of the dynamics, in various individual places, that gave rise to and sustained (or did not sustain) movements in different parts of the region.

13. Bill Maurer (2004) cites heavy tourism, offshore finance in St. Lucia, and the creation of a Goods Distribution Free Zone coordinated by the St. Lucian state and the Chinese as the very reasons why it is challenging to categorize St. Lucia strictly as a Caribbean locale. For him, St. Lucia's boundaries extend to China and Hong Kong due to the island's centering within these differing frameworks of global capital.

14. Here I am using the racial/ethnic classifications as denoted in the census, according to de Albuquerque and McElroy (1999). It is important to note that the authors use the term "East Indian" to refer to those St. Lucian residents who have ancestry through India. East Indian has been a term commonly used as an identifier of people of this ancestry who reside in the Caribbean, and it has its origins in the distinction drawn between India and the Caribbean. Columbus believed he had arrived in India during his first voyage to the Americas in 1492 and, once it was realized that he had not, the Caribbean thereafter became popularly referred to as the "West" Indies (with India considered to be in the East, the East Indies). However, recently, academics have replaced their usage of "East Indian" with the terms "Indian" or "Indo-Caribbean," in recognition of the problematic origins of the term East Indian. Throughout this book I use the

more recent terminology adopted by Caribbean academics and thank Terenecia Kyneata Joseph for pointing out to me the development in thinking on this issue.

15. It is important to note that, in the community where I conducted my research, Indians' farms were among the largest. Thus, while they were represented in agricultural fields within the census, it is likely that they are classified as large-scale farmers. This likely dates to the history of Indian indentured servants being granted large tracts in lieu of their return passage to India following the end of their indenture. Many Indians, especially in Guyana and Trinidad, opted to stay in the West Indies and became more of a Caribbean class than did Afro-West Indians.

16. In St. Lucia, banana farming was an occupation that crossed class boundaries to some extent. The bulk of producers were indeed the smallest farmers on the island and banana production was, I would argue, by and large an occupation associated with rurality and lower class status. Still, some large scale growers who might have had other primary and higher-paying occupations also farmed bananas. This included, for example, the country's prime minister whose identity as a banana grower was often profiled publicly in an attempt to situate him among the non-elite St. Lucian citizenry. Some of the SLBGA administrators also held this dual and seemingly contradictory identity of banana grower and middle level professional.

17. Mabouya Valley is an actual location. It is not a pseudonym.

CHAPTER 2

1. Since the 1990s especially, a vast literature on globalization (specifically, the global economy) and neoliberal policies has emerged that cites these features in its analyses. Hirst and Thompson (1996), Brecher and Costello (1994), and Harvey (1989) are important sources here. For work on this topic within the Caribbean more specifically, see especially Klak (1998) and Watson (1993). In addition, some key sources discuss and analyze whether globalization as a new phenomenon of worldwide connections and new proportions actually exists (Robertson 1992; Hirst and Thompson 1996); whether the nation-state has lost its footing in the contemporary world economy (Hirst and Thompson 1996); and the extent, history, dimensions, and implications of various neoliberal policies and global connections (Harvey 1989; Featherstone 1990; King 1991; Hannerz 1992; Hirst and Thompson 1996; Appadurai 1996).

2. Alan Scott (1997) discusses the preponderance of the idea of globalization in current times (and its connection to long-standing models of neoliberalism), as do Hirst and Thompson (1996) and Lazarus (1998). Critical work on development (such as Escobar 1995; Crush 1995; and Arce and Long 2000) also addresses development discourses and the neoliberal model of development. The discourse approach has not been applied to studies of the banana industry although Bourgois (1989), Moberg (1997), Raynolds and Murray (1998), and Striffler (2002) consider constructions of race, ethnicity, class, and gender within the context of the organization and resistance to banana production.

3. Striffler's (2002) work on Ecuador, Euraque's (1996) work on Honduras, Purcell's (1993) study of Costa Rica, and Forster's (2003) study of Guatemala provide accounts of the historical development of specific banana industries in a national context. Together, these reveal the far-reaching and diverse developments of various Latin American banana industries under United Fruit from the late nineteenth to the mid-twentieth century.

4. At least in the St. Lucian and Dominican cases, peasant production of bananas for export included shipments to North America through Canadian and U.S. distributors during the early part of the twentieth century. Banana shipments to Europe began in the middle of the century. Thus, the "Caribbean/European system" of which Raynolds (2003) writes did not develop in St. Lucia and Dominica until around the 1950s, when a British shipping company, Geest Industries, inserted itself as both plantation owner and distributor in the islands and began exporting Windward Islands bananas to the United Kingdom. For detailed discussions of early exporting arrangements in these cases, see Trouillot (1988); Biggs, Bennett, and Leach (1963); and Slocum (1996).

5. For work that discusses the contexts in which these companies have operated, see especially Bourgois (1989); Purcell (1993); Striffler (2002); and Striffler and Moberg (2003).

6. Bananas traded from other parts of the Caribbean have operated under arrangements that differ from those of the Windward Islands, which all are former British colonies. For example, while Jamaica was covered by the Lomé accord it worked with a different transnational shipping company than the one shipping Windward Islands' bananas. Bananas produced and exported from Martinique and Guadeloupe have been shipped to France, since these two countries are external "departments" of France. The Dominican Republic, which was not a part of Lomé, has sold bananas to Germany and Italy.

7. In addition to allowing for a preferential trade arrangement between ACP and EU nations, Lomé also included the provision of development aid and a price-stabilizing mechanism for agricultural products traded to the EEC.

8. Although the United States had obvious interests in the Latin American case, U.S. representatives formally stayed out of the GATT negotiations and the largest dispute at this point. Instead, the United States participated as an "interested observer" by staying on the sidelines and following Latin Americans' preference that the issue not become a fight between the EU and the United States (Stovall and Hathaway 2003: 152).

9. The European Economic Community or EEC is the term used for the EU in the panel transcripts. I employ them interchangeably.

10. Government of St. Lucia (GOSL). 1991. *Annual Agricultural Statistical Digest*. A publication of the statistical Unit of the Ministry of Agriculture, Lands, Fisheries, and Forestry.

11. All-inclusive resorts were on the rise in St. Lucia by the early 1990s. This included the controversial building of the high-end Jalousie Plantation, which opened in 1992 (Pattullo 1996). In addition to critiques of the exclusive

and exclusionary practices around such resorts, some St. Lucians argued that the Jalousie Plantation also compromised St. Lucia's environment since it was constructed within the island's Piton Mountains. Around the same time that Jalousie was built, St. Lucia also acquired a foreign-owned Sandals Resort in the northern part of the island, where other major hotels and resorts already existed. See Pattullo (1996) for a discussion of the controversies and implications of this branch of tourism on St. Lucia.

12. While "the British housewife" was referenced in correspondence from the Banana Growers' Association to banana producers, she also was called up in discussions among producers I encountered. To explain how they needed to make sure that their bananas were not bruised or why sales might have dropped, banana growers appealed to the British housewife as someone whose tastes dictated the possibilities for the sale of their bananas in Europe. With obvious constructions and pairings of gender and domesticity, it was as if she was *the* consumer purchasing household foods and thus the person who made the most important decisions impacting the possibilities for St. Lucian banana sales in overseas markets.

13. Based on the setup of the industry after 1977, Geest provided the Windward Islands, including St. Lucia, with information (directly inaccessible to the average grower) on the quality demands of the UK market. Decisions regarding production practices were built out of this market information, and, Michel-Rolph Trouillot (1988) has argued, the company was therefore able to set the quality standards in the Windward Islands, and also to change those standards on a continual basis, without being questioned. For further discussion of this arrangement, especially the implications of relying on market information from one source, the buyer of a product, see Trouillot (1988).

14. A British commission of inquiry (United Kingdom 1897: 116), for instance, noted that more than thirty St. Lucian estates were abandoned between the years 1887 and 1897. This was the mark of the first exit from sugar production, particularly by the smaller estates.

15. The involvement of colonial administrators in peasant production during this period reflected a developing role of the state in organizing and overseeing peasant production, an interest that appears not to have been as much a focus of the colonial before. For a longer discussion of administrators' 1950s report on peasant production, see Slocum (2003). Barrow (1992: 6) also relates this report to the perspectives of other researchers and development specialists claiming to observe and consider correcting risk aversion and low productivity among peasants and peasant uses of land in particular. For a general discussion of the late-nineteenth- and early-twentieth-century St. Lucian peasantry, see Marshall (1968); Acosta and Casimir (1985); and Adrien (1996).

16. During the early 1950s, the plantations had also moved toward a new form of privatization. Three of the four shifted from being operated through family-run enterprises to being held by Sugar Manufacturers Limited. Thus, the shift toward privatization of the SLBA mirrored a shift occurring on the large estates that also were slowly beginning to transition out of sugar. For a slightly

longer discussion of this period and the shift in the plantations, see Slocum (forthcoming).

17. Before acquiring estates in St. Lucia, Geest had already owned plantations in nearby Dominica, and it also had an agreement with the Dominican Banana Association to purchase and distribute Dominican bananas. Thus, by the time the company arrived in St. Lucia it was already playing a role elsewhere in the region, much like it would play in St. Lucia. Trouillot (1988: 128) argues that Geest was successful in its estate production and banana distribution, partially due to support for its activities from the Colonial Office. That success and experience in Caribbean banana production and distribution likely shaped the path the company pursued in other Windward Islands, including St. Lucia.

18. For a history of Geest Industries, see Trouillot (1988).

19. Evidence of smallholders' rapid climb to the forefront of banana production, and their quick abandonment of cane cultivation, was provided in the testimony of Jan van Geest, owner of the Roseau and Cul-de-Sac Estates and proprietor of the Geest Industries shipping company. In the 1960s, during his discussions with government officials, he addressed the status of sugar estates and the possibilities for maintaining sugar production on them amid government concern that sugar not be abandoned entirely (GOSL 1960). Yet, to the dissatisfaction of government representatives, Geest underscored the factors that rendered the regression of cane cultivation beyond the power of the estate owner, specifically, the work of independent cane growers, known as *contributors*, who cultivated and supplied large estates with sugarcane. According to Geest, bananas had enticed cane growers out of sugar, beyond the control of estate owners to reverse the trend. In Geest's opinion, expressed at a meeting with St. Lucia's then chief minister: "I do not know whether it will be possible to get the cane farmers to grow more canes because the banana industry is very attractive and I think that already some of them are growing more bananas than cane" (GOSL 1960: 2).

20. *Métayage* was common and an important social and economic feature of St. Lucia's agricultural landscape. Beginning in the mid-nineteenth century, it lasted almost one hundred years and involved a farmer-tenant bearing responsibility to grow export crops (primarily sugarcane, coffee, or cocoa) and then sell them to the planter-landlord, who kept a portion of the returns (Louis 1981). *Métayers* also could use the land to plant other crops for their own use or sale, without any further obligation to the owner. According to Louis (1981), ex-slaves preferred this arrangement because other means of holding land were not available to them. Adrien (1996) notes that *métayage* helped stratify the poor, nonplanter classes that existed in plantation regions. Laborers worked fully on plantations while small *métayers* did so partially (working part time as *métayer* tenants), while large *métayers* worked fully as tenants. Thus, *métayage* became a means by which *métayer*-tenants could begin to move out of a sole dependence on waged employment on plantations.

21. By the 1960s, independence and postcolonial possibilities were on the minds of many West Indians in British colonies. St. Lucia had achieved univer-

sal suffrage in 1951, which opened up the development of local political parties led by a local black elite. Like elsewhere in the region, local formal politics became deeply connected to trade unionism built around lobbying on behalf of plantation workers in the sugarcane and banana industries. Thus, the transition to the SLBGA from the SLBA was steeped in these dynamics as they unfolded in St. Lucia, responding to a growing divide around politics, the plantation economy, class, and race. For a discussion of these dynamics in the 1950s period in St. Lucia, see Slocum (forthcoming).

22. Trouillot (1988) has also made this point, arguing that banana growers actually function like wage laborers rather than independent producers given the terms of the contract with Geest, which does not allow them bargaining power.

23. Trouillot (1988) has argued that various contract clauses were unclear, leaving room for interpretation, to Geest's benefit. For example, a clause claimed that Geest would purchase only bananas of "exportable quality" but left undefined how that quality was to be measured or determined, allowing the company, Trouillot argues, to reject bananas at its own discrimination.

24. Since 1967, the act has undergone several amendments, which include changes in the board's composition. In 1979, the board was made up of thirteen persons of which seven were appointed by the minister of agriculture, giving government a majority representation. This distribution was undone in 1983, and growers held a majority at six elected members compared to three appointees. However, by 1990, the tide appeared to shift back. Representation of government appointees on the board rose to 46% (up from the 33% set in 1983), when an eleven-member board was reconstituted to include five government appointees and six elected members. Thus, growers maintained a majority but to a lesser extent.

25. The Banana Act was developed in the 1960s but, according to some sources, lay dormant for several decades. It was resurrected in 1986.

26. To my knowledge, there are no instances of WINBAN officials or the police actually coming onto farmers' fields to direct their activities. The point is, however, that the law was established in 1986, allowing for this to be a possibility. Other laws regarding the banana industry that *seemingly* lie dormant on the books have been used unexpectedly, as when the government dissolved the SLBGA board of directors in 1988 and again in 1993. This is a point made by the leaders of the BSC.

27. Looking at these and other later reports on the status and future of the Windward Islands' banana industries, Patsy Lewis (2000: 55) notes that, despite the projections of poverty for the future of the industries given market changes, the reports contended that no "'viable' alternative to bananas existed" and that "therefore banana production should continue." The solution proposed here was to reduce the size of the farming population to include those whose income from banana sales was higher and better able to withstand the costs of production and service overhead.

CHAPTER 3

1. Here, I borrow from Ferguson and Gupta's (2002) discussion of the ways in which the state transgresses spatiality. The authors argue that state representatives' prerogative to transgress space in order to carry out its goals of disciplining state subjects is a feature of "spatializing states."

2. The work here draws heavily on the ideas of Michel Foucault (1977), who explored the assertion of power through surveillance and knowledge systems. Cooper and Packard (2005) point out that this set of scholars offered a counterposition to the work of "ultramodernists," who are against policy interventions in development so that economic laws can and will successfully guide development.

3. Trouillot (1988) has argued that banana producers in neighboring Dominica served as wage laborers rather than independent producers because the contract with the Banana Growers' Association set many of the terms of production. Trouillot highlights especially the fact that the contract denied growers the ability to bargain for the worth of their product.

4. Elsewhere (Slocum 2001) I have discussed how the intersection of my nationality, class, and gender identities shaped my experiences doing fieldwork among rural women traders in neighboring St. Vincent, in ways that differed from my own expectations around a politicized race and gender identity that I might have shared with the women participating in my study. This is a theme that has been well explored in anthropological literature considering insider-outsider dimensions of ethnographic research. For literature on insider-outsider negotiations in the Caribbean context see Bolles (1985); Harrison (1991); McClaurin (1996).

5. Breen's book, *St. Lucia: Historical, Statistical, Descriptive,* is one of the most referenced and consulted sources for historical information on St. Lucia. Covering the early seventeenth to mid-nineteenth century, it provides a fairly detailed—and skewed—description of life on the island in the areas of history, climate and geology, population, religion, morality, agriculture, legal institutions, and administration. Throughout his discussion, Breen's perspective as someone affiliated with the dominant European colonial administration stands out particularly when he describes the practices of Afro-St. Lucians by using terms such as "the lower orders." He also describes St. Lucia as a landscape of beauty (in contrast to the descriptors of the Afro-Caribbean population), akin to the ways that Sheller (2003) argues early European writing characterized the region as a type of tropic playground and paradise.

6. In his memoir, Charles (1994) provides a useful discussion of the development of political parties in St. Lucia, as does DaBreo (1981) for the 1970s period of political activity. A description of the developing political scene on the island, specifically in the 1950s, is also provided partially by Jackson, Pounder, and Leacock (1957) and Malone, Hagley, and Pearson (1952).

7. Names of St. Lucian estates, such as the Dennery Estate, are actual names.

8. Denis Barnard was the actual owner of the Dennery Estate. His name used here is not a pseudonym.

9. This model of development, coordinating state resources and private capital in the coordination of production, existed elsewhere in the Caribbean during the mid- to late 1970s (Crichlow 1997).

10. Trouillot (1988) points out that WINBAN's research efforts were guided by market information supplied by Geest Industries, again reflecting the strong role of the transnational, not merely in the legal setup of production on St. Lucia but also in the company's less visible but important insertion in the weekly arrangement of production activities within individual farming communities and for individual producers.

11. When harvested bananas were processed at SLBGA centers before the early 1970s, they were washed in large fungicidal baths. However, once postharvest processing shifted to individual producers' fields, the baths were replaced with the use of a fungicidal pad applied to the crown of banana clusters. This was known as the crown pad.

12. The shift to the Mini Wet Pack system also led to a higher degree of labor segmentation since the various tasks falling under Mini Wet Pack were considered the domain of specific individuals marked by gender and class (e.g., packers and washers, carriers, and cutters), unlike the systems that preceded it. For a discussion of the gendering of postharvest processing tasks, see Slocum 1996.

13. No date exists for this interview, which was obtained from the SLBGA files.

14. In particular, Garrett (forthcoming) calls attention to the insertion of programming in Kwéyòl after independence.

15. An example of the intersection of radio as a medium for airing discussions about the industry and the wider consumption of radio programming was the period of the October 1993 banana producers' strike. During this event, radio became an important and active medium for listeners—growers and non-growers alike—to call in and discuss their thoughts on the strike developments. It also was how images of the strike activities were displayed, as callers from various farming communities called in to describe what was occurring in their areas. Television also covered the strike, but radio appeared to be a more constant medium for airing strike developments, sometimes brought out by non-banana-grower observers residing in banana-farming communities. Interestingly, the state's role in mass media also was made clear during this event when the radio station aired callers' critical views of how government representatives handled the strikes. In response, the government shut down the radio station for several weeks for allowing such views to be heard.

16. While the Banana Act, as a St. Lucian law, may appear to be the work of the independent state, I would argue that it is actually the work of Geest Industries and the St. Lucian government together. As Trouillot (1988) has argued, Geest worked through local institutions (such as the SLBGA) and exerted a disguised means of control over internal aspects of the national banana industry. I am amending Trouillot's point by suggesting that the company worked through

and *with* local institutions *and* the state. Indeed, the Banana Act is an excellent example of Geest's power, *hidden* behind the state.

17. During the 1990s in St. Lucia, the Ministry of Agriculture, Lands and Fisheries employed extension agents, who, much like SLBGA field officers, were charged with visiting farmers' fields to advise them on *non-banana* crop production. However, very few growers in Morne Verte stated that they received visits from the Ministry's agents, while more said they were apt to have visits from SLBGA field officers. Further, the regularity of SLBGA officer visits (whether announced or not) was something that the Ministry could not apply to agents' work. That is, they did not make unannounced visits or work with farmers on a regular basis. I heard more farmers express to me that they made appointments with Ministry agents. For information on the differential structural support available to Caribbean producers of banana and non-banana crops, see Andreatta 1997.

18. Some growers in Morne Verte had this formal training. At least two persons from my sample of interviews identified themselves as banana growers and also as employees of the SLBGA with training in agriculture. The bulk of interviewees, however, did not fit this category.

19. Because, according to the SLBGA Act, all bananas of particular varieties were required to be sold to the SLBGA, only bananas rejected by the association could be sold in domestic or regional markets.

20. The price was set each week through a complex formula based on the wholesale market price for the week (a value communicated by Geest Industries), the price that Geest then offered to the SLBGA after extracting deductions for its own expenses, and the amount that the SLBGA then offered to farmers after accounting for member service and association costs. In the 1990s, Geest calculated the price it would offer to the Windward Islands banana growers' associations according to a value known as the Green Wholesale Price. This was calculated based on the price Geest received in Europe for its sale of bananas and the Green Market Price—the price the company paid to importers of the unripened, "green" fruit. Before 1983, only the Green Market Price was calculated to determine the price offered to island BGAs (Grossman 1998). For a more detailed discussion, see Grossman (1998) and Trouillot (1988).

21. There were rumors in St. Lucia that inspectors illegally helped growers to get higher fruit quality scores by fixing their papers.

22. In his analysis of Caribbean banana industries, Trouillot (1988) assigns weight to the role of Geest Industries over the state, and provides a useful analysis of transnational corporate power.

23. This would not be true for all farming regions of St. Lucia since producers in other areas worked on lands leased by Geest Industries and thus dealt more directly and visibly with the company (see Crichlow 1997).

CHAPTER 4

1. These questions were posed to me by audience members after I had given lectures on my research at Duke University and the University of North Carolina-Chapel Hill.

2. All names are pseudonyms. I have altered some details about specific people in this chapter to protect their identities.

3. *Share* practiced in Morne Verte resembled the métayage system that has been noted by Adrien (1996), Acosta and Casimir (1985), and Marshall (1965) from the postemancipation period (1838) to the late 1950s in St. Lucia. *Métayage* was more commonly applied to the cultivation and sale of sugarcane. I am unaware of what might account for the change in nomenclature for this arrangement.

4. See Dujon (2002) for a discussion of the Land Registration and Titling Project, funded by the U.S. Agency for International Development (USAID), whose goal was to "correct" peasant communal land-tenuring systems that were deemed counterproductive.

5. One U.S. dollar is equivalent to 2.7 Eastern Caribbean (E.C.) dollars, making the average labor cost in Morne Verte $15 U.S./day. One day was meant to be eight hours long, but based on my research a day's work could be as little as five hours and as much as ten. The wage (not contingent on hourly input) was agreed upon before the work was performed and thus the rate one was paid did not vary with the length of time a person worked. The farmer-employer provided lunch. Further, an average production level in Morne Verte brought in an approximate gross figure of $500 E.C. ($185 U.S.) per harvest. Three laborers (the average) at $40 E.C. each, would mean that close to 25% of growers' *gross* income went to labor costs. This, however, does not account for the SLBGA deduction of fees and taxes, as well as growers' other production costs, nor does it take into account the sharp differences in income and labor uses by classes of growers and by gender. See Slocum 1996 for a detailed discussion of growers' expenses and incomes in 1993–95.

6. Debates on the origins of family land have been taken up between Besson (1987b) and Carnegie (1987a). Besson argues for family land as a peasant adaptive creation within the plantation context, while Carnegie argues for the possibility of an African heritage to family land. By attempting to trace facets of family land practices to land tenure arrangements among the Ashanti, Clarke (1966) argued most strongly for viewing family land as an example of the survival of African cultural traits.

7. Crichlow (1994) questions the use of the "plantation economy framework" to explain the persistence of family land, arguing that it narrowly views people's actions and social practices as merely resistance to the plantation and thereby does not permit us to account for change. For a debate on this topic, see Crichlow (1994) and Besson (1995).

8. Charles Carnegie's (1983) notion of "strategic flexibility" contrasts with others' notions of Caribbean flexibility. Smith (1956), Clarke (1966), and Gonzalez (1969) argued that flexibility emerged in the region due to economic stress or the impact of historically contextualized social marginalization experienced by Afro-West Indians. They examine changing residential and romantic partner relationships as well as patterns of migration that illustrate a degree of flexibility among and between Afro-Caribbean men and women. The notion of mar-

ginalization has been applied especially to Afro-West Indian males deemed to be distant from domestic life, whereas women are considered culturally more significant and powerful. In this case, flexible family and household trends result from a cultural pattern contextualized by both history and economy. This idea, as well as more recent iterations of the marginalization thesis, has been critiqued (see Barriteau 2003).

9. The literature on higglering and its related fields of "huckstering," "trafficking," and "speculating" has been vastly extended over the past fifty years. For discussions of higglering during slavery, see especially Olwig (1981); and Mintz (1957). For discussions of the ways in which higglers link producers to consumers through informal relations, see Mintz (1957). For more recent studies addressing intersections of beauty, fashion, femininity, and entrepreneurship among higglers, see Freeman (1997, 2002); and Ulyssee (1999).

10. My delineations of small, medium, and large growers do not correspond to the SLBGA's categories. Mine are drawn from my own division of growers within Morne Verte, according to production level and land size.

11. Among the growers I interviewed there were only two single older men, above the age of seventy who lived neither with a common law or legal spouse nor with his adult children. Only John, as a single younger male in his twenties, also fit this description, although John was a de facto household head given his godmother's absence due to migration. The older men (and John) thus headed the farm and their households but did not have a female domestic partner with whom they shared farm duties. This was in contrast to the bulk of men who I interviewed yet much like the ten women who I describe as having a double responsibility to farm and household. Thus, age (especially older age) and life-cycle might have shaped the likelihood that a male bore this dual role, especially since the number of men fitting this description was restricted to a few who were at a certain age level.

12. *Koudeman,* as a cooperative laboring arrangement (not restricted to agriculture), was quite rare in Morne Verte. Betty's comment about giving up the practice after banana production was introduced suggests that this form of cooperative work may have eroded with the transition into smallholder banana production.

13. Most residents of Morne Verte are African descendants. Of the fifty-four farmers I interviewed, only three were Indo-St. Lucian like Lynette.

14. During the nineteenth century, Indians who had contracts for indentured servitude were, in some cases, given the option of taking plots of land in the places of their servitude rather than returning to India (Richardson 1992). Such an option for access to land was not provided to African descendants who labored on sugar plantations during the same time. However, while land distribution to Indian contract workers existed in Trinidad and Guyana, it appears that it did not occur in St. Lucia, where financial and land resources did not exist for such distribution (Joseph 2004). However, Joseph notes that Indians in the late nineteenth century were active in purchasing lands escheated by small-scale planters who abandoned their estates when the sugar industry went into decline.

15. According to Trouillot (1988: 4), the peasant labor process is "an institutionalized process through which a household performs agricultural labor on a unit over which it exerts a form of control . . . with instruments of work which it also controls and which generally represent less of an input than the labor itself." Similar work on Caribbean peasant forms of production, their intersection with the organization of labor on plantations, and the origins of peasant production within the plantation context can be found in Mintz (1989) and Tomich (1990).

16. In this argument, Rodney (1981) takes on other scholars who have argued that Afro-West Indians developed themselves as a peasantry immediately following emancipation. For him, freed slaves became proletarians who worked part and full time on the plantations, yet Rodney also claims that they were proletarians asserting and making use of their newfound bargaining power through their labor.

17. See Mindie Lazarus-Black's (1994) book for a discussion of the ways in which family formations and male-female relationships deemed illegal by colonial law were nonetheless part of everyday practice in Antigua and Barbuda. She argues (1994: 3) that the "interplay of legalities and illegalities challenged each other."

18. The work on the Indo-St. Lucian population is very scant, and comments here are as yet inconclusive. However, Joseph's (2004) research is useful in beginning to orient us toward an understanding of the historical establishment of Indians on the island during and following the indentureship period. Her research suggests that, unlike in other Caribbean territories, where Indo-West Indians settled separately from the Afro-West Indians, this was not necessarily the case in St. Lucia, where both groups appear to have settled as peasants around the periphery of the island's major plantations. When Joseph's work is considered with Meliczek's (1975) and Acosta and Casimir's (1985), the one distinction that appears between the two ethnic groups, however, may be with respect to the acquisition of Crown Lands as a vehicle for community establishment. Indians appear to have purchased relatively large Crown Land plots and used these to form settlements (Joseph 2004). By contrast, former African slaves appear to have acquired land most often by squatting (Acosta and Casimir 1985).

19. During my initial research in 1993–94, U.S. media that was popular and widely watched in Morne Verte included talk shows (e.g., the *Ricky Lake Show*, the *Jenny Jones Show*, *Oprah*) as well as soap operas. As in the other parts of the Caribbean (see for example, Miller 1992), the *Young and the Restless* was the most popular soap opera that Morne Vertians watched. During my research, it came on at 8 PM every weeknight and adult males, adult females, and children gathered around to watch the show. On a given day, it was common to hear people referencing and analyzing the last night's episode. Similarly, because daytime and evening programming was piped in from the United States, when special reports aired in the United States they did so simultaneously in Morne

Verte. Thus, the arrest and subsequent trial of O. J. Simpson was breaking television news in Morne Verte in 1994 and also the subject of much public discussion. Upon my return to St. Lucia in 1998, I was also asked about the events of the Columbine school shootings in Colorado that Morne Vertians had watched unfold live in their living rooms.

CHAPTER 5

1. The movement for federation, which grew out of the collective work of trade unions and political activists across the British West Indies, resulted in the formation of the West Indies Federation in 1958. This body represented the political integration of the British West Indian colonies and was led by Afro-West Indian political figures, many of whom had been politically active in their individual colonies. Due to internal power struggles, the federation was short-lived and ended in 1962. For work on the activist precedent for the formation of the Federation, see Bolland (2001). For work on the formation and disintegration of the Federation, see Proctor (1962); Wallace (1977); and Braithwaite (1957).

2. In the 1952 and 1957 commissioned inquiries, as well as through the newspapers in the 1950s, it was cited that tension between estate owners and trade union leaders centered on whether the trade unionists actually represented and had the support of the laborers on whose behalf they claimed to lobby. Estate owners often claimed that many of their workers did not belong to the unions and that the leaders therefore misrepresented themselves as the voice of workers in labor negotiations (see Malone, Hagley, and Pearson 1952; and Jackson, Pounder, and Leacock 1957).

3. The 1960s and 1970s marked a period of major transformation in the British Caribbean. Independence first occurred in Jamaica and Trinidad in 1962 but continued in other places through the early 1980s, ending in 1983 with St. Kitts. During this period, there was also heightened political activism around racial, economic, and political issues in the region. For accounts of specific political movements in the region during this time, see especially Bennett (1989) for Trinidad's February Revolution, Palmer (1989) for a discussion of race and black power in Jamaica; Westmaas (2004) for an analysis of Guyana's Working People's Alliance; and Bishop (1984) and Payne, Sutton, and Thorndike (1984) on the socialist revolution in Grenada.

4. Josie's and Odlum's critiques of the Compton administration reflect a long history of discord between the two "sides." By the 1970s, Compton's administration was considered to be more conservative compared to the anti-colonial labor organizing and socialist perspective that formed part of the 1970s' trade union activism that Josie and Odlum helped spawn. The 1950s trade union activity did not try to undo the plantation structure, but only attempted to garner better conditions for workers. By contrast, the 1970s' activity was focused on chipping away at plantations as an example of colonialism's continuation.

5. Although the SLP should have been in power for five years, exposed

corruption within the party led to its overthrow after only two years. This led to Comptons party, the UWP, regaining power. See Wayne (1986) and DaBreo (1981) for accounts of this event.

6. A reason why the BSC might not have connected with trade unions was that the group represented independent producers, solely, compared to the workers *and* producers around which the SLP and the St. Lucian Workers and Cooperative Union had rallied. However, active and former trade unionists in the country during the 1990s told me they had approached the BSC to assist them in their struggle but had not met with reception to the idea. There was a sentiment that the group was interested in working on its own for its own political gain rather than joining forces with existing unions or even those that had experience organizing during earlier decades.

7. It was rumored that the BSC's activities were financed by Chiquita. While I have no conclusive information to support this, the group suggested on occasion that the offer from Chiquita should be considered as a compliment to working with Geest rather than relying on the sole-buyer arrangement with Geest. They justified this position with the claim that all possibilities should be considered and that the best option should be taken. At the same time, I would argue that the issue of Chiquita's offer was not a primary component of the BSC's rally discourse.

8. Unless otherwise noted, quotations from the farmers' group leadership were recorded or noted at public rallies or during interviews with the author.

CHAPTER 6

1. The debate was between proponents of resource mobilization theory and proponents of new social movement theory. The former theory especially considered the pre-civil-rights period (see Morris 1984) of mobilization during which material resource disparity was a motivator for social movements. By contrast, "new" social movements were seen to be a late-twentieth-century phenomenon in which identity and culture were at the basis of collective action (see Laclau and Mouffe 1985; Touraine 1988; and Melucci 1989, 1996). Thus, there was often a periodization to the different positions, even if culture and class were conceptualized as opposing or "either-or" dynamics, giving rise to protests. Although the arguments regarding new social movements typically were applied to the North American and European context (Edelman 2001), some scholars refuted this narrow application by examining cultural identity and representation within social movements especially in Latin America but also in other areas (Escobar 1992a; Escobar and Alvarez 1992; Alvarez, Dagnino, and Escobar 1998; Fox and Starn 1997).

2. During the labor strikes of the 1950s, managers and investors in the sugar industry's corporations made critical reference to trade union activists' organizing on the Castries' market steps. In one 1957 instance, a shareholder in Sugar Manufacturers' Ltd. insinuated that it was from the market steps that trade unionists could launch their politically and socially controversial plat-

forms and positions. The comment implied that the market steps were considered an unofficial but politically charged space (see Slocum forthcoming).

3. Widespread burning of banana sheds was one of the activities associated with the October 1993 strike. It continued during subsequent strikes as well. There were often official allegations that the BSC was responsible for these events, but the group always denied the charge and claimed that these were government measures undertaken to discredit the BSC. It is interesting to note that burning structures was also associated with earlier strikes in the 1950s and 1970s (see, e.g., Jackson, Pounder, and Leacock 1957). In these cases, plantation fields and buildings on plantations were burned rather than structures belonging to individual small farmers, as was the case during the 1990s events.

4. In Slocum (2003), I point out that the BSC's strategic decision (what some call "strategic essentialism") to present farmers as an undifferentiated group resulted in the denial of important gender and race differences that mark banana growers' experiences.

5. Influenced by personal communication with Paul Garrett regarding the transition in uses of terminology for the language and common practice and preferences among activists in St. Lucia, I use the spelling Kwéyòl for the English word "Creole."

6. The expression of some of these newer ideas about creolization can be found in literature especially out of Martinique (see, e.g., Chamoiseau 1998) where Bernabé, Chamoiseau, and Confiant (1989) *creolité* movement emerged. Ethnomusicologists have also looked at the expression *creolité* in West Indian music (see Guilbault 1997). For critiques of the *creolité* movement see Price and Price (1997) and Taylor (1998).

7. As a colony that had a longstanding French presence before settling in the hands of the British, St. Lucia shows evidence of cultural, social, and political influence from the French as well as the British. The French influence appears in the realm of: religion with Catholicism being very strong on the island while most other British West Indian islands have a stronger Anglican (British) presence; the prevalence of the French-based Kwéyòl language while English is the national language; and certain popular (revitalized) dance forms such as the Quadrille dance, a dance with French roots that historically was adapted by African descendants in parts of the Caribbean.

8. In his work, Paul Garrett (2000) argues that a "High Kweyol" language has emerged in St. Lucia. Here, upper-class St. Lucians who have adopted the idea of Kwéyòl as a symbol of national and cultural pride, speak and use a type of Kwéyòl that differs from "Ordinary Kweyol." "High Kwéyòl" is more commonly used in public, particularly in the media and political speeches. The BSC's Kwéyòl, however, appears to fall under what Garrett would term "Ordinary Kwéyòl."

CHAPTER 7

1. For discussions of the area studies-global studies debate, Harootunian and Miyoshi's (2002) work has been influential. In anthropology, recent partic-

ipants in this discussion include Guyer (2004), Maurer (2004), and Slocum and Thomas (2003).

2. Maurer (2004) discusses the presence of the Chinese mission that has been situated in St. Lucia's economy through its role in the country's Goods Distribution Free Zone conceived as a plan to bring Chinese goods into the Caribbean. The work of the Chinese has replaced the previous Taiwanese mission to the island.

References

ARCHIVES

Office of Mortgages and Deeds, St. Lucia

Office of the United States Trade Representative, Washington, DC

St. Lucia Banana Growers' Association, St. Lucia

St. Lucia National Archives, St. Lucia

Sugar Manufacturers Ltd. Draft Minutes of an Extraordinary Meeting of the Shareholders of the Company. Wednesday, April 24, 1957.

Windward Island Banana Growers Association, St. Lucia

PERIODICALS

The Crusader, St. Lucia

The Vanguard, St. Lucia

The Voice, St. Lucia

The Weekend Voice, St. Lucia

SPEECHES

Address to the Nation, the Prime Minister, the Rt. Hon. John Compton, October 4, 1993.

Address to the Nation, the Prime Minister, the Rt. Hon. John Compton, October 7, 1993.

Address to the Nation, the Prime Minister, the Rt. Hon. John Compton, October 11, 1993.

Speech, Banana Salvation Committee, February 1994.

Speech, Banana Salvation Committee, March 1994.

Speech, Banana Salvation Committee, April 1994.

Speech, Banana Salvation Committee, October 1994.

Speech, Banana Salvation Committee, November 1994.

Statement by the Prime Minister, the Rt. Hon. John Compton, on the Reorganisation of the Banana Industry 1994 and Beyond, January 1994.

Statement by the Honourable Ira d'Auvergne, Minister of Agriculture, Lands, Fisheries and Forestry, on the Banana Situation, February 22, 1994.

Press Statement by Honourable Ira D'Auvergne, Minister of Agriculture, Lands, Fisheries and Forestry, on the Banana Industry, March 17, 1994.

BOOKS, ARTICLES, AND REPORTS

Acosta, Yvonne, and Jean Casimir. 1985. Social origins of the counter-plantation system in St. Lucia. In *Rural Development in the Caribbean*, ed. P. I. Gomes, 34–59. New York: St. Martin's; London: C. Hurst.

ACP-EEC Council of Ministers. 1979. Second ACP-EEC Convention of Lomé. Compilation of texts.

———. 1992. *Fourth ACP-EEC Convention Signed at Lomé on 15 December 1989*. Luxembourg: Office for Official Publications of the European Communities.

Adams, Paul C., Steven Hoelscher, and Karen E. Till. 2001. Place in context: Rethinking humanist geographies. In *Textures of Place: Exploring Humanist Geographies*, ed. P. C. Adams, S. Hoelscher, and K. E. Till, xii–xxxiii. Minneapolis: University of Minnesota Press.

Adrien, Peter. 1996. *Metayage, Capitalism, and Peasant Development in St Lucia, 1840–1957*. Mona, Jamaica: Consortium Graduate School of Social Sciences, University of the West Indies Press.

Advisory Committee for Dennery Basin Development. 1985. Report of Advisory Committee for Dennery Basin Development. Draft report.

Alvarez, Sonia E., Evelina Dagnino, and Arturo Escobar, eds. 1998. *Cultures of Politics, Politics of Culture: Re-visioning Latin American Social Movements*. Boulder: Westview Press.

Amit-Talai, Vered. 1997. In pursuit of authenticity: Globalization and nation building in the Cayman Islands. *Anthropologica* 39:53–63.

Anderson, Benedict. 1991. *Imagined Communities: Reflections on the Origin and Spread of Nationalism*. London: Verso.

Anderson, Rachel, Timothy Taylor, and Timothy Josling. 2003. The Caribbean and the banana trade. In *Banana Wars: The Anatomy of a Trade Dispute*, ed. T. Josling and T. Taylor, 123–50. Oxon, UK: CABI Publishing.

Andreatta, Susan L. 1997. Bananas: Are they the quintessential health food? A global and local perspective. *Human Organization* 56 (4): 437–49.

———. 1998. Transformation of the agro-food sector: Lessons from the Caribbean. *Human Organization* 57 (4): 414–29.

Appadurai, Arjun. 1988a. Introduction: Place and voice in anthropological theory. *Cultural Anthropology* 3:16–20.

———. 1988b. Putting hierarchy in its place. *Cultural Anthropology* 3:36–49.

———. 1990. Disjuncture and difference in the global cultural economy. *Public Culture* 2 (3): 1–24.

———. 1996. *Modernity at Large: Cultural Dimensions of Globalization*. Minneapolis: University of Minnesota Press.

Arce, Alberto, and Normal Long. 2000. Reconfiguring modernity and development from an anthropological perspective. In *Anthropology, Development, and Modernities: Exploring Discourses, Counter-tendencies, and Violence*, ed. A. Arce and N. Long, 1–31. London: Routledge.

Arias, Pedro, Cora Dankers, Pascal Liu, and Paul Pilkauskas. 2003. *The World Banana Economy, 1985–2002*. FAO Commodity Studies, no. 1. Food and

Agriculture Organization of the United Nations, Raw Material, Tropical and Horticultural Products Service Commodities and Trade Division. Rome: Food and Agriculture Organization of the United Nations.

Atkinson, Henry, George Devaux, Kerde Severin, and Christopher Cox. 1991. *Report of Review Committee, St. Lucia Model Farms.* Cited in Crichlow 1997.

Atkinson, H. V., Calixte George, David Demacque, Geoff Devaux, Richard Peterkin, Michael Joseph, Octave Fevriere, and Cyrus Reynolds. 1993. Report of the Banana Review Committee. Report commissioned by the St. Lucia Banana Growers' Association.

Barriteau, Eudine. 2003. Requiem for the male marginalization thesis: Death to a non-theory. In *Confronting Power, Theorizing Gender,* ed. E. Barntau, 324–53. Kingston, Jamaica: University of the West Indies Press.

Barrow, Christine. 1986. Finding the support: A study of strategies for survival. *Social and Economic Studies* 35 (2): 131–76.

———. 1992. *Family Land and Development in St. Lucia.* Cave Hill, Barbados: Institute of Social and Economic Research (Eastern Caribbean), University of the West Indies Press.

Basch, Linda, Nina Glick Schiller, and Christina Szanton Blanc. 1994. *Nations Unbound: Transnational Projects, Postcolonial Predicaments, and Deterritorialized Nation-States.* New York: Gordon and Breach.

Beckford, George L. 1972. *Persistent Poverty: Underdevelopment in Plantation Economies of the Third World.* London: Zed Books.

Beneria, Lourdes, and Martha Roldán. 1987. *The Crossroads of Class and Gender: Industrial Homework, Subcontracting, and Household Dynamics in Mexico City.* Chicago: University of Chicago Press.

Bennett, Herman L. 1989. The challenge to the post-colonial state: A case study of the February Revolution in Trinidad. In *The Modern Caribbean,* ed. F. W. Knight and C. A. Palmer, 129–46. Chapel Hill: University of North Carolina Press.

Bernabé, Jean, Patrick Chamoiseau, and Raphäel Confiant. 1989. *Éloge de la Creolité.* Paris: Gallimard.

Berry, Brian. 1989. Comparative geography of the global economy: Cultures, corporations, and the nation-state. *Economic Geography* 65 (1): 1–18.

Besson, Jean. 1979. Symbolic aspects of land in the Caribbean: The tenure and transmission of land rights among Caribbean peasantries. In *Peasants, Plantations, and Rural Communities in the Caribbean,* ed. M. Cross and A. Marks, 86–116. Guilford: University of Surrey; Leiden: Royal Institute of Linguistics and Anthropology.

———. 1984a. Land tenure in the free villages of Trelawny, Jamaica: A case study in Caribbean peasant response to emancipation. *Slavery and Abolition* 5:3–23.

———. 1984b. Family-land and Caribbean society: Toward an ethnography of Afro-Caribbean peasantries. In *Perspectives on Caribbean Regional Identity,* ed. E. M. Hope, 57–83. Liverpool: Center for Latin American Studies, University of Liverpool.

————. 1987a. A paradox in Caribbean attitudes to land. In *Land and Development in the Caribbean*, ed. J. Besson and J. Momsen, 13–45. London: Macmillan.

————. 1987b. Family land as a model for Martha Brae's new history: Culture building in an Afro-Caribbean village. In *Afro-Caribbean Villages in Historical Perspective*, ed. C. V. Carnegie, 100–132. Kingston: African-Caribbean Institute of Jamaica.

————. 1992. Freedom and community: The British West Indies. In *The Meaning of Freedom: Economics, Politics, and Culture after Slavery*, ed. F. McGlynn and S. Drescher, 183–219. Pittsburgh: University of Pittsburgh Press.

————. 1993. Reputation and respectability reconsidered: A new perspective on Afro-Caribbean peasant women. In *Women and Change in the Caribbean*, ed. Janet Momsen. Bloomington: Indiana University Press.

————. 1995. Land, kinship and community in the post-emancipation Caribbean: Regional perspectives and societal variations. In *Small Islands, Large Questions: Society, Culture and Resistance in the Post-Emancipation Caribbean*, ed. K.F. Olwig, 73–99. London: Frank Cass.

Besson, Jean, and Janet Momsen, eds. 1987. *Land and Development in the Caribbean*. London: Macmillan Caribbean.

Biggs, Henry, Michael Bennett, and Robert Leach. 1963. *Report of the Commission of Inquiry into the Banana Industry of St. Lucia*. Castries: Government Printer at the Government Printing Office.

Bolland, O. Nigel. 1981. Systems of domination after slavery: The control of land and labour in the British West Indies after 1838. *Comparative Studies in Society and History* 23 (4): 591–619.

————. 1992. The politics of freedom in the British Caribbean. In *The Meaning of Freedom: Economics, Politics, and Culture after Slavery*, ed. F. McGlynn and S. Drescher, 113–46. Pittsburgh: University of Pittsburgh Press.

————. 2001. *The Politics of Labour in the British Caribbean: The Social Origins of Authoritarianism and Democracy in the Labour Movement*. Kingston, Jamaica: Ian Randle; Oxford: James Currey; Princeton: Markus Wiener.

Bolles, A. Lynn. 1983. Kitchens hit by priorities: Employed working class Jamaican women confront the IMF. In *Women, Men, and the International Division of Labor*, ed. J. Nash and M. P. Fernandez-Kelly, 138–60. Albany: State University of New York Press.

————. 1985. Of mules and yankee gals: Struggling with stereotypes in the field. *Anthropology and Humanism Quarterly* 10 (4): 114–19.

————.1996. Paying the piper twice: Gender and the process of globalization. *Caribbean Studies* 29 (1): 106–19.

Bond, Patrick. 2001. *Against Global Apartheid: South Africa Meets the World Bank, IMF, and International Finance*. Landsdowne: University of Cape Town Press.

Bourgois, Philippe I. 1989. *Ethnicity at Work: Divided Labor on a Central American Banana Plantation*. Baltimore: Johns Hopkins University Press.

Boyne, Roy. 1990. Culture and the world system. In *Global Culture: Nationalism, Globalization, and Modernity*. Vol. 7: *Theory, Culture, and Society*, ed. M. Featherstone, 57–65. London: Sage Publications.

Braithwaite, Lloyd E. 1957. Progress toward federation, 1938–1956. Part A: The federal negotiation. *Social and Economic Studies* 6 (2): 133–64.

Brathwaite, Kamau. 1971. *The Development of Creole Society in Jamaica, 1770–1820*. Oxford: Clarendon.

Brecher, Jeremy, and Tim Costello. 1994. *Global Village or Global Pillage: Economic Reconstruction from the Bottom Up*. Boston: South End.

Breen, Henry. [1844] 1970. *St. Lucia: Historical, Statistical, and Descriptive*. London: Frank Cass.

Brenes, Esteban R., and Kryssia Madrigal. 2003. Banana trade in Latin America. In *Banana Wars: The Anatomy of a Trade Dispute*, ed. T. E. Josling and T. G. Taylor, 97–121. Cambridge, MA: CABI Publishing.

Bruce, John W. 1983. *Family Land Tenure and Agricultural Development in St. Lucia*. Madison: University of Wisconsin-Madison, Land Tenure Center.

Callinicos, Alex. 2003. *An Anti-capitalist Manifesto*. Cambridge: Polity.

Caribbean Development Bank. 1993. Development of a Time-Phased Action Programme to Improve the International Competitiveness of the Banana Industry of the Windward Islands. Final report. Submitted by Kairi Consultants Ltd. and Agrocon Ltd. April.

Carnegie, Charles V. 1983. Strategic flexibility in the West Indies: A social psychology of Caribbean migration. *Caribbean Review* 11 (1): 10–13, 54.

———, ed. 1987a. *Afro-Caribbean Villages in Historical Perspective*. Kingston: African-Caribbean Institute of Jamaica.

———. 1987b. Introduction to *Afro-Caribbean Villages in Historical Perspective*, ed. C. V. Carnegie, iv–x. Kingston: African-Caribbean Institute of Jamaica.

———. 2002. *Postnationalism Prefigured: Caribbean Borderlands*. New Brunswick, NJ: Rutgers University Press.

Carney, Judith. 1988. Struggles over crop rights and labour within contract farming households in a Gambian irrigated rice project. *Journal of Peasant Studies* 15 (3): 334–49.

Central Bureau of Statistics. 1946. *West Indian Census, 1946: Census of Agriculture in Barbados, the Leeward Islands, the Windward Islands, and Trinidad and Tobago*. Kingston, Jamaica: Government Printer.

Chamberlain, Mary. 1997. *Narratives of Exile and Return*. New York: St. Martin's.

———. 1998. Family and identity: Barbadian migrants to Britain. In *Caribbean Migrations: Globalised Identities*, ed. M. Chamberlain, 148–61. London: Routledge.

Chamoiseau, Patrick. 1998. *Texaco*. New York: Vintage Books International.

Charles, Embert. 1985. Media and language: The Kweyol alternative. Paper presented at the seminar The State of Media in St. Lucia, University Centre, St. Lucia.

Charles, George F. 1994. *The History of the Labour Movement in St. Lucia, 1945–1974: A Personal Memoir*. Castries, St. Lucia: Folk Research Centre.

Chase, Jacquelyn, ed. 2002. *The Spaces of Neoliberalism: Land, Place, and Family in Latin America*. Bloomfield, CT: Kumarian Press.

Chin, Christine B. N., and James H. Mittelman. 2000. Conceptualizing resistance to globalization. In *Globalization and the Politics of Resistance*, ed. B. K. Gills, 29–45. London: Macmillan.

Clarke, Edith. 1966. *My Mother Who Fathered Me: A Study of the Family in Three Selected Communities in Jamaica*. London: George Allen and Unwin.

Clegg, Peter. 2002. *The Caribbean Banana Trade: From Colonialism to Globalization*. New York: Palgrave Macmillan.

Collins, Jane. 1993. Gender, contracts, and wage work: Agricultural restructuring in Brazil's Sao Francisco Valley. *Development and Change* 24:53–82.

Cooper, Frederick, and Randall Packard. 2005. The history and politics of development knowledge. In *The Anthropology of Development and Globalization: From Classical Political Economy to Contemporary Neoliberalism*, ed. M. Edelman and A. Haugerud, 126–39. Malden, MA: Blackwell Publishers.

Crichlow, Michaeline. 1994. An alternative approach to family land tenure in the anglophone Caribbean: The case of St. Lucia. *New West Indian Guide* 68:77–99.

———. 1997. The limits of maneuver: Caribbean states, small farmers, and the capitalist world economy, 1940s–1995. *Comparative Studies of South Asia, Africa and the Middle East* 17 (1): 1–18.

———. 2005. *Negotiating Caribbean Freedom: Peasants and the State in Development*. Lanham, MD: Lexington Books.

Crush, Jonathan. 1995. *The Power of Development*. London: Routledge.

DaBreo, D. Sinclair. 1981. *Of Men and Politics: The Agony of St. Lucia*. Castries, St. Lucia: Commonwealth Publishers International.

Daisley, Lennoz E. A. 1991. Bananas, Windward agriculture, and a perception on the future security of the region's farming sector. Unpublished document. November.

Darnovsky, Marcy, Barbara Epstein, and Richard Flacks. 1995. *Cultural Politics and Social Movements*. Philadelphia: Temple University Press.

de Albuquerque, Klaus and Jerome McElroy. 1999. Race, ethnicity, and social stratification in three Windward Islands. *Journal of Eastern Caribbean Studies* 24 (4): 1–29.

de Certeau, Michel. 1984. *The Practice of Everyday Life*. Berkeley and Los Angeles: University of California Press.

Deere, Carmen Diana. 1990. *Household and Class Relations: Peasants and Landlords in Northern Peru*. Berkeley: University of California Press.

Deere, Carmen Diana, Peggy Antrobus, Lynn Bolles, Edwin Melendez, Peter Phillips, Marcia Rivera, and Helen Safa. 1990. *In the Shadows of the Sun: Caribbean Alternatives and U.S. Policy*. Boulder: Westview Press.

De Guiran, L. 1986. Elements of the agrarian history of the island of St. Lucia:

From the Caribs to the morrow of independence. National Research and Development Foundation, St. Lucia. Mimeograph. Cited in Adrien 1996, 27.

della Porta, Donatella, and Hanspeter Kriesi. 1999. Social movements in a globalizing world: An introduction. In *Social Movements in a Globalizing World*, ed. D. della Porta, H. Kriesi, and D. Rucht, 3–22. New York: St. Martin's Press.

Development and Welfare Organisation of the West Indies. 1951. *The Agricultural Development of St. Lucia: Report of Team of Experts on Visit in March and April, 1951*. Published in Barbados.

Dirlik, Arif. 2001. Placed-based imagination: Globalism and the politics of place. In *Places and Politics in an Age of Globalization*, ed. R. Prazniak and A. Dirlik, 15–51. Lanham, MD: Rowman and Littlefield.

Duany, Jorge. 1997. Reconstructing racial identity: Ethnicity, color, and class among Dominicans in the United States and Puerto Rico. *Latin American Perspectives* 25 (3): 147–72.

Dujon, Veronica. 1995. National actors against world market pressures: Communal land, privatization, and agricultural development in the Caribbean. Ph.D. diss., University of Wisconsin-Madison.

———. 2002. Local actors, nation-states, and their global environment: Conceptualizing successful resistance to the anti-social impacts of globalization. *Critical Sociology* 28 (3): 371–88.

Dupuy, Alex. 2001. The new world order, globalization and Caribbean politics. In *New Caribbean Thought: A Reader*, ed. B. Meeks and F. Lindahl, 521–36. Jamaica: University of West Indies Press.

Dwyer, Daisy, and Judith Bruce, eds. 1988. *A Home Divided: Women and Income in the Third World*. Stanford: Stanford University Press.

Eastern Caribbean News and Views. 1997. Statement of the permanent representative of St. Lucia to the WTO at a press conference on the occasion of the meeting of the WTO Dispute Settlement Body. Eastern Caribbean News and Views. http://www.caribisles.org/news-01a.htm. October 16.

Economist. 1990. Yellow peril. *Economist* 317 (7678): 72.

———. 1997a. Expelled from Eden. *Economist* 345 (8048): 35–39.

———. 1997b. Banana row: The eastern Caribbean. *Economist* 343 (8019): 36.

Edelman, Marc. 1990. When they took the 'muni': Political culture and anti-austerity protest in rural northwestern Costa Rica. *American Ethnologist* 17 (4): 736–58.

———. 1996. Reconceptualizing and reconstituting peasant struggles: A new social movement in Central America. *Radical History Review* 65 (spring): 26–47.

———. 1999. *Peasants against Globalization: Rural Social Movements in Costa Rica*. Stanford: Stanford University Press.

———. 2001. Social movements: Changing paradigms and forms of politics. *Annual Review of Anthropology* 30:285–317.

Escobar, Arturo. 1992a. Culture, economics, and politics in Latin American social movements theory and research. In *The Making of Social Movements in Latin America: Identity, Strategy, and Democracy,* ed. A. Escobar and S. E. Alvarez, 62–85. Boulder: Westview Press.

———. 1992b. Culture, practice, and politics: Anthropology and the study of social movements. *Critique of Anthropology* 12 (4): 395–432.

———. 1995. *Encountering Development: The Making and Unmaking of the Third World.* Princeton: Princeton University Press.

———. 2001. Culture sits in places: Reflections on globalism and subaltern strategies of localization. *Political Geography* 20 (2): 139–74.

Escobar, Arturo, and Sonia Alvarez. 1992. *The Making of Social Movements in Latin America: Identity, Strategy, and Democracy.* Boulder: Westview Press.

Euraque, Dario A. 1996. *Reinterpreting the Banana Republic: Region and State in Honduras, 1870–1972.* Chapel Hill: University of North Carolina Press.

———. 2003. The threat of blackness to the mestizo nation: Race and ethnicity in the Honduran banana economy, 1920s and 1930s. In *Banana Wars: Power, Production, and History in the Americas,* ed. S. Striffler and M. Moberg, 229–49. Durham: Duke University Press.

Featherstone, Mike. 1990. Global culture: An introduction. In *Global Culture: Nationalism, Globalization and Modernity: A Theory, Culture and Society Special Issue,* ed. M. Featherstone, 1–14. London: Sage Publications.

Feld, Steven, and Keith Basso. 1996. Introduction to *Senses of Place,* ed. S. Feld and K. Basso, 3–12. Santa Fe: School of American Research.

Ferguson, James, and Akhil Gupta. 2002. Spatializing states: Toward an ethnography of neoliberal governmentality. *American Ethnologist* 29 (4): 981–1002.

Fisher, William F., and Thomas Ponniah. 2003. *Another World Is Possible: Popular Alternatives to Globalization at the World Social Forum.* London: Zed Books.

Fitzpatrick and Associates. 1990. Trade policy and the EC Banana market: An economic analysis. Paper prepared for Dole Europe Ltd.

Food and Agriculture Organization of the United Nations. 1983. *World Banana Economy: Statistical Compendium.* Rome: Food and Agriculture Organization of the United Nations.

———. 2001. Banana statistics. U.N. Doc. CCP: BA/TF 01/2. Second session of the Intergovernmental Group on Bananas and Tropical Fruits, December 4–8, 2001.

Forster, Cindy. 1998. Reforging national revolution: Campesino labor struggles in Guatemala, 1944–1954. In: *Identity and Struggle at the Margins of the Nation-State: The Laboring Peoples of Central America and the Hispanic Caribbean,* ed. A. Chomsky and A. Lauria-Santiago, 196–226. Durham: Duke University Press.

———. 2003. "The Macondo of Guatemala": Banana workers and national revolutions in Tiquisate, 1944–1954. In *Banana Wars: Power, Production, and History in the Americas,* ed. S. Striffler and M. Moberg, 191–228. Durham: Duke University Press.

Foucault, Michel. 1977. *Discipline and Punish: The Birth of the Prison.* New York: Pantheon Books.

Fox, Richard G., and Orin Starn, eds. 1997. *Between Resistance and Revolution: Cultural Politics and Social Protest.* New Brunswick, NJ: Rutgers University Press.

Freeman, Carla. 1997. Reinventing higglering in a transnational arena: Barbadian women juggle the triple shift. In *Daughters of Caliban: Caribbean Women in the 20th Century Caribbean,* ed. C. Lopez-Springfield, 68–95. Bloomington: Indiana University Press.

———. 2000. *High Heels and High Tech in the Global Economy: Women, Work, and Pink-Collar Identities in the Caribbean.* Durham: Duke University Press.

———. 2002. Mobility, rootedness, and the Caribbean higgler: Production, consumption and the gender of transnational livelihoods. In *Work and Migration: Life and Livelihoods in a Globalizing World,* ed. K. F. Olwig and N. Nygberg-Sorensen, 61–82. New York: Routledge.

Friedman, Jonathan. 1994. *Cultural Identity and Global Process.* London: Sage Publications.

———. 2000. Globalization, class, and culture in global systems. *Journal of World-Systems Research* 6 (3): 636–56.

———. 2003. Globalization, dis-integration, re-organization: The transformations of violence. In *Globalization, the State, and Violence,* ed. J. Friedman, 1–34. Walnut Creek, CA: Altamira.

Fruit Quality Task Force. 1989. Final report of the Fruit Quality Task Force, March 30.

Garrett, Paul. 2000. "High" Kwéyòl: The emergence of a formal Creole register in St. Lucia, West Indies. In *Language Change and Language Contact in Pidgins and Creoles,* ed. J. McWhorter, 63–101. Amsterdam: John Benjamins.

———. Forthcoming. Say it like you see it: Radio broadcasting and the mass mediation of Creole nationhood in St. Lucia. In *Identities: Global Studies in Culture and Power.*

GATT (General Agreement on Tariffs and Trade). 1993. EEC—member states' import regimes for bananas. Report of the panel (DS32/R), June 3.

———. 1994. EEC—import regimes for bananas. Report of the panel (DS38/R), February 11.

Genovese, Eugene D. [1974] 1976. *Roll Jordan Roll: The World the Slaves Made.* New York: Vintage.

Gibson-Graham, J. K. 1996. *The End of Capitalism (as We Knew It): A Feminist Critique of Political Economy.* Cambridge, MA: Blackwell.

Giddens, Anthony. 1996. *The Consequences of Modernity.* Stanford: Stanford University Press.

Glick Schiller, Nina, and George Eugene Fouron. 2001. *Georges Woke up Laughing: Long Distance Nationalism and the Search for Home.* Durham: Duke University Press.

Glissant, Edouard. 1989. *Caribbean Discourse: Selected Essays.* Charlottesville: University Press of Virginia.

Goffman, Erving. [1959] 1990. *The Presentation of Self in Everyday Life*. New York: Doubleday.

Gonzalez, Nancie. 1969. *Black Carib Household Structure: A Study of Migration and Modernization*. Seattle: University of Washington Press.

GOSL (Government of St. Lucia). 1946. *Revised Development Sketch Plan, 1946–1956*. Castries, St. Lucia: Voice Printers, by Authority of the Government of Saint Lucia.

———. 1960. Proceedings of discussion with government representatives and Geest Industries representatives concerning the sugar industry, February 6.

———. 1963. Government announcement regarding sugar industry, August 12.

———. 1967. St. Lucia Banana Growers' Association Act of 1967 and Amendments.

———. 1973–74. *The Agricultural Census Data of St. Lucia*. Castries, St. Lucia: Ministry of Agriculture.

———. 1980. Inquiry into the banana industry, final report. Report commissioned by the Government of St. Lucia, August.

———. 1986. Banana Protection and Quality Control Act of 1986.

———. 1990. Comprehensive audit of the Ministry of Agriculture, Lands, Fisheries and Cooperatives: Diversification and extension.

———. 1991. *Annual Agricultural Statistical Digest*. A publication of the Statistical Unit of the Ministry of Agriculture, Lands, Fisheries and Forestry.

———. 1993. *Economic and Social Review, 1992*. Castries, St. Lucia: Ministry of Finance, Statistics and Negotiating.

———. 1994. Proceedings of the Mount Coubaril summit meeting on the banana industry. Video recording, Government Information Service.

GOSL and OAS (Government of Saint Lucia and the Organization of American States). 1983. Report on the land registration activities of the Morne Panache pilot project. Land Reform Unit, Castries, October.

Grasmuck, Sherri, and Petricia R. Pessar. 1991. *Between Two Islands: Dominican International Migration*. Berkeley: University of California Press.

Gregory, Steven. 1998. *Black Corona: Race and the Politics of Place in an Urban Community*. Princeton: Princeton University Press.

Grossman, Lawrence. 1993. The political ecology of banana exports and local food production in St. Vincent, eastern Caribbean. *Annals of the Association of American Geographers* 83 (2): 347–67.

———. 1998. *The Political Ecology of Bananas: Contract Farming, Peasants, and Agrarian Change in the Eastern Caribbean*. Chapel Hill: University of North Carolina Press.

Guidry, John A., Michael D. Kennedy, and Mayer N. Zald, eds. 2000. *Globalizations and Social Movements: Culture, Power, and the Transnational Public Sphere*. Ann Arbor: University of Michigan Press.

Guilbault, Jocelyne. 1997. "Creolité" and "Francophonie" in music: Sociomusical repositioning where it matters. *Cultural Studies* 11 (2): 207–35.

Gupta, Akhil, and James Ferguson. 1997. *Culture, Power, Place: Explorations in Critical Anthropology*. Durham: Duke University Press.

Haarer, A. E. 1963. News about bananas. *Windward Island Annual* 8:28–31.

Hall, Douglas. 1978. The flight from the estates reconsidered: The British West Indies, 1838–1842. *Journal of Caribbean History* 10 (11): 7–24.

Hall, Stuart. 1991. The local and the global: Globalization and ethnicity. In *Culture, Globalization, and the World-System: Contemporary Conditions for the Representation of Identity*, ed. A. King, 19–39. Binghamton: State University of New York Press and Department of Art and Art History; London: Macmillan Education.

Hamel, Pierre, Henri Lustiger-Thaler, Jan Nederveen Pieterse, and Sasha Roseneil. 2001. Introduction: The shifting global frames of collective action. In *Globalization and Social Movements*, ed. P. Hamel, H. Lustiger-Thaler, J. N. Pieterse, and S. Roseneil, 1–18. New York: Palgrave.

Hannerz, Ulf. 1989. Notes on the global ecumene. *Public Culture* 1 (2): 66–75.

———. 1992. *Cultural Complexity: Studies in the Social Organization of Meaning*. New York: Columbia University Press.

———. 1996. *Transnational Connections: Culture, People, Places*. New York: Routledge.

Harootunian, Harry, and Masao Miyoshi, eds. 2002. *Learning Places: The Afterlives of Area Studies*. Durham: Duke University Press.

Harrison, Faye. 1991. Ethnography as politics. In *Decolonizing Anthropology: Moving Further toward an Anthropology for Liberation*, ed. Faye V. Harrison, 88–110. Arlington, VA: American Anthropological Association.

Harvey, David. 1989. *The Condition of Postmodernity: An Enquiry into the Origins of Cultural Change*. Oxford: Blackwell Publishers.

———. 1991. Flexibility: Threat or opportunity? *Socialist Review* 21 (1): 65–78.

———. 1993. Class relations, social justice, and the politics of difference. In *Place and the Politics of Identity*, ed. M. Keith and S. Pile, 41–66. London: Routledge.

Hastrup, Kirsten, and Karen Fog Olwig. 1997. Introduction. In *Siting Culture: The Shifting Anthropological Object*, ed. K. F. Olwig and K. Hastrup, 1–14. London: Routledge.

Hebdige, Dick. 1979. *Subculture: The Meaning of Style*. London: Methuen.

Herskovits, Melville. 1937. *Life in a Haitian Valley*. New York: Knopf.

Highmore, Ben. 2002. Introduction: Questioning everyday life. In *The Everyday Life Reader*, ed. Ben Highmore, 1–34. London: Routledge.

Hintzen, Percy. 2001. *West Indian in the West: Self-Representations in a Migrant Community*. New York: New York University Press.

Hirst, Paul, and G. Thompson. 1996. *Globalization in Question: The International Economy and the Possibilities of Governance*. Cambridge: Polity.

Horowitz, Michael M. 1967. *Morne-Paysan: Peasant Village in Martinique*. New York: Holt, Rinehart and Winston.

Inda, Jonathan Xavier, and Renato Rosaldo. 2002a. Introduction: A world in motion. In *The Anthropology of Globalization: A Reader*, ed. J. X. Inda and R. Rosaldo, 1–34. Malden, MA: Blackwell Publishers.

———, eds. 2002b. *The Anthropology of Globalization: A Reader*. Malden, MA: Blackwell Publishers.

Jackson, Donald, Martin Pounder, and D. G. Leacock. 1957. Report of the commission of inquiry into the stoppage of work at the sugar factory in St. Lucia in March 1957.

Jenkins, J. Craig, and Bert Klandermans. 1995. The politics of social protest. In *The Politics of Social Protest: Comparative Perspectives on States and Social Movements*, ed. J. C. Jenkins and B. Klandermans, 3–13. Minneapolis: University of Minnesota Press.

Joseph, M., and C. A. Borton. 1989. Field packing in the Windward Islands: Opportunities and constraints. In *Proceedings of the Ninth Re-union Meeting of ACORBAT, Venezuela. September 24–29.*

Joseph, Terenecia Kyneata. 2004. The indentureship experience in St. Lucia: The second phase from central factories to permanent settlement (1878–1903). Unpublished paper.

Josling, Timothy. 2003. Bananas and the WTO: Testing the new dispute settlement. In *Banana Wars: The Anatomy of a Trade Dispute*, ed. T. Josling and T. Taylor, 169–94. Oxon, UK: CABI.

Kairi Consultants and Agrocon Ltd. 1993. Development of a time-phased action programme to improve the international competitiveness of the banana industry of the Windward Islands. Vol. 2. Final Report submitted to Caribbean Development Bank, Barbados, West Indies, April.

Kasinitz, Philip. 1992. *Caribbean New York: Black Immigrants and the Politics of Race*. Ithaca: Cornell Univesity Press.

Kearney, Michael. 1992. The local and the global: The anthropology of globalization and transnationalism. *Annual Review of Anthropology* 24:547–65.

———. 1996. *Reconceptualizing the Peasantry: Anthropology in Global Perspective*. Boulder: Westview Press.

Keck, Margaret E., and Kathryn Sikkink. 1998. *Activists beyond Borders: Advocacy Networks in International Politics*. Ithaca: Cornell University Press.

Kelley, Robin. 2002. *Freedom Dreams: The Black Radical Imagination*. New York: Beacon.

Kelly, Philip. 1999. The geographies and politics of globalization. *Progress in Human Geography* 23 (3): 379–400.

Kepner, Charles D. 1936. *Social Aspects of the Banana Industry*. New York: Columbia University Press.

King, Anthony D., ed. 1991. *Culture, Globalization, and the World System: Contemporary Conditions for the Representation of Identity*. Basingstoke: Macmillan Education.

Klak, Thomas. 1998. Thirteen theses on globalization and neoliberalism. In *Globalization and Neoliberalism: The Caribbean Context*, ed. T. Klak, 3–24. Lanham, MD: Rowan and Littlefield.

Knight, Franklin, and Colin Palmer. 1989. The Caribbean: a regional overview.

In *The Modern Caribbean,* ed. F. Knight and C. Palmer, 1–20. Chapel Hill: University of North Carolina Press.

Laclau, Ernest, and Chantal Mouffe. 1985. *Hegemony and Socialist Strategy: Towards a Radical Democratic Politics.* London: Verso.

Lash, Scott, and John Urry. 1987. *The End of Organized Capitalism.* Cambridge, U.K.: Polity.

Lazarus, Neil. 1998. Charting globalisation. *Race and Class* 40 (2–3): 91–109.

Lazarus-Black, Mindie. 1994. *Legitimate Acts and Illegal Encounters: Law and Society in Antigua and Barbuda.* Washington, DC: Smithsonian Institution.

Leacock, Eleanor, and Helen Safa, eds. 1986. *Women's Work, Development, and the Division of Labor by Gender.* South Hadley, MA: Bergin and Garvey.

Lefebvre, Henri. [1947] 1991. *Critique of Everyday Life.* London: Verso.

LeFranc, Elsie. 1989. Petty trading and labour mobility: Higglers in the Kingston metropolitan area. In *Women and the Sexual Division of Labour in the Caribbean,* ed. K. Hart, 99–132. Kingston, Jamaica: Consortium Graduate School of Social Sciences.

Lewis, Patsy. 2000. A future for Windward Islands' bananas? Challenge and prospect. *Commonwealth and Comparative Politics* 38 (2): 51–72.

Lewis, Sir Arthur. 1936. The evolution of the peasantry in the British West Indies. Colonial Office, pamphlet no. 656.

Little, P. D., and M. J. Watts, eds. 1994. *Living under Contract: Contract Farming and Agrarian Transformation in Sub-Saharan Africa.* Madison: University of Wisconsin Press.

Louis, Michael. 1981. "An equal right to the soil": The rise of a peasantry in St. Lucia, 1838–1900. Ph.D. diss., Johns Hopkins University.

Lovell, Nadia. 1998. *Locality and Belonging.* London: Zed Books.

Low, Setha M., and Denise Lawrence-Zúñiga. 2003. Locating culture. In *The Anthropology of Space and Place: Locating Culture,* ed. Setha Low and Denise Lawrence-Zúñiga, 1–47. Malden, MA: Blackwell Publishers.

Lowenthal, David. 1967. Race and color in the West Indies. *Daedalus* 96 (2): 580–626.

———. 1972. *West Indian Societies.* London: Oxford University Press.

Malins, A., and M. St. Rose. 1994. Review of development of Windward Islands banana postharvest handling technologies to meet the challenges of competitive international marketing. Paper presented at the international conference Advances in Tropical Agriculture in the 20th Century and Prospects for the 21st Century: TA 2000. Port-of-Spain, Trinidad. September 4–9.

Malone, Clement., W. G. Hagley, and N. Pearson. 1952. *Report of the Commissions Appointed by His Excellency the Governor to Enquire into the Stoppage of Work at Sugar Factories in St. Lucia and into the Adequacy of the Existing Wage-Fixing Machinery in That Colony.* Government House, Government of the Windward Islands.

Marshall, Woodville K. 1965. Metayage in the sugar industry of the British Windward Islands, 1838–1865. *Jamaican Historical Review* 5:26–55.

————. 1968. Notes on peasant development in the West Indies since 1838. *Social and Economic Studies* 17 (3): 252–63.

————. 1988. Provision ground and plantation labour: Competition for resources. Paper presented at the twentieth annual conference of the Association of Caribbean Historians, St. Thomas, Virgin Islands. Cited in Bolland 1992, 113–46.

Massey, Doreen. 1993. Power-geometry and a progressive sense of place. In *Mapping the Futures: Local Cultures, Global Change*, ed. J. Bird, B. Curtis, T. Putnam, G. Robertson, and L. Tickner, 59–69. London: Routledge.

Massiah, Joycelin. 1983. *Women as Heads of Households in the Caribbean: Family Structure and Feminine Status*. Paris: United Nations Educational, Scientific, and Cultural Organization.

Mathurin, D. C. E. 1967. An unfavourable system of land tenure: The case of St. Lucia. In Proceedings of the Second West Indian Agricultural Economics Conference, University of the West Indies, Trinidad, 139–52. Cited in Barrow 1992.

Maurer, Bill. 2004. Ungrounding knowledge offshore: Caribbean studies, disciplinarity and critique. *Comparative American Studies* 2 (3): 324–41.

McClaurin, Irma. 1996. *Women of Belize: Gender and Change in Central America*. New Brunswick, NJ: Rutgers University Press.

Meliczek, Hans. 1975. *Land Tenure, St. Lucia: Project Findings and Recommendations*. Rome: United Nations Development Programme, Food and Agricultural Organization of the United Nations. Report prepared for the Government of St. Lucia, the United Nations Development Programme, and the Food and Agriculture Organisation.

Melucci, Alberto. 1989. *Nomads of the Present: Social Movements and Individual Needs in Contemporary Society*. Philadelphia: Temple University Press.

————. 1996. *Challenging Codes: Collective Action in the Information Age*. Cambridge: Cambridge University Press.

Melville, Gary. N.d. Case study of the Windward Islands. Online report for Agricultural Economics and Agribusiness Management. http://www.unc tad.org/en/docs/ditctncd20031p3_en.pdf.

Mintz, Sidney. 1957. The role of the middleman in the internal distribution system of a Caribbean peasant economy. *Human Organization* 15 (2): 18–23.

————. 1960. *Worker in the Cane: A Puerto Rican Life History*. New Haven: Yale University Press.

————. 1989. *Caribbean Transformations*. New York: Columbia University Press.

————. 1996. Enduring substances, trying theories: The Caribbean region as oikoumene. *Journal of the Royal Anthropological Institute* 2 (2): 289–312.

————. 1998. The localization of anthropological practice: From area studies to transnationalism. *Critique of Anthropology* 18 (2): 117–33.

Mintz, Sidney, and Richard Price. [1976] 1992. *The Birth of African-American Culture*. Boston: Beacon.

Moberg, Mark. 1997. *Myths of Ethnicity and Nation: Immigration, Work, and Identity in the Belize Banana Industry.* Knoxville: University of Tennessee Press.

Momsen, Janet. 1972. Land tenure as a barrier to agricultural innovation: The case of St. Lucia. In Proceedings of the seventh West Indian Agricultural Economics Conference, University of the West Indies, St. Augustine, Trinidad, 103–9.

Moore, Donald. 1997. Remapping resistance: "Ground for struggle" and the politics of place. In *Geographies of Resistance,* ed. S. Pile and M. Keith, 87–106. London: Routledge.

Morris, Aldon. 1984. *The Origins of the Civil Rights Movement: Black Communities Organizing for Change.* New York: Free Press; London: Collier Macmillan.

Morris, Aldon, and Carol McClurg Mueller, eds. 1992. *Frontiers in Social Movement Theory.* New Haven: Yale University Press.

Morrissey, Marietta. 1989. *Slave Women in the New World: Gender Stratification in the Caribbean.* Lawrence: University Press of Kansas.

Mueller, Carol McClurg. 1992. Building social movement theory. In *Frontiers in Social Movement Theory,* ed. A. D. Morris and C. M. Mueller, 3–25. New Haven: Yale University Press.

Munasinghe, Viranjini. 2001. *Callaloo or Tossed Salad? East Indians and the Cultural Politics of Identity in Trinidad.* Ithaca: Cornell University Press.

Nash, June C. 2001. *Mayan Visions: The Quest for Autonomy in an Age of Globalization.* New York: Routledge.

National Development Corporation. 1987. *Roseau Valley Smallholders Crop Diversification Project.* Castries, St. Lucia: St. Lucia Model Farms Ltd.

Neff, Liana, and Terri Raney. N.d. EC 1992: Caribbean and Central American competition in the banana market. Unpublished paper.

Newsweek. 1997. Brawl over bananas. *Newsweek* 129 (17): 43–45.

New York Times. 1999a. What bananas? Tariff fight baffles Europe. *New York Times,* March 5.

———. 1999b. An outpost in the banana and marijuana wars. *New York Times,* March 4.

Nurse, Keith, and Wayne Sandiford. 1995. *Windward Islands Bananas: Challenges and Options under the Single European Market.* Kingston, Jamaica: Freidrich Ebert Stiftung.

Olwig, Karen Fog. 1981. Women, "matrifocality" and exchange: An ethnohistorical study of the Afro-American family on St. John, Danish West Indies. *Ethnohistory* 28 (1): 59–78.

———. 1985. *Cultural Adaptation and Resistance on St. John: Three Centuries of Afro-Caribbean Life.* Gainesville: University of Florida Press.

———. 1993. *Global Culture, Island Identity: Continuity and Change in the Afro-Caribbean Community of Nevis.* Chur, Switzerland: Harwood Academic Publishers.

———. 1997. Cultural sites: Sustaining a home in a deterritorialized world. In

Siting Culture: The Shifting Anthropological Object, ed. K. F. Olwig and K. Hastrup, 17–37. London: Routledge.

Ong, Aihwa. 1987. *Spirits of Resistance and Capitalist Discipline: Factory Women in Malaysia.* Albany: State University of New York Press.

———. 1999. *Flexible Citizenship: The Cultural Logics of Transnationality.* Durham: Duke University Press.

Organization of American States. 1991. Integrated land development: The case of the Mabouya Valley in Saint Lucia. Prepared by the Department of Regional Development and Environment, Executive Secretariat for Economic and Social Affairs, Organization of American States, Washington, DC, June.

Palmer, Colin A. 1989. Identity, race, and Black Power in independent Jamaica. In *The Modern Caribbean,* ed. F. W. Knight and C. Palmer, 111–28. Chapel Hill: University of North Carolina Press.

Pappin, Francis. 1987. Assessment of the Roseau Resettlement and Diversification Project. Central Planning Unit, Ministry of Finance and Planning, St. Lucia, June.

Pattullo, Polly. 1996. *Last Resorts: The Cost of Tourism in the Caribbean.* London: Monthly Review Press.

Persaud, B. 1967. Economic problems of the Windward Islands banana industry. In Proceedings of the second West Indian Agricultural Economics Conference, University of the West Indies, St. Augustine, Trinidad, 35–55.

Pile, Scott. 1997. Introduction: Opposition, political identities, and spaces of resistance. In *Geographies of Resistance,* ed. S. Pile and M. Keith, 1–32. London: Routledge.

Polanyi, Karl. 1944. *The Great Transformation: The Political and Economic Origins of Our Time.* New York : Farrar and Rinehart.

Prazniak, Roxann, and Arif Dirlik, eds. 2001. *Places and Politics in an Age of Globalization.* Lanham, MD: Rowman and Littlefield.

Pred, Allan, and Michael J. Watts. 1992. *Reworking Modernity: Capitalisms and Symbolic Discontent.* New Brunswick, NJ: Rutgers University Press.

Price, Richard, and Sally Price. 1997. Shadowboxing in the mangrove. *Cultural Anthropology* 12:3–36.

Proctor, Jesse Harris. 1962. British West Indian society and government in transition, 1920–1960. *Social and Economic Studies* 11 (4): 273–304.

Purcell, Trevor. 1993. *Banana Fallout: Class, Color, and Culture among West Indians in Costa Rica.* Los Angeles: University of California, Center for Afro-American Studies.

Radcliffe, Sarah. 1993. Women's place/*el lugar de mujeres:* Latin America and the politics of gender identity. In *Place and the Politics of Identity,* ed. M. Keith and S. Pile, 102–16. London: Routledge.

Radcliffe, Sarah, and Sallie Westwood. 1996. *Remaking the Nation: Place, Identity, and Politics in Latin America.* London and New York: Routledge.

Raynolds, Laura T. 1994a. The restructuring of third world agro-exports:

Changing production relations in the Dominican Republic. In *The Global Restructuring of Agro-food Systems*, ed. P. McMichael, 214–37. Ithaca: Cornell University Press.

―――. 1994b. Institutionalizing flexibility: A comparative analysis of Fordist and post-Foridst models of third world agro-export production. In *Commodity Chains and Global Capitalism*, ed. G. Gereffi and M. Korzeniewicz, 143–61. Westport, CT: Praeger.

―――. 1998. Harnessing women's work: Restructuring agricultural and industrial labor forces in the Dominican Republic. *Economic Geography*. 74 (2): 149–69.

―――. 2003. The global banana trade. In *Banana Wars: Power, Production, and History in the Americas*, ed. S. Striffler and M. Moberg, 23–47. Durham: Duke University Press.

Raynolds, Laura T., and Douglas Murray. 1998. Yes, we have no bananas: Re-regulating global and regional trade. *International Journal of Sociology of Agriculture and Food* 7:7–44.

Reddock, Rhoda. 2004. Women's workers' struggles in the British Colonial Caribbean in the 1930s. In *Revisiting Caribbean Labour: Essays in Honour of O. Nigel Bolland*, ed. Constance Sutton, 19–40. London, Miami: Ian Randle Publishers.

Richardson, Bonham. 1989. Caribbean migrations, 1838–1985. In *The Modern Caribbean*, ed. F. W. Knight and C. Palmer, 203–28. Chapel Hill: University of North Carolina Press.

―――. 1992. *The Caribbean in the Wider World, 1492–1992*. Cambridge: Cambridge University Press.

1955. The rise of the banana industry of the Windward Islands. In *The Windward Islands Annual, 1955*, 32–35. Sussex, England: House Magazine.

Riviere, W. Emmanuel. 1972. Labour shortage in the British West Indies after emancipation. *Journal of Caribbean History* 4:1–30.

Robertson, Roland. 1992. *Globalization: Social Theory and Global Culture*. London: Sage.

Rodman, Margaret C. 1992. Empowering place: Multilocality and multivocality. *American Ethnologist* 94 (3): 640–56.

Rodney, Walter. 1981. Plantation society in Guyana. *Review* 4 (4): 643–66.

Safa, Helen. 1974. *The Urban Poor of Puerto Rico: A Study in Development and Inequality*. New York: Holt Rinehart and Winston.

Sassen, Saskia. 1998. *Globalization and Its Discontents: Selected Essays, 1984–1998*. New York: New Press.

Sawyer, Suzana. 2001. Fictions of sovereignty: Prosthetic petro-capitalism, neoliberal states, and phantom-like citizens in Ecuador. *Journal of Latin American Anthropology* 6 (1): 156–97.

―――. 2004. *Crude Chronicles: Indigenous Politics, Multinational Oil, and Neoliberalism in Ecuador*. Durham: Duke University Press.

Scarano, Francisco. 1989. Labor and society in the nineteenth century. In *The*

Modern Caribbean, ed. F. W. Knight and C. Palmer, 51–84. Chapel Hill: University of North Carolina Press.

Scott, Alan. 1997. Introduction—Globalization: social process or political rhetoric? In *The Limits of Globalization: Cases and Arguments*, ed. A. Scott, 1–24. London: Routledge.

Scott, James. 1985. *Weapons of the Weak: Everyday Forms of Peasant Resistance.* New Haven: Yale University Press.

———. 1989. *Domination and the Arts of Resistance: Hidden Transcripts.* New Haven: Yale University Press.

———. 1998. *Seeing Like a State: How Certain Schemes to Improve the Human Condition Have Failed.* New Haven: Yale University Press.

Severin, Kerde. 1989. Mabouya Valley Development Project: Brief project profile. Prepared by Mabouya Valley Development Project Program Officer, St. Lucia.

Sheller, Mimi. 2003. *Consuming the Caribbean: From Arawaks to Zombies.* London: Routledge.

Shephard, C. Y. 1947. Peasant agriculture in the Leeward and Windward Islands. *Tropical Agriculture* 24 (4–6): 61–71.

Shepherd, Verene. 1993. *Transients to Settlers: The Experience of Indians in Jamaica, 1845–1950.* Leeds: Peepal Tree.

Sklair, Leslie. 2001. Social movements and global capitalism. In *The Cultures of Globalization*, ed. F. Jameson and M. Miyoshi, 291–311. Durham: Duke University Press.

Slocum, Karla. 1991. Managing markets and households: The case of women inter-island traders in St. Vincent. M.A. thesis, State University of New York at Binghamton.

———. 1996. Producing under a globalizing economy: The intersection of flexible production and local autonomy in the work, lives, and actions of St. Lucian banana growers. Ph.D. diss., University of Florida Press.

———. 2001. Negotiating essentialism, group politics, and black feminism. Paper presented at the annual meeting of the American Anthropological Association, Washington, DC.

———. 2003. Discourses and counterdiscourses on globalization and the St. Lucian banana industry. In *Banana Wars: Power, Production, and History in the Americas*, ed. S. Striffler and M. Moberg, 253–85. Durham: Duke University Press.

———. Forthcoming. Situating sugar and politics: Regionality, race, and nationhood in the transition from colonialism in St. Lucia. *Identities: Global Studies in Culture and Power*.

Slocum, Karla, and Deborah A. Thomas. 2003. Rethinking global area studies: Insights from Caribbeanist anthropology. *American Anthropologist* 105 (3): 553–65.

Smith, Raymond T. 1956. *The Negro Family in British Guiana.* London: Routledge and Kegan Paul.

Starn, Orin. 1992. "I dreamed of foxes and hawks": Reflections on peasant protest, new social movements, and the Rondas Campesinas of northern

Peru. In *The Making of Social Movements in Latin America: Identity, Strategy, and Democracy*, ed. A. Escobar and S. E. Alvarez, 89–110. Boulder: Westview Press.

St. Lucia Mirror. 1996. Pats and chides for the B.S.C.: Pressure group told no-cut strikes "senseless" but urged to keep pressuring gov't. *St. Lucia Mirror* (Castries), March 29, 4.

Stovall, John, and Dale Hathaway. 2003. U.S. interests in the banana trade controversy. In *Banana Wars: The Anatomy of a Trade Dispute*, ed. T. Josling and T. Taylor, 151–68. Oxon, UK: CABI Publishing.

Striffler, Steve. 2002. *In the Shadows of State and Capital: The United Fruit Company, Popular Struggle, and Agrarian Restructuring in Ecuador, 1900–1995*. Durham: Duke University Press.

Striffler, Steve, and Mark Moberg, eds. 2003. *Banana wars: Power, production and history in the Americas*. Durham, NC: Duke University Press.

Sutton, Constance. 2004. Continuing the fight for economic justice: The Barbados sugar workers' 1958 wildcat strike. In *Revisiting Caribbean Labour: Essays in Honour of O. Nigel Bolland*, ed. Constance Sutton, 41–64. London: Ian Randle Publishers.

Sutton, Paul. 1997. The banana regime of the European Union, the Caribbean, and Latin America. *Journal of Inter-American Studies and World Affairs* 39 (2): 5–36.

Taylor, Lucien. 1998. Créolité bites: A conversation with Patrick Chamoiseau, Raphael Confiant, and Jean Bernabé. *Transition*, no. 7 (2): 124–61.

Thomas-Emeagwali, Gloria, ed. 1995. *Women Pay the Price: Structural Adjustment in Africa and the Caribbean*. Trenton, NJ: African World Press.

Tomich, Dale. 1990. *Slavery in the Circuit of Sugar: Martinique and the World Economy*. Baltimore: Johns Hopkins University Press.

Touraine, Alain. 1988. *The Return of the Actor: Social Theory in Postindustrial Society*. Minneapolis: University of Minnesota Press.

Trouillot, Michel-Rolph. 1988. *Peasants and Capital: Dominica in the World Economy*. Baltimore: Johns Hopkins University Press.

———. 1992. The Caribbean region: An open frontier in anthropological theory. *Annual Review of Anthropology* 21:19–42.

———. 1997. Between the cracks. *Crosscurrents in Culture, Power, and History* 4 (2): 1.

———. 2001. The anthropology of the state in the age of globalization. *Current Anthropology* 42 (1): 125–33.

———. 2002. The otherwise modern: Caribbean lessons from the savage slot. In *Critically Modern: Alternatives, Alterities, Anthropologies*, ed. B. M. Knauft, 220–40. Bloomington: Indiana University Press.

———. 2003. *Global Transformations: Anthropology and the Modern World*. New York: Palgrave Macmillan.

ULG Consultants Ltd. 1975. The Windward Islands Banana Industry Consultancy draft final report. Report compiled under assignment from the Ministry of Overseas Development.

Ulyssee, Gina. 1999. Uptown ladies and downtown women: Female representations of class and color in Jamaica. In *Representations of Blackness and the Performance of Identities*, ed. J. M. Rahier, 147–72. Westport, CT: Bergin and Garvey.

United Kingdom. 1897. *Report of the West India Royal Commission*. London: Her Majesty's Stationery Office.

————. 1930. *Report of the West Indian Sugar Commission*. Presented by the State for the Colonies to Parliament by Command of His Majesty, March. London: Her Majesty's Stationery Office.

————. 1945. *West India Royal Commission Report*. London: Her Majesty's Stationery Office.

————. 1948. *Colonial Annual Reports, St. Lucia, 1948*. London: Her Majesty's Stationery Office.

————. 1951–52. *Saint Lucia: Report for the Years 1951 and 1952*. London: Her Majesty's Stationery Office.

————. 1955–56. *Saint Lucia: Report for the Years 1955 and 1956*. London: Her Majesty's Stationery Office.

U.S. Department of State, Bureau of Public Affairs, Office of Public Communication. 1994. *Background Notes: Saint Lucia*. Washington, DC.

USEU (United States Mission to the European Union). 1996. U.S. Trade representative position paper on the banana industry. December 17. http://www.useu.be/archive/bana.html.

————. 1998. A new EC banana regime: WTO-consistent alternatives. Brussels, November. http://www.useu/be/issues/ bananaalt.html.

United Workers' Party. 1964. *Manifesto for the 1964 General Elections*. Castries, St. Lucia: Art Printery.

Wallace, Elizabeth. 1977. *The British Caribbean: From the Decline of Colonization to the End of the Federation*. Toronto: University of Toronto Press.

Warren, Kay B. 1998. *Indigenous Movements and Their Critics: Pan-Maya Activism in Guatemala*. Princeton: Princeton University Press.

————. 1993. Globalization, liberalism, and the Caribbean: Deciphering the limits of nation, nation-state, and the sovereignty under global capitalism. *Caribbean Studies* 26 (3–4): 213–64.

————, ed. 1994. *The Caribbean in the Global Political Economy*. London: Lynne Rienner.

Watts, M. 1994. Life under contract: Contract farming, agrarian restructuring, and flexible accumulation. In *Living under Contract: Contract Farming and Agrarian Transformation in Sub-Saharan Africa*, ed. P. D. Little and M. J. Watts, 21–77. Madison: University of Wisconsin Press.

Wayne, Rick. 1986. *Foolish Virgins*. Los Angeles: Star Publications.

Welch, Barbara M. 1996. *Survival by Association: Supply Management Landscapes of the Eastern Caribbean*. Montreal: McGill-Queen's University Press.

West Indian Commission. 1993. *Time for Action: Report of the West Indian Commission*. Kingston, Jamaica: University of the West Indies Press.

Williams, Eric E. 1942. *The Negro in the Caribbean*. Washington, DC: Associates in Negro Folk Education.

———. 1944. *Capitalism and Slavery*. Chapel Hill: University of North Carolina Press.

Willis, Paul. 1990. *Common Culture: Symbolic Work at Play in the Everyday Cultures of the Young*. Boulder: Westview Press.

Wilson, Peter J. 1973. *Crab Antics: The Social Anthropology of English-Speaking Negro Societies of the Caribbean*. New Haven: Yale University Press.

WINBAN (Windward Island Banana Growers' Association). 1989. Fruit Quality Task Force final report. Windward Island Banana Growers' Association.

Wolf, Eric. 1982. *Europe and the People without History*. Berkeley and Los Angeles: University of California Press.

World Trade Organization. 1997. *Dispute Settlement Reports, 1997*. Vol. 2. Cambridge: Cambridge University Press.

Yankey, Bernard, Thomas Henderson, Nicholas Liverpool, D. R. Aitchison, and George Eaton. 1990. Review of the banana industry of St. Lucia. Report prepared for the Government of Saint Lucia, Castries.

Yelvington, Kevin. 2000. Caribbean crucible: History, culture, and globalization. *Social Education* 64 (2): 70–77.

Index

ACP (African, Caribbean and Pacific) territories, 36, 37, 41
Adrien, Peter, 22, 24, 128, 209n20
African, Caribbean, and Pacific (ACP) territories, 36, 37, 41
Afro-Caribbean free villages, 126–27
Afro-Caribbeans and rural places, 18
Afro-St. Lucians: freedom of work discourse among, 112–19, 121–23; historical perspective on, 20, 24; and Indo-St. Lucians, 120–21, 127–28, 216n18; occupational/class positions of, 22–23; political activism of, 67, 140–43, 205n12, 217n2, 218n6; and socioeconomic mobility of farming, 24–25; and trade union leadership, 139, 140; and urban/rural dichotomy, 23, 65–66
Afro-West Indians and land-use patterns, 125–27
age and freedom of work discourse, 111–23
agriculture: diversification program of, 55–56, 68; flexible production strategies in, 11; personal rewards of, 3–4; socioeconomic mobility in, 24–25; and St. Lucia's economic bases, 43–44; state's role in, 12–13. *See also* banana industry; sugar industry

Albuquerque, Klaus de. *See* de Albuquerque, Klaus
Anthony, Kenny, 201
Appadurai, Arjun, 130
associyé (society), 105, 107
autonomy. *See* freedom of work discourse

Banana Framework Agreement (BFA), 42
Banana Growers' Association Act (1967), 51–53, 70, 210nn24–25, 212–13n16
banana industry: and class, 23, 206n16; Compton's role in transition to, 142; decentralization of production in, 12, 35, 74; and demographic shifts, 21–22; and globalization, 19–20, 31–33, 34, 44, 45, 208nn12–13, 210n27; harvesting processes in, 59–60, 76–77, 86; historical background on, 33–43, 207n6, 208–9nn15–16; hurricanes' impact on, 199; peasants as backbone of, 24, 35, 47–48, 123–24; policy shifts in St. Lucia in, 46–53; postcolonial growth of, 66–68; postharvest techniques in, 71–72, 74, 77, 212nn11–12; recent St. Lucian developments in, 199–202; and socioeconomic mobility,

ment and Exporting Company
(WIBDECO), 200–201
Windward Island Banana Growers'
Association (WINBAN), 53–54,
61, 70, 71–72, 81–82, 84–85
Windward Islands, banana trading
role of, 10, 35–36, 41, 55, 207n6;
position of, at GATT panels, 39,
41–42. *See also* nation, the
women: and attitudes toward banana

growing, 114–19; as higglers,
109–10; income differential of, vs.
men, 214n5; as single heads of
household, 115; and use of unpaid
labor, 105. *See also* gender
World Social Forum, 14
World Trade Organization (WTO),
199
written communication,
SLBGA/grower, 81–83